POPULATION, SETTLEMENT AND DEVELOPMENT IN ZAMBIA

So geographers in Afric maps,
With savage pictures fill their gaps,
And O'er unhabitable downs,
Place elephants instead of towns.

From: E.P. Mathers, *Zambesia*, Kins, Sell & Railton Ltd. London, 1918, p. 17.

POPULATION, SETTLEMENT AND DEVELOPMENT IN ZAMBIA

PRITHVISH NAG

CONCEPT PUBLISHING COMPANY, NEW DELHI-110 059

ISBN 81-7022-268-0

First Published 1990

Prithvish Nag (*b.* 1951)

Published by
Ashok Kumar Mittal
Concept Publishing Company
A/15-16, Commercial Block, Mohan Garden
NEW DELHI-110 059 (India)

Lasertypeset by
Microtech Advance Printing Systems (P) Ltd.
H-13, Bali Nagar
NEW DELHI-110 015

Printed in India by
Taj Press
New Delhi-110 006

Dedicated to my father
Professor Pradyumna Chandra Nag

G.V. Sc. (Calcutta),
D.V.M. (Munich).

FOREWORD

AFRICA is a suffering continent with many problems. Although it contains far fewer people than India, it has been politically divided into 56 countries, most of whose boundaries reflect the late nineteenth century scramble by European powers and the subsequent decolonisation since the middle of this century. Many of the countries of tropical Africa are among the poorest in the world, with low social and economic development, high population growth, a profusion of ethno-linguistic groups and frequent disasters both human and man-made. Millions of migrants have political motives as well as those with economic ones.

Some of the most difficult problems are faced by the 14 landlocked countries in Africa which have no direct access to the sea and which experience high costs, political and economic, of transportation across neighbouring territories. Zambia the former Northern Rhodesia, falls into this category, and its vulnerability was emphasised during Rhodesia's unilateral declaration of independence (UDI). However, despite its curious bow-tie shape, it is more fortunate than most other landlocked countries, particularly because it has profited from the extraction of one major mineral resources, copper. A lower middle income country with only six million inhabitants and a per capita GNP of $580 (1983), it has closer economic parallels to southern Africa than to most of the countries to the north. Its modest economic and considerable demographic growths have provoked changes in the spatial patterns of population and settlement, especially rapid urbanization with all its numerous attendant problems, such as those of housing, employment and the provision of facilities and amenities.

The Zambian government, aiming at economic diversification, regional and rural development and redistribution of wealth, is one of an increasing number of African governments giving serious attention to the spatial patterns of population and settlement in their national development plans, and therefore, this country constitutes a valuable case study.

Hence, I am very happy to welcome this volume on population, settlement and development in Zambia by Prithvish Nag, an Indian population geographer who has spent some time in Zambia and is now a Deputy Director in the National Atlas and Themátic Mapping Organisation, Government of India. He has been associated with me for some years as a member of the International Geographical Union Commission on Population Geography, and I am pleased that he has been able to complete this book among his other duties. I wish it well.

Durham
27th January, 1986

JOHN I. CLARKE

CONTENTS

Foreword vii
Abbreviations Used x
List of Figures xi
Preface xiii

1. Introduction 1
2. Growth of Population and Settlements 14
3. Spatial Analysis of Population 32
4. Settlements in Rural Areas 62
5. Rural Development and Population Redistribution 87
6. Urban Settlements, Urbanization and Urban Development 108
7. Housing Problems and Squatter Population 141
8. Development of Population and Settlements 176
9. Retrospect and Prospect 197

Select Bibliography : *Related to Zambia* 209
(a) Published work
(b) Unpublished, Government and U.N.Reports.
Index 229

ABBREVIATIONS USED

A.A.A.G.	–	Annals of the Association of American Geographers
A.S.C.O.	–	African States Consulting Organisation
A.S.R	–	American Sociological Review
C.S.O.	–	Central Statistical Organisation
D.T. & C.P.	–	Department of Town and Country Planning
E.D.C.C.	–	Economic Development and Cultural Change
E.G.	–	Economic Geography
F.R.N.	–	Federation of Rhodesia and Nyasaland
G.J.	–	Geographical Journal
G.P.	–	Government Printers
G.R.Z.	–	Government Republic of Zambia
I.S.R.	–	Institute of Social Research
I.S.R.C.	–	Institute for Social Research Communication
L.E.	–	Land Economics
M.L.G.H.	–	Ministry of Local Government and Housing
M.R.D.	–	Ministry of Rural Development
M.U.P.	–	Manchester University Press
L.U.S.	–	Land Use Services
N.G.S.I.	–	National Geographical Society of India
N.I.P.A.	–	National Institute for Public Administration
N.R.J.	–	The Northern Rhodesia Journal
P.G.	–	Professional Geographer
Pr.G.	–	Progress in Geography
P.R.S.A.	–	Papers, Regional Science Association
R.L.C.	–	Rhodes Livingstone Communication
R.L.J.	–	Rhodes Livingstone Journal
R.L.P.	–	Rhodes Livingstone Papers
Tr.I.B.G.	–	Transactions of the Institute of British Geographers
Z.G.A.	–	Zambia Geographical Association
Z.I.S.	–	Zambia Information Service
Z.P.	–	Zambian Paper

LIST OF FIGURES

1.1 Drainage Basins and Settlements 3
1.2 Distribution of Settled Areas 5
1.3 Environmental Hazards of Zambia 6
1.4 Province, District and Chief's Territory 8

2.1 Tribal Settlement 16
2.2 Evolution of Settlements in Swahili Reserve Area 25

3.1 Population Distribution and Density, 1969 34
3.2 Population Growth, 1969-80 36
3.3 Sex Ratio 37
3.4 Migration Pattern, 1969 49
3.5 Traffic Flow 52
3.6 Human Movement by Bus Service 53

4.1 Waterlogged Areas of Northern Zambia 68
4.2 Settlement Types 69
4.3 Distribution of Rural Settlements 74
4.4 Sandalya and Ndongo Villages 77
4.5 Mubila and Pemba Villages 78
4.6 Chief Chiwala's Village 79
4.7 Kasama Village 81
4.8 Mutamino and Nakonga Villages 82

5.1 Mungwi Scheme 91
5.2 Miengwe Village Regrouping Scheme 94
5.3 Kafubu Block 95
5.4 Kalichero Area 97
5.5 Chifwile Scheme 99

6.1 Early Town plans 110
6.2 Distribution of Urban Centres, 1969 112
6.3 Distribution of Urban Centres, 1980 117
6.4 Urban and Mining Complex of Copperbelt 118
6.5 Ndola 123
6.6 Low and High Density Areas of Lusaka 124
6.7 Mwinilunga 126
6.8 Chipata 127
6.9 Livingstone 129
6.10 Mansa 130
6.11 Kasama 131
6.12 Mongu 132
6.13 Lusaka 133

7.1 Nguluwe/Chaisa Squatter Settlement 142
7.2 Garneton 150
7.3 Malota 152
7.4 Distribution of Squatter Settlements in Kitwe 164
7.5 Lusaka : Planned and Unplanned Areas 171

8.1 Distribution of Central Places 184
8.2 Planning through growth poles 188
8.3 Proposed Railway lines 193

9.1 Types of areas 104
9.2 Rail-road accessibility 106
9.3 Likely Diffusion Pattern of Population 107

PREFACE

THE idea of studying Zambia came to mind during my two months hurricane visit to the country in 1969. Then I was a graduate student of geography in the Banaras Hindu University. This study was undertaken in response to the appeal of the then President of India, Dr. V.V. Giri. After his return from Zambia in 1972, he made an appeal to the Indian scientists to help Zambia in planning and development. By then I completed my post-graduation in geography from the same university, and I acceded to take up research work related to planning and development of this friendly African country. Further, I received an encouraging response from the office of the Zambian President. I was graciously granted permission to carry out the project, and at the time of field-work all possible assistance was extended to me. I was attached to the Cabinet Office, Lusaka during my stay there. The Indian High Commission in this city co-operated with me in all possible ways.

In completing this research work I was benefited greatly from my father's experience of the country. He was attached to the Ministry of Agriculture and later Ministry of Rural Development for several years. It is however, disheartening that he died before this work could be completed. It was due to his encouragement that I took up the challenge of studying this lesser known country of the world. In Banaras Hindu University, I was associated with Professor A.S. Jauhari who had a long experience of teaching African geography. My dissertation was entitled *Zambia : A Geographical Analysis of Settlement Planning*. In 1977, I was awarded the Ph.D. degree based on this work which became the first Ph.D. dissertation on African geography from an Indian university.

This book is not the printed version of my Ph.D. dissertation. However, I have been greatly benefited by my earlier experience. In 1978, Professor R.W. Steel, then Director of the Commonwealth Geographical Bureau came to know about my research work. He was particularly impressed by the fact that a geographer of one Commonwealth country has been working on another Commonwealth country. It was due to his encouragement I applied for the Commonwealth Geographical Bursary. Fortunately in 1982, I was awarded this Bursary which was granted on the occasion of 150th anniversary of the Royal Geographical Society. Under this scheme, I went to England as a visiting Member of Staff to the School of Oriental and African Studies, University of London from June 1982 to January 1983. During this visit, I started working on this book. The whole idea was discussed with my colleagues there. It was Professor B.W. Hodder an eminent Africanist geographer of this school who suggested the topic of the book as entitled here.

Books and papers on Africa are scarcely available in the Indian libraries. However, some of the libraries proved to be very useful for the present study. These are National Library (Calcutta), Banaras Hindu University Central Library (Varanasi), Jawaharlal Nehru University Library (New Delhi), and the library of the National Atlas and Thematic Mapping Organisation (Calcutta). In Zambia, I found the libraries of the University of Zambia, National Archives (both in Lusaka) and National Museum of Zambia (Livingstone) most useful for this work. The libraries of the Royal Geographical Society, School of Oriental and African Studies, Senate House of London University, London School of Economics, Foreign and Commonwealth Office (all in London). Sydney Jones Library, University of Liverpool and Department of Geography Library of the University of Durham maintain a good collection of books, maps and reports on Africa. These libraries have been consulted for the preparation of this book. I have to depend on a lot of my geographer friends in England, U.S.A., Zambia and in The Netherlands for keeping track of the recent work done in Zambian geography or in sister disciplines. I am indebted to Prof. R.W. Steel (Swansea), Dr. W. van Spengen (Amesterdam) and Mr. Dhubo Gupta (Calcutta) for giving me access to their private collection of books, maps and papers on south-central Africa. Dr. Paul White of the University of Sheffield was kind enough to send me the recent Publications about Zambia. Dr. G.E. Chisanga of the National Council for Scientific Research, Lusaka provided me with demographic data and maps when they were required the most. I am grateful to him for this favour. These contacts have helped in keeping me informed about Zambia, and about the research work being done on this country as well. While staying in India, maintaining these contacts have been difficult and expensive but very useful. However, I do admit that there is a scope to consult many more work being done on Zambia in different parts of the world.

This book is also based on intensive field-work carried out in Zambia from August 1973 to April 1974. During this period I visited several places in the country and carried out sample studies of cities, towns, rural development schemes, squatter settlements, mission settlements and villages. These sample studies could not have been completed without the help of the authorities concerned. I am grateful to the council authorities of Lusaka, Ndola, Kitwe, Kasama, Chipata, Mongu and Mansa; District Governor's Offices of Mansa, Kasama, Mwinilinga, Chipata, Mongu, Lusaka Rural and Livingstone; and Senior Chief Chiwala and St. Francis Mission (Solwezi). The Director of the Central Statistical Organisation (CSO), Lusaka kindly provided me all the relevant data of 1969 census and data related to labour and industries; and later, I received the 1980 Census data from C.S.O. as well. This favour has facilitated my work. I have also been helped by the Ministry of Rural Development and its provincial offices, especially the Land Use Services in several ways. I owe much to the Ministry of Local Government and Housing and Ministry of Lands and Natural Resources for permitting me to use maps, data and air photos. My work could not have been completed without the help of the Ministries of Planning and National Guidance, Education, and Health, and Post and Telegraph Department, National Housing Authority, United Bus Service, Roads Department, Department of Town and Country Planning, and National Agricultural Marketing Board.

From 1978, I had been sent as a Government of India official delegate to several international conferences around the world. As a result I presented my findings based on my study on Zambia in the Benin city, Calcutta, Dhaka, Lagos, London, Nagoya, Sao Paulo, Tokyo and elsewhere. My participation to the 1978 African Regional Conference of the International Geographical Union was particularly useful. The focal theme of this conference was *Resources and Development in Africa.* It was in this conference where I became fully aware of the common issues and challenges involved in the development of the African countries. In the present book some of these issues have been included. Further, I have been closely associated with the I.G.U. Commission on Population Geography and I.G.U./MAB Working Group on Perception of the Environment. Both the I.G.U. bodies have been particularly interested in African problems. My participation in their activities kept me abreast with the fast changing African scene.

Such associations proved to be very useful because academic interest in Africa has not fully developed in the Indian Universities. Under the aegis of the I.G.U. Commission on Population Geography and I.C.A. Commission on Census Mapping, I was entrusted in organising an international survey on census mapping where national reports on several African countries including Zambia were presented. This survey greatly helped me in estimating the current population related issues in Africa.

From the time I completed my field-work in Zambia, I have been continuously publishing papers on different aspects of the problems related to population, settlement and development in Zambia. These papers have been published in India and elsewhere, and referred in this book. Some of the papers are under publication as well.

During last 12 years, I kept in touch with the members of the Department of Geography of the University of Zambia, particularly Prof. G.J. Williams and Dr. A.P. Wood. Though I was never attached to the famous Institute for African Studies in Lusaka, I keep in touch with its activities with a great interest and in the past I have regularly sent my published papers to the library of this institute. Similarly, I have also been interested in the activities of the Indian Centre for Africa of the Indian Council for Cultural Relations, New Delhi. This Centre brings out Journal called *Africa Quarterly* where two of any important papers on Zambia have been published. Mrs. Shanti Sadiq Ali, once Executive Editor of this journal has been a source of inspiration for me for continuing my academic interest on Africa. Prof. S.P. Chatterjee, the former President of the International Geographical Union and founder Director of my Organisation has always been encouraging me for taking up a challenging work. I owe much to both of them.

Personally, I would like to thank Mr. N.N. Mubwelelera, Mr. L.M. Sililo and Mr. P.P. Musungwa of the Cabinet Office, Dr. R.K. Sharma, former Senior Economist of the Ministry of Finance, Dr. B. Debroy of the Flying Doctor Service, Dr. R.P.L. Sinha of the Kitwe City Council, and Mr. Y.K. Shamapande of Lusaka City Council. I have my special thanks to Mr. A.K. Mazumdar and his family for helping me in several ways during my field-work. I take this opportunity to acknowledge the kind assistance of several translators, messengers, clerks in different offices and the members of the Indian community in Zambia in completing my field-work and making my stay homely there.

This work would not have been completed without the help of my colleagues in the Ministry of Science and Technology, New Delhi and the National Atlas & Thematic Mapping Organisation, Calcutta, more particularly to Dr. G.K. Dutt, Mr. A.K. Kundu and Mr. A.K. Sengupta. My wife Sutapa was always ready to assist me in completing this book in all possible ways.

This work was completed with the financial assistance of the University Grants Commission, Council for Scientific and Industrial Research and the Union Department of Science and Technology (all in New Delhi); and the Royal Geographical Society, Commonwealth Foundation, and Commonwealth Geographical Bureau. I would like to acknowledge them with thanks, particularly Dr. John Hemming of the Royal Geographical Society.

I would like to acknowledge with gratitude the favour accorded to me by Mr. Naurang Rai, Concept Publishing Company, New Delhi for agreeing to undertake my another publication and completing it so magnificently.

Finally, I owe my deep gratitude to Prof. John I. Clarke, Pro-Vice-Chancellor of Durham University, for having agreed to write the foreword of this volume. He has been a constant source of inspiration to me.

Calcutta PRITHVISH NAG
22nd October, 1989

1

INTRODUCTION

SINCE Mahatma Gandhi visited southern Africa, a movement has started all over for independence, equality and dignity of labour. It was in this part of the world where the fight against colonialism, racialism and apartheid was initiated. In 1947, when India got independence, it was considered as a watershed in the world history. Following this, territories in Asia and Africa achieved independence. Zambia got independence in 1964 and became a frontline state. Its national philosophy of humanism has been appreciated all over. India and Zambia joined their efforts in order to eradicate colonialism from the world and from Africa in particular. As a result, several countries around Zambia got independence in the last decade. However, the task still remains incomplete. Perhaps, more determined efforts have to be made in the future in this regard.

It was not the imperial powers which brought the two territories closer. There are several evidences explaining the close association of Indian and East African (including Sofala) coasts.[1] The European colonizers and missionaries came to India, collected detailed information about the Indian Ocean, East African coast and the interior of Africa, and then left for African exploration sometimes with Indians as well.[2] A detailed investigation has yet to be made about the role of Indians in providing the world with the knowledge about Africa. It was in the colonial period that Indians migrated with their colonial masters as railway workers, soldiers, clerks or traders. After independence, a new group of Indians came to the African countries. They were teachers, doctors, accountants, engineers and other professionals. The Indian population, either settlers or expatriates, make their presence felt in African towns including that of Zambia.

Zambia and Africa

Zambia (8° to 18° S and 24° 40′ to 33° 40′E) is landlocked country surrounded by Tanzania, Malawi, Mozambique, Zimbabwe, Botswana, Namibia, Angola and Zaire. Several geographers have suggested regionalization schemes consisting of some of these countries.[3] Location of Zambia in south-central Africa, consisting of other four independent States of Malawi, Mozambique, Angola and Zimbabwe appears to acceptable. It is not only due to the common pre-colonial and colonial pasts, but due to a lot of similarities among these countries which are still conspicuous. While regionalising the whole of Africa into eight regions, Prothero and his colleagues considered that each of the region including south-central Africa possesses an accepted locational reality which was thought to be brought out clearly in their treatment, each has both elements and factors which contribute to some degree of cohesion and integration, though at the same time within each there is a great diversity.[4]

Physiography

Population distribution and settlements have been largely influenced by physical and environmental factors. Human activities are closely associated with such factors. The relief consists mainly of a series of gently undulating to flat plateau, occasionally broken by isolated hills or low ranges of resistant rocks.[5] The highest elevation is on Nyika Plateau in the north-east, while lowest is in the south where river Zambezi enters Mozambique. The western portion of this country is covered by Kalahari sands. River Luwangwa and Muchinga escarpments run northeast to southwest. Large lowlying areas and waterbodies are covered by lake Tanganyika, Lake Mweru (shared by Tanzania and Zaire, respectively), Bangweulu lake and swamp, Kafue Flats and Lukanga swamp. Lake Kariba is man-made and shared by Zimbabwe. Apart from these waterbodies, there are innumerable ill-drained lowlying areas locally known as *dambos*. The whole country can be divided into (a) Zambezi system, having outlet in the Indian Ocean, and (b) Congo System, with an outlet in the Atlantic Ocean. Major part of the former system lies in the western Zambia, while sizable part of the latter system in northern Zambia. The Congo-Zambezi watershed runs almost parallel to the Muchinga Escarpment in the north (Fig 1.1). The settlement proliferation is stimulated by the headwaters on undulating surfaces. Principal settlements at the headwaters are connected by roads and tracts which follow watersheds. These settlements are generally of social importance as well, such as chiefs' headquarters or missions. The expansion of settlements is along the downflow of the streams or rivers. Boundaries of chiefs or wards follow the watersheds. On the other hand, ill-drained lowlying areas along big rivers like Kafue and Luangwa have ecological consequences to fetch tropical diseases, such as glossina morsitans, glossina fuscipes, glossina brevipalpis, glossina pallidipes and human sleeping sickness. The ill-drained areas below 5,000 feet (1325m) suffer from such diseases which discourage human settlements and animal population. Tsetse flies or glossina spp. are the insect vectors for the infections.[6] However, due to population pressure particularly in the Eastern Province, human settlements are found in tsetse fly infested areas of Luangwa Valley. The lowlying, ill-drained and a tsetse fly infested areas are generally occupied by large game and forest reserves, which are not available for human settlements by statutory laws. Such reserves are elsewhere as well (Fig. 1.2).

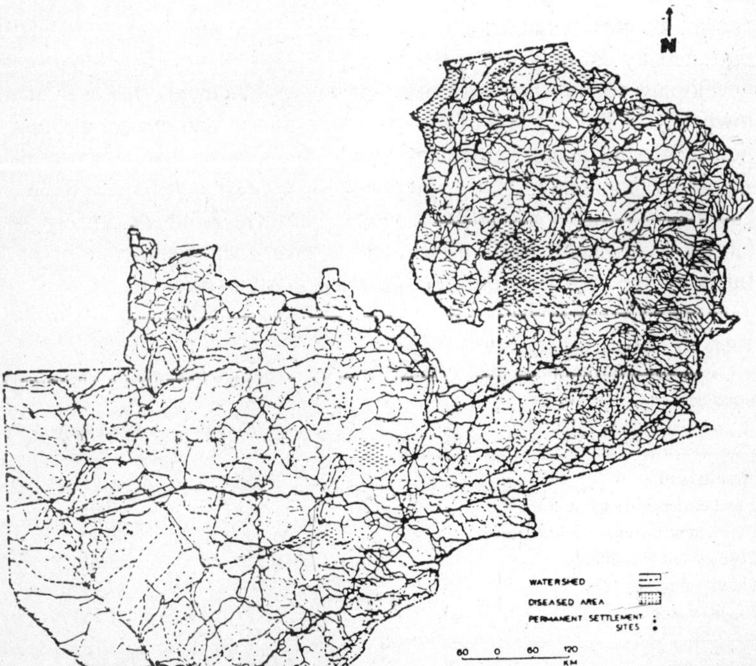

Fig. 1.1: Drainage Basins and Settlements

General Landuse and Social Set-up

The total area available for agriculture is about 5050 thousand ha (6.71%) which is less than the area covered by the forest and woodlands (Table 1.1).[7] The human settlements covers approximately 25 per cent of the area, while extension services for rural development through agricultural camps and other centres is made available to about forty-six per cent of the country's area. This clearly indicates that the development infrastructure is already available in unfavourable rural areas (Fig. 1.3). However in spite of governments sincere efforts, enterprising population continues to move towards the old line-of-rail. The rural-urban migration was so voluminous that several districts away from this line-of-rail recorded negative growth during 1963-69. The percentage of urban population has increased from 20.5 in 1963, 29.4 in 1969, 35.6 in 1974 (sample census) to 43 in 1980. But the growth rate of urban population has decreased from 8.9 per cent during the period 1963-69 to 6.7 per cent in 1969-80. Rural population has increased its growth rate from 0.5 to 1.1 during the same period. Population density is only 7.5 persons per sq km. This underpopulated developing country has a lot of scope for development. However, the towns along the old line-of-rail are overcrowded and sizable population reside in squatter settlements there. Another significant aspect of Zambia's population is the preponderance of females over males, having 962 males per 1000 females. Further, Zambian society is largely matrilineal. Both these factors have been significant in influencing the socio-economic set-up, particularly in rural areas.

Table 1.1 : Broad Landuse, 1979

Landuse	*Area in '000 ha*	*Percentage*
Arable land	5,050 *	6.71
Land under permanent crops	8 *	0.01
Permanent meadows and pastures	35,000 *	46.50
Forests and woodlands	20,550 **	27.31
Other nd	13,464	17.89
Inland water	1,189	1.58
Total Area	75,261	100.00

*FAO estimates; ** Unofficial estimates.

Source : FAO Production Yearbook

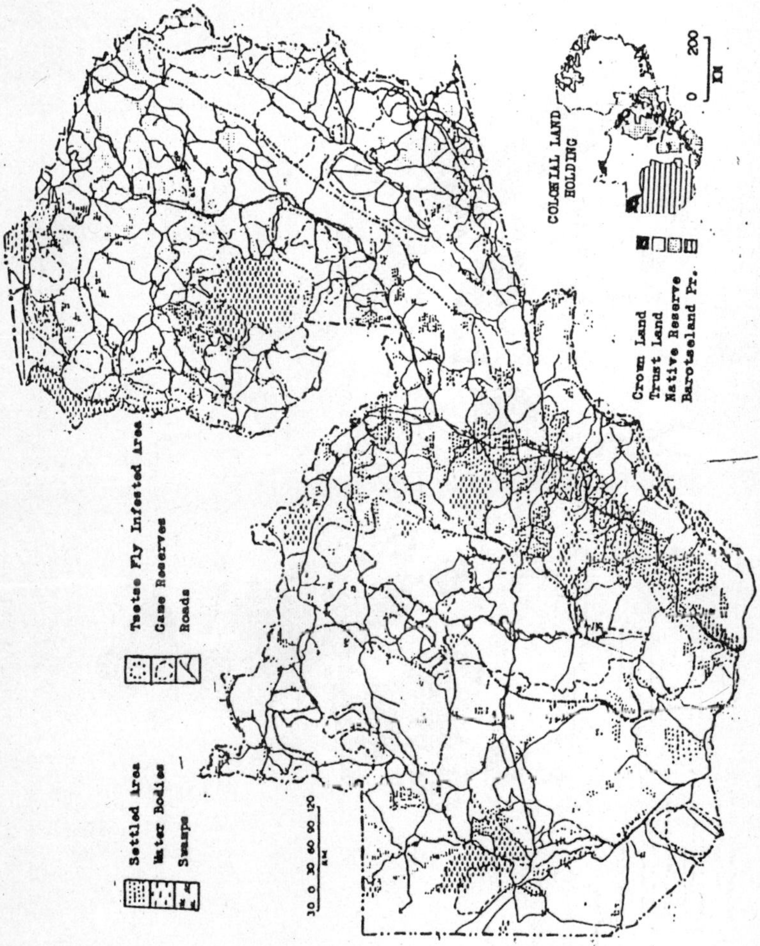

Fig. 1.2: Distribution of Settled Areas

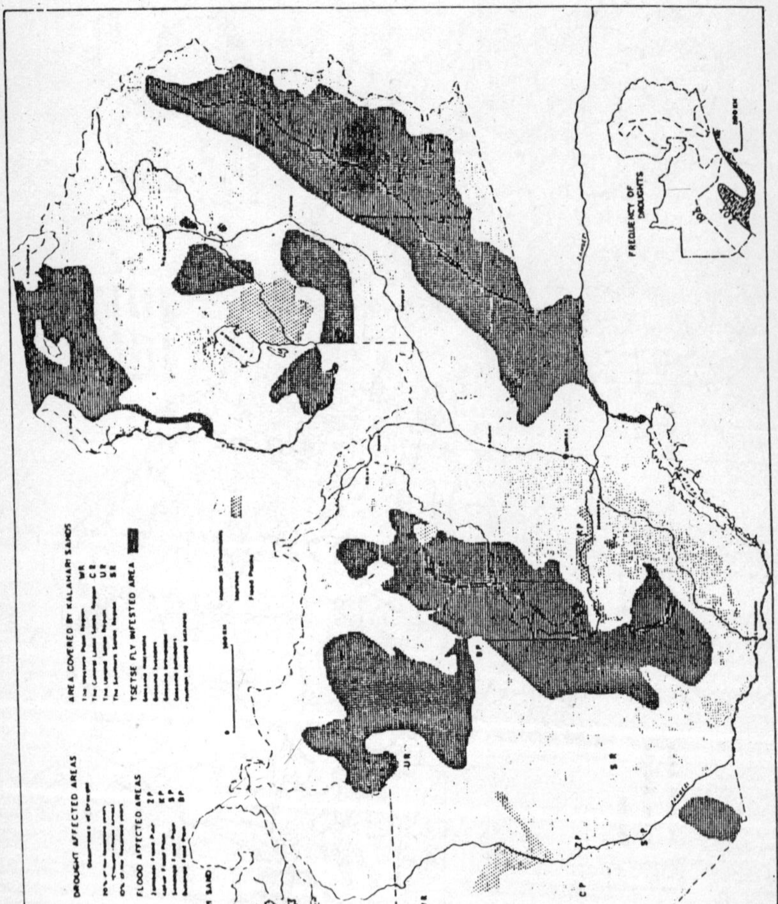

Fig. 1.3: Environmental Hazards of Zambia

Zambian society has about 73 ethnic groups. Bemba in the Northern Province, Tonga (Bantu) in Southern Province, Lozi in Western Province, Nyanja and Ngoni in the Eastern Province are important African ethnic groups. There are seven recognised languages named after prominent ethnic groups (Table 1.2). In addition, English is the language of the government. The non-African ethnic groups are of Europeans and Asians (Table 1.3). Christianity is the religion of the African population. However, there are three pockets of African population of Muslim religious faith. These are Muslim outposts in the interior of Africa.

In 1972 villages were registered throughout the country. Their number was 32,472 in 273 chiefs' territories. These villages frequently change their location after the exhaustion of the local resources. Owing to this reason, government's efforts for extension of services and facilities and rural development in general are not fully rewarding. In densely populated provinces such as Eastern or Luapula, the rural settlements are permanent in nature.

Table 1.2 : Major Language Groups, 1969-1980

Language Group	*Percentage of total Population*	
(Mother Tongue)	*1969*	*1980*
Bemba	33.6	36.2
Tonga	15.2	15.1
North-Western	10.6	10.1
Barotse	9.2	8.2
Nyanja	17.0	17.6
Mambme	5.2	4.6
Tumbuka	4.7	4.6
Non-Zambian	4.5	3.6

Source : Census of 1969 and 1980.

In the last census which was taken in 1980, there were 85 towns out of which 33 were new. All the 'large urban areas' lie along the old line-of-rail from Livingstone in the south to Copperbelt in the north. Copperbelt has seven large urban centres and with the other urban centres along this line, makes an urban corridor in pre-dominantly rural Zambia (Fig.1.4). This urban system has been so conspicuous that one cannot avoid referring to it frequently while writing on Zambia. All the three national development plans have been aiming to reduce dependency on this line-of-rail based urban system by providing facilities and opportunities in vast rural areas.[8] But, even after the government's sincere efforts for rural upliftment, population continues to migrate along the old line-of-rail. It is only in 1980 Census that the provincial headquarters towns away from this line have recorded a reasonable size. The developmental infrastructure suffers from both having a viable population base in rural areas, while the crowding in urban areas has lead to strain the urban amenities, as a result, squatter settlements are found in every town along the line-of-rail.

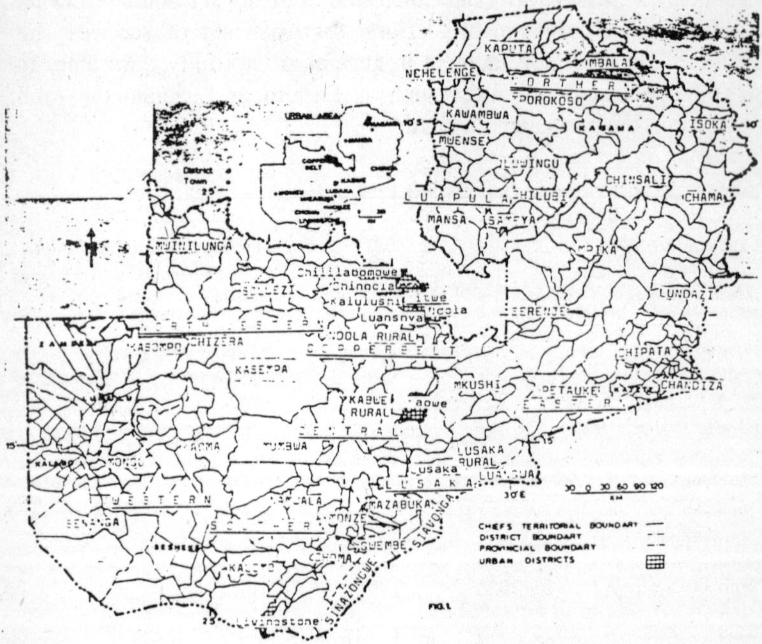

Fig. 1.4: Province, District and Chief's Territory

Administrative Framework

Only after independence, 'policy measure were taken to put the rural and urban local governments on an equal footing'. Small tribal authorities were amalgamated into more viable district councils and principals of elected majority was established.[9] The rural councils are now organised for administration, development and planning in rural areas. In urban districts, such as, Kitwe or Livingstone, these councils are not in existence. In general, a district has rural council and township or municipal council for the towns.

Table 1.3 : Ethnic Population (%)

Ethnic Groups	*1961*	*1969*	*1980*
African	97.3	98.6	99.3
European	2.4	1.1	0.3
Asian	0.2	0.3	0.3
Coloured	0.1	0.1	0.1
Total	100.00	100.00	100.00

Source : C.S.O. Lusaka.

The significant change in administration was under the banner of 'One Party Participatory Democracy'. The decision-making bodies were to decentralised at grass-root level. Organizational structure of the decentralised government under the President of the Republic and Secretary-General of the party is through three institutions : (a) party, (b) elected institutions, and (c) government. The 'party' has the most sound hierarchical organization and in the recent years it has proved to be a significant instrument for diffusion and implementation of the national philosophy and goals.

In theory, provisions were made to interlink the 'Elected Institutions' (EI) and Government (G). The village headman (G) becomes chairman of the village productivity committee (E.I.), while the 'chief' (G) is supposed to implement effective and efficient administration and oversee the functioning of the V.P.C. This administrative organisation, based on Ward Development Committees (WDC) and V.P.C. was likely to dilute the authority of chiefs and headman, as the functions which are at present done by them were to be performed by the E.I. Villages still remain the basic unit of administration.[10]

The Government thought of a parallel and homogeneous administrative units based on W.D.C. and V.P.C. The wards are approximately of equal population size twenty in each district, which are carved out based on the chief's areas. Census units are also based on 'chiefs' areas". As a result the different boundaries largely coincide with each other.[11] The wards are in towns as well as in rural areas. Mbala or Kasama towns have twelve wards each. However, these committees are no longer functioning. District councils have taken over the functions of such development committees.

Development Constraints

Zambia is fortunate in having rich natural resources. Pressure on land is less and a variety of crops can be grown there. Forests and games are valuable resources. Lakes, rivers and other water bodies have provided superb fishing sites. Minerals have been exploited for a long time. Copper has dominated the mining activities. Fluctuations of its price in the international markets have several times effected the development of the country adversely. In this landlocked country with heavy export based economy. Proper transportation system has been crucial. Its rail outlets to sea passes through countries which had different colonial set-up in the past. Being a frontline state, its relationship with the neighbouring colonial territories were not always congenial. As a result, Zambia had suffered a lot by frequent boundary closers with the neighbours. It has been claimed repeatedly that due to the unilateral declaration of independence by the then Southern Rhodesia, the First National Development Plan could achieve some of its targets. The others valuable minerals are lead, zinc and coal. There are deposits of iron ore, and radio-active minerals as well.

In the early post-independence days, Zambian economy was in much better shape than many of the African countries. This was due to copper prices which increased substantially during the period, 1964-69. But, after 1970 this picture became more complex due to recession on the price and demand for copper. This was followed by Mufulira mine disaster in late 1970. Share of copper production fell from nearly 12 per cent in 1969 to 8 per cent in 1981. The government was forced to find out alternative strategies, such as development of agriculture and industry. Agricultural output increased in 1976 and 1977 and later in 1980 and 1981. During the latter years, agriculture accounted for only 13 per cent of the G.D.P., of which subsistence output contributed about two-third and commercial sector about one-third (of which about half came from European farms).[12] There has been a growing number of small scale emergent farmers in rural areas as well. However, the industrial situation did not improve much. Government made certain changes by establishing parastatal holding companies in order to provide an organisational and financial base. But the results have not been commensurate with the efforts.

Constraints to development were not only due to falling copper prices or transport dislocation or due to Zambia's involvement in the liberation struggle of the neighbouring countries, but also due to scarcity of skilled and educated manpower. The enrollment in primary and secondary schools has increased several times since independence. University education and technical training have been given due importance in the successive national development plans. Zambianization of jobs depends on the success of the outcome of such efforts. There has been all round scarcity of skilled Zambians and owing to this reason dependence on expatriates is still continuing. Employment in mining and quarrying activities has reduced slightly during the period 1973-80; while in construction activities there has been a drastic reduction during the same period. On the other hand, employment in agriculture, forestry and fishing activities has increased from 31.7 thousand employees in 1973 to 39.6 thousand in 1980. In addition to the above problems, lack of development infrastructure and population base especially off the line-of-rail, shortage of foreign exchange, major cutback in expenditure and inflation have repeatedly come in the way of development activities.

Even with all these constraints, Zambia has a great potentiality for development. It has a very low population density and rich mineral reserves. The pressure of population is limited to some specific areas only. Earlier experiences in agriculture indicate that with more determined efforts the diversification of the economy from copper, and development away from the line-of-rail are possible. The objectives of the Third National Development Plan are meant to make a break through in this direction.

REFERENCES

1. Nag, P., Asian Settlement in Zambia, *Africa Quarterly*, Indian Centre for Africa, Vol. 18 (4), 1979, pp. 59-75.
2. Nag, P., India, Indian Ocean and Africa : Historical and Geographical Aspects, in Chandra, Satish (ed), *Indian Ocean : Exploration in Commerce, Politics and History*, Sage International, New Delhi, 1987. See also Simpson, D.H., the part taken by Africans in the European Exploration of East and Central Africa, proceedings of a seminar on *The Exploration of Africa in the Eighteenth and Nineteenth Centuries*, Centre of African Studies, University of Edinburgh,

1971, pp. 87-112. This paper also shows the involvement of Indians in exploration of Africa, particularly in Dr. David Livingstone's expeditions.

3. In the book Hance, William A., *Population Migration and Urbanisation in Africa*, Columbia University Press, New York and London, 1970, p. 34, (Map 2) Zambia has been shown in Eastern Africa alongwith Rhodesia, Mozambique, Malawi, Tanzania, Uganda, Kenya, Somalia and even Ethiopia. This is based on U.N. Deliniation. In an another book Hodder, B.W. and D.R. Harris (ed) *Africa in Transition*, Methuen & Co.Ltd., London, 1967, Zambia has been included in Southern Africa, pp.1-4, also ch. 6 by Board, C. Southern Africa, pp. 295-364, Fordham Paul has placed Zambia in Central Africa alongwith Rhodesia and Malawi in his book on *The Geography of African Affairs*, Penguin Books, 1972, ch. 9, pp. 173-191. Similarly, L. Dudley Stamp has included this country in Central Africa in *Africa: A Study in Tropical Development*, John Willy & Sons, Inc., New York and Chapman & Hall Ltd., London 1953, Fig. 1. In a book by Hance, William, A., *The Geography of Modern Africa*, Columbia University Press, New York and London, 1975 Zambia has been included in South-Central Africa along with Rhodesia, Malawi, Angola and Mozambique (ch.12 : Zambia, pp. 457-76). Further Fitzerald has included Northern Rhodesia in East Africa with Nyasaland, Kenya, Uganda and Tanzania (pp. 214-64), while Central Africa including Congo (Katanga), Angola, Gabun and Cameroons (pp. 277-321). See Fitzerald, Walter, *Africa : A Social, Economic and Political Geography of its Major Regions*, Methuen & Co. Ltd., London and E.P. Dutton & Co. Inc. New York 1952. In his book on Southern Africa, Hull has excluded Zambia from Southern Africa, but Namibia, Botswana, Zimbabwe, Malawi, Mozambique and South Africa. Vide Hull, Richard, W., *Southern Africa : Civilisation in Turmoil*, New York University Press, New York and London, 1981. According to Prothero, South-Central Africa consists of Angola, Zambia, Rhodesia, Malawi and Mozambique, and this idea has lately been widely accepted. See Prothero, R. Mansell (ed), *A Geography of Africa*, Routledge & Kegan Paul, London and Boston, 1969.

4. Prothero, *op. cit*, pp. 3-4, also see ch. 6 by Kay, G., South-Central Africa, European settlement and economic development, pp. 264-324.

5. Archer, D.R. Relief, in Davies, D.H.(ed), *Zambia in Maps*, University of London Press Ltd. 1971, p. 14. Carinaldi has recognised five erosion surface between Jurasic to Late Tertiary. During Late Tertiary, the formation of Lake Bangweulu, Victoria Falls and Batoka Gorges took place over Zambian landscape. This period was also responsible for 'dambos' which is a flat depression system. Vide Carinaldi, V., Zambia: The natural background, in Fagan, B.M. (ed), *A Short History of Zambia*, Oxford University Press, 1970, pp. 20-1.

6. Paddock, Williams, Tropical population ecology, in Farnworth, E.G. and F.B. Galley (eds), *Frasile Ecosystems*, Springer Verlag, New York, 1974, p. 46

7. Ziche, J.B. Beharrel and T.T. Hartman, Relative importance of labour input in agricultural development : The Zambia case. *Journal of Rural Development*, 1974, pp. 111-41. According to a recent study, 8 per cent of the country's area is under national parks while another 30 per cent outside these areas is heavily infested with tsetse flies or is seasonally flooded. Vide Wood, A.P., Zambia, in Nag, P. (ed), *Census Mapping Survey*, IGU Commission on Population Geography, Concept Publishing Company, New Delhi, 1984, pp. 232-51.

8. Smith, W., Crisis and Response : Agricultural Development and Zambia's Third National Development Plan, *Geography*, Vol. 66, 1981, pp. 134-6.
9. *Report of the Working Party Appointed to Review the System of Decentralised Administration*, Cabinet Office, Lusaka, May, 1972, p. 99.
10. Registration and development of villages Millner, A.M., Secretary-General to the Government, Paper for discussion at Solwezi on 26 September, 1972.
11. In fact the ward boundaries are supplied by the Local Government Electoral Commission to the Surveyor General who is responsible for preparing Zambian maps.
12. Jolly, Richard, Zambia-Economy, in *Africa: South of the Sahara, 1982-83*, Europa Publication Ltd. 12th ed. pp. 1185-91.

2

GROWTH OF POPULATION AND SETTLEMENTS

ZAMBIA is a landlocked country in south central Africa. Though it is at a considerable distance from the coasts of the Indian and Atlantic Oceans, processes of change have reached this territory. Its human and mineral resources have attracted early trade and commerce from the sea coasts. The activities at the coasts have influenced the population, settlement and the economy of this region. The peopling of this region, the creation of settlements and formation of territories were not only influenced by the external forces mentioned above, but also by local resources, level of technology attained by population groups, inter-tribal conflicts and the socio-political control of land. The study of the growth of population and settlement is divided into five historical phases : (a) first : before 1500 A.D.; (b) second: 1500-1850 A.D.; (c) third: 1850-1890 A.D.; (d) fourth: 1890-1964 A.D.; and (e) fifth: after 1964 A.D.

First Phase : Before A.D. 1500

The records and evidences of the prehistorical period are extremely rare. However, some evidences indicate the pattern of human occupation of space at that time. There were no well defined territories as we understand them today. The spatial nature of human activities indicates that the area was under control of some population groups. During the *Early Stone Age*, as in other parts of Central Africa, there were no permanent settlements. The population groups of no significant identity moved to new places after the environmental resources were exhausted. However, at a later stage the population increased and distinctive population groupings emerged. During the *Middle Stone Age*, the diffusion of settlements took place from the major river valleys and lake basins. The new foci for settlements were the smaller *dambos* and caves.[1] The sphere of human activity became somewhat limited and this made possible more clear regional variation of population groupings. There was prolonged occupation of caves and rock-shelters during the *Late Stone Age*. Water bodies continued to be favoured sites for settlements. Different types of hunting tools were introduced during this age, and hunting-gathering some became the area of influence of these settlements.

Archaeologists have differentiated the *Late Stone Age* with *Early Iron Age* regarding (a) the methods of food production; (b) animal domestication; (c) metallurgical techniques; (d) pottery; (e) construction of houses; and (f) nature of settlements. The above criteria have been used to identify the distinct population groups and settlements during the *Early Iron Age*. Settled life in permanent and semi-permanent villages was for the first time introduced in Zambia. During this age large scale migration with distinct cultural entities took place. Moreover, there was a scope for higher population density due to better farming techniques and due to industries, such as, melting and for forging of iron. This made possible a further shrinking of the spatial nature of the human activity. However, such changes were localised. Permanent or semi-permanent villages with some area associated with them was the main feature of the *Early Iron Age*.

The *Early Iron Age* was replaced by the 'Kalomo Culture' of the *Later Stone Age* (A.D. 800). The fresh migration to this region produced higher population density than before, leading to the segregation of the land according to socio-political grouping of tribes and clans. For the first time the settlements of Zambia were territorially identified. Kingdoms, states and territories were formed, however, their boundaries remained imprecise. There are sufficient evidences to prove that extensive trading contacts were established during this period. The Zambezi Valley not only had trade links with the East African Coast but even with the west Indian Coast.[2] However, the commencement of *Iron Age Culture* did not take place at the same time in all parts of Zambia.

Second Phase : A.D. 1500-1850

During the period A.D. 1500-1750 great migration from *Luba* and *Lunda* kingdoms of *Katanga (Zaire)* took place (Fig 2.1). Many scholars have indicated the then growing population and diminishing resources in those areas which forced peoples to diffuse.[3] As a result,

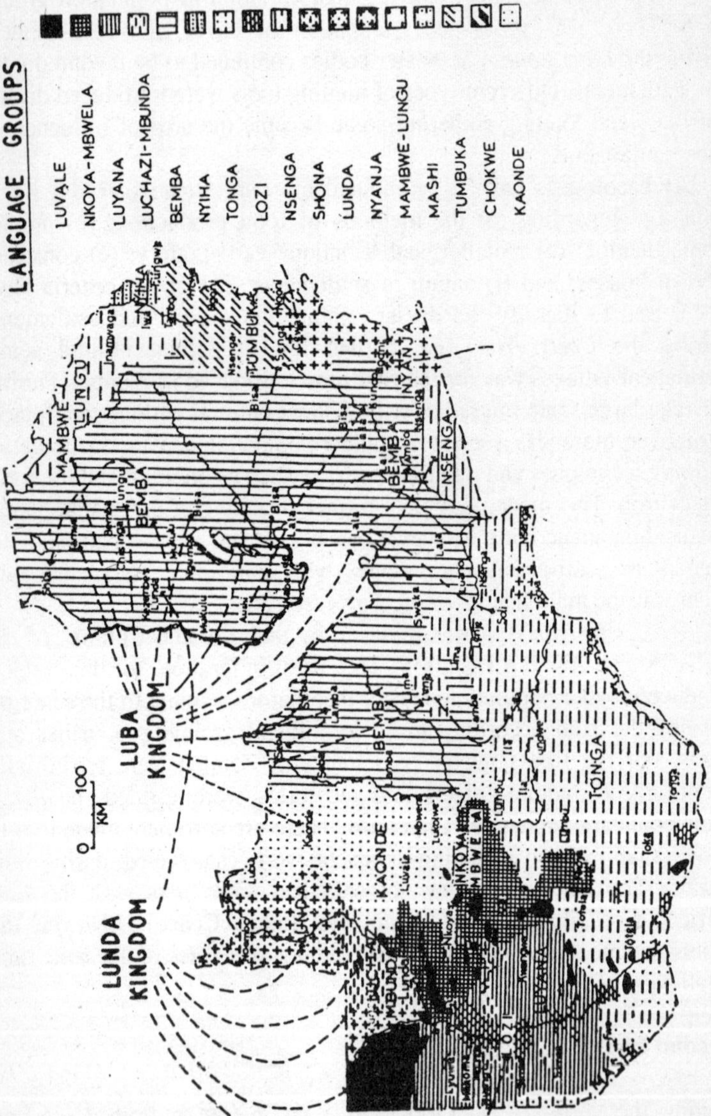

Fig. 2.1: Tribal Settlement

the 'hop-and-jump' pattern of spreading to the areas where best resources were available and the centralised states patterns came into existence which seems to have been inherited from the place of origin, but they were modified according to local conditions.[4] The settlements in the unfavourable areas indicate the weakness in political organization. *Lamba, Ushi* and *Lala* territories in the areas handicapped by nature, are examples of weak political organisation. Permanent villages with stable population provided a base for the development of socio-political nuclei. These nuclei become important settlements in the tribal occupance of space. Subsequently, these socio-political centres became the headquarters of the territory under each tribe. Around A.D. 1750, Zambia was occupied by such tribal territories. The village as a basic unit with vague boundaries was governed by the headman of same tribe and in most cases of the same clan. They controlled the population, settlement, land and resources of the village. In larger territories, sub-chiefs, councillors and the like were appointed. The territories were divided into small manageable units. Following examples will indicate the organisation of settlements during the early pre-colonial period.

In the east of the river *Luapula, Lunda* kingdom of *Kazembe* was established around A.D. 1725. However, the *Lunda* kingdom and chiefdoms in Zambia were under the central control of *Lunda* chief (*Mwata Yamvo*) in *Katanga*. There was close family relationship among the *Lunda* chiefs. Honorary *Lundahood* was granted to the subject chiefs and this made possible for the settlements in the subject areas to be identified with the overall territorial administration of *Lundas*. In *Lunda* politico-territorial organisation, after the conquest, the local chiefs were incorporated as the owners of the land and they continued to rule over their original areas.[5] *Nkuba; Bisa* and *Chibwe* chiefdoms were included in the Lunda hierarchy and a system of indirect rule was practiced. The settlements and their hierarchy were not disturbed. A sense of personal attachment, kin relationships and redistribution of tributes played a vital role in organising the settlements under the *Lunda* supremacy. However, all the *Lunda* territories and the settlements of the present day Zambia, were not associated with the *Lunda* chief *Kazembe*. This was owing to the factor of distance. *Ishinde, Kanongesha* and *Musokantanda* were the other *Lunda* chiefs who established tributary kingdoms in the north-western Zambia. The settlements in these territories were less organised owing to fewer number of settlements, lack of environmental resources and away from the main trade routes. In the same region of Zambia, *Luvale* chiefs (probably arrived from the *Lunda Kingdom* in the seventeenth century) never established a state structure; and even today more Luvale villages are outside the areas of *Luvale* chiefs. They acquired special power by recruiting men from each village recognising their jurisdiction; and they strengthened their local ties through marriage.[6] The bond of kinship played an important role in organising the settlements.

The *Bemba*, most significant *Luba* tribe, migrated to Zambia after A.D. 1600 and they settled in the areas on a high plateau with poor soil, lying between the *Luapula* and *Luangwa* valleys. Several highly organised chieftainships diffused from *Lubemba* (the Bemba heartland near present-day Kasama), who were highly organised. By A.D. 1800, *Bembas Bembas Bembas* 1800 were able to develop as one of the significant territorial system of the pre-colonial Zambia. During the same period, the *Bisa* were able to develop as one of the significant territorial system of the pre-colonial Zambia. During the same period, the *Bisa* tribe also migrated into Zambia and developed similar territorial structures. The element of clan was the most significant factor in organising the *Bemba* and *Bisa* territories. The senior chiefs of both the tribes had only ritual and religious power over these tribal territories and the settlements falling within them. However, there was a marked difference between the settlements in these territories. 'The soil of the *Bemba* plateau are not particularly fertile so villages must frequently shift their sites in search of productive land. Large areas are poorly watered making settlements and the support of a dense population impossible'.[7] Bisa villages have better economic advantages. Their economy is based on relatively on fertile soil, salt marshes and long distance trade. There are other *Luban* territories and settlements in central Zambia, such as, *Lumba, Soli, Lenge, Ushi, Lala* and *Ambo*. Some of these territories had accepted and *Bemba* paramountcy. The whole territorial system was a loose confederacy. Though, *Lubemba* was the religious and ritual capital of this confederation, the individual territories had their own organisation, of settlements.

In the western Zambia, the Luvana kingdom developed out of the central Bulozi flood plain of the upper *Zambezi*. This area was rich in fishing and cattle pasture.[8] Lozi administration is an example of highly-centralised territorial system of the pre-colonial Zambia. This kingdom was divided into small administrative territorial units under induanas was were directly appointed by the Lozi King, Litunga. These functionaries have similar authority regarding land and settlements as that of the chiefs in other parts of Zambia. In Lozi colonisation of the fertile Zambezi valley, the villages appeared to be more man-centred and man-land relationships seems to be much stronger.[9] 'In Bulozi the villages settlement was basic; ... villages or cluster of villages became the fundamental unit of administration and justice'.[10] The seasonal migrations and temporal rule of the Kalolo tribe did not affect the hereditary occupance of land. In the flood plains, the settlements were made on artificial mounds. The isolated settlements were connected by canals. This brought different settlements and territories closer to the centre of the Lozi power. The centralised administration was possible in Lozi kingdom due to rich resources, better soil, external trade and transportation, organisation of space; and these were the reasons that the waves of settlements which once created regional and functional differences could be brought into a single territorial organisation.

In the east, Chewa and Nsenga tribes came and even settled before their chiefs. Chewas had three levels of hierarchy of rulers with the king, Undi, then subordinate rulers of tributary kings and chiefs, and finally headmen at the village level.[11] The different territorial chiefs were of Phiri clan. However, people of other class were assimilated through marriage and were subsequently made chiefs. The population and settlements in the tributary kings' or chiefs' area were independent of central power. Separate hierarchies of settlements developed in each territory. The settlements of other tribes were somewhat integrated in such decentralised set-up.

In Zambia, the traditional village system, as in most part of Africa, was influenced by a particular clan or tribe, which took over a certain territory (mostly nebulous) and emerged as the power elite which then had clean domination over a chief's area.[12] The typical form of the indigenous political organisation is the non-centralised system such as we find in Northern Rhodesia among the Plateau Tonga and the Luvale.[13] The settlements which are not in the fold of centralised territorial and political organisation, the kingship, clan and tribal ties are most stronger. Some of the settlements fall in the independent clan territories. Here the political organisation of settlement is weak. However, these territories are economically, ritually and sentimentally in allegiance with the territorial powers at their neighbourhoods. It is not always felt that these independent or semi-independent territories would like to remain autonomous, but the superior powers have also permitted them to retain such a character.

Though the polity varied from highly centralised administration to indirect rule, yet at the village level the headman who might be head of an extended family system or a man or woman highly placed in society, was recognised throughout Zambia.[14] Pre-colonial history clearly reveals that the external agencies connected with the trade of slave or ivory or cattle has little to do with the holding of land. Whenever the village shifted or diffused there was no change in the village administration of headman who continued to hold their right over land. Any change in the polity at the top hardly affected the village administration or constitution and village always remained as a basic unit.[15]

Third Phase : A.D. 1850–1890

This phase of forty years was full of events and hence it is separated out of the pre-colonial period. The historical processes which were responsible for creating such events started from the 18th century. During this phase Zambia suffered from a fresh threat from south Africa kingdoms. The slave-trade, the scramble for land and mineral resources by the colonial powers missionary activities and long distance trade affected state formation. Such processes, directly or indirectly, have influenced the territorial organisation of settlements. In some cases these processes were combined to modify the territorial control on settlements. However, in other cases, external trade and slave-trade became the economic back-bone of prospering territories. The shifting importance owing to the trading activities reoriented the territorial set-up; and this contributed to the reorganisation of the hierarchy settlements.

The well established Lozi state in the western Zambia was attacked by Kololo people of south African origin. The settlements in the newly formed Kololo kingdom were organised by unifying the Kololo, Lozi and other tribes and by giving subject tribes a chance in the affairs of the kingdom. However, administration was organised by spreading Makololo families in villages as lords of land.[16] The Kololo king had common touch with the people under his rule. This pattern of organisation of settlements extended into adjoining regions in the present day Southern Province of Zambia and in Angola, Bechuanaland and Rhodesia. After Kololo rule was overthrown, their central organisation was weakened and the settlements became independent under separate chiefs. In A.D. 1864, Lozis were again able to regain their paramountcy over the territories and settlements of western Zambia, however, dynastic quarrels for another fourteen years continued to threaten the stability of this kingdom.

The second major attack was of Ngoni people from the south. They raided eastern Zambia and Malawi for food and cattle. Their politico-territorial organisation was based on the creation of age-regiments and assimilation of non-Ngoni tribes. The territorial organisation of settlements was through family and marriage ties and 'segmentation system'. Chiefs would attach their followers to the households of their various wives so that these households would have substantial population. Further, 'the continuous inflow of captives which leads to the constant proliferation of satellite settlements attached to royal households (or royal segment) resulted in these households becoming the centres of powerful territorial chiefdoms'.[17] They captured weaker tribes and forced them to accept their overlordship. The Ngonis have the largest villages of the pre-colonial Zambia.

Zambian settlements were also disturbed by the slave-trade. Portuguese and Swahili people joined hands with the local tribes, such as, Chikundu from Mozambique, Yeke from Tanzania and Mambari from Angola in this transcontinental trade of human resources. Guns and gunpowder became the decisive factor in the tribal wars. The captives were made the victims of slave-trade.[18] Portuguese, Swahilies and their allies were 'responsible for depopulation, knowingly weakening kingdoms such as *Kazembe* (Lunda), and unknowingly causing kingdoms such as *Bemba* to flourish'.[19] On the other hand, the missionaries resisted the flourishing slave-trade. The British missionaries did not have any territorial ambitions of their own but they showed the way to the colonialisation of Zambia by the imperial powers. Missions developed as important settlements in rural Zambia.

This period of pre-colonial Zambia was under the influence of external forces. The hierarchy of settlements and their organisation were disturbed. The development and degeneration of the territories had its roots in slave-trade, guns, raids, tribal wars, ivory and the like. The changes in the political and territorial organisations created fertile grounds for European colonisation. The Europeans arrested some of the processes mentioned above and the present territorial organization of settlement is to some extent the outcome of the conditions prevailing at the end of the pre-colonial era.

Fourth Phase : A.D. 1890–1964

With the turn of the century, a new type of economic activity started in this part of Africa. It was the mineral and natural wealth of Zambia which attracted the colonial powers. Royal character and award of concessions for mineral exploration sowed the seed of colonial territorial interests in central Africa. New types of territories were carved out keeping into consideration of mineral exploration and European settlement. The life line of the territory under the *British South African Company* (BSAC) and *North Charterland Exploration Company* (NCEC) was the railway line running south to north. The territories and settlements serving the colonial interest were along this line-of-rail and around the mining areas. However, in June 1904 proposals were formulated with a view to a final settlement of the questions outstanding between the people of Rhodesia and the BSA Company.[20] Subsequently, B.S.A.C. identified different types of land for lease and sale around Livingstone town. As a policy measure no land on which natives were settled were leased. Farming land was divided into three classes : (a) farms intended mainly for agriculture of about 500 acres, near townships, with good water and suitable or partly suitable for irrigation; (b) farms of from 500 to 3000 acres suitable for general farming, and (c) farms of from 3,000 to 10,000 acres away from towns and railways and only suitable for ranching.[21]

In 1924, the colonial office took over the administration of the territory. The pre-colonial territorial structure was somewhat retained. Barotseland under the Lozi king remained as protectorate. Paramount chiefs, senior chiefs and chiefs of various tribes were recognised. However, the land of the then Northern Rhodesia was divided into two types : (a) Crown Land - For European settlers ;and (b) Reserves - for African population. The crown lands were mostly along the 'line-of-rail' and were earmarked for 'a great influx of European settlers'. The African population was forced to settle in 39 Reserves (138,880 km^2) amounting to 19.2 per cent of the total area. In the early forties, it was felt that the Reserves were getting overpopulated and in 1947 a new category of land was carved out of the Crown Land which was granted to the African.This was the Native Trust Land which, like the Reserves, also came under African customary laws and not for further expatriate development unless it was in the interest of all the races.[22]

This division of land produced three types of territories within a district. However, some districts were exclusively Crown Land. The settlements in the Crown Land were in the form of cities, towns and large farms. These settlements were along both sides of the line-of-rail. Europeans interests were safeguarded and the African was only permitted in the townships meant for them which were of high density and away from the city/town centres. The new government turned its attention to the problems arising from the rapidly developing urban communities, and passed a Township Ordinance in 1922 and Municipal corporations ordinance in 1927. These ordinances must be considered in the light of British colonial policy in the 1920's. The indirect rule was not considered to be appropriate for urban communities.[23] After 1930 A.D., the towns along this line including that of the Copperbelt developed at a faster rate and almost all the social and economic activities of the territory concentrated in the zone along the 'line-of-rail'. The attraction of the urban centres was so strong that even the African population became sizeable in every urban centres. These settlements were free from customary laws. In the Copperbelt, the mine townships existed along side of the municipal township. The twin townships were the notable feature in the mining areas. In total, such corridor development functioned as a divorced settlement system on the Crown Land. Except for the migration of labour, the settlements in the Crown Land and Reserves were hardly interlinked. In the Copperbelt, the Europeans were successful in creating "little englands" - secure island of civilization with in a primitive and underdeveloped country.[24] In other places Europeans made settlements for themselves.[25]

The reserves were under the administration of traditional chiefs of various orders. Chiefs became the apparatus of indirect rule as they were included in local government. Each reserve was ruled by the chief of a particular tribe and the headmen of the villages mostly belong to the same tribe and even the same clan as that of the chief. The density of settlement was reasonable high in comparison to the surrounding areas. This arrangement has adverse effects on the rural settlement fabric of the country which brought about concentration in some areas and vast empty spaces with almost no settlements, though environmental factors were not largely unfavourable for their development.[26] There was virtually no development in the reserves except for a few missions, their schools and clinics, which were of course with a different motive and the government of the day was least concerned with it.[27]

Settlement and farming schemes were planned in the Native Trust Land comprising of 56.3 per cent of Zambia's area and villages were resettled from the crowded Reserves.[28] In these territories, the extension of the settlement fabric originated from the neighbouring reserves. The new settlements were included in the hierarchy of settlements of the reserves. However, the Native Trust Land remained undersettled and can clearly be identified from the reserves nearby. For all practical purposes this land was not encroached by the settlement initiated from the Crown Lands.

The case of Swahili Native Reserve presents an example of settlement and population pattern during this period. Swahili people of East African origin have three reserves in Zambia, one in the east of Ndola city and the other two in northern Zambia. Earlier settlements of Swahilis were at the present site of the National Monument in Ndola City from where they were pushed towards the east in the Ndola Rural district by the colonial administration with the establishment of Ndola town. The Swahili villages are in the north of the reserve and can be recognised by their Arabic names (Fig. 2.2). The chief's headquarters shifted to the present site in A.D. 1931.

Prior to 1945 only the northern area was populated. After releasing more lands to the traditional authority, i.e. the chief, the reserve was expanded to the present extent. The southern portion was settled after 1945 and is very sparsely population. The settlement fabric, similar to other places, starts from the headwaters of streams and further extends in the direction of the flow. The old road leading to Copperbelt passes through the southern part of the area. Owing to unfavourable conditions this part could not be developed. However, the pressure of land in the reserve prior to the creation of Native Trust Lands was high. The process of colonization is from north to south. The Munkulunge area in the middle of this reserve is better linked with the west.

In 1964 the chief was promoted to Senior Chief and no more villages were created. The old villages in the densely settled area in the north shifted to south but the village structure remained the same. This reserve, apart from Swahili population, consists of people of Lamba, Lala and Swaka tribes. At present there about 190 villages in the reserve. Swahilis are Muslims but there is a sizable Christian population in this territorial unit, even in the chief's headquarters.

The Crown Lands, Reserves and Native Trust Lands were included in the district framework under the colonial administration. The 43 districts were organised into seven provinces and the protectorate of Barotseland. The provincial headquarters towns, even away from the line-of-rail, such as, Fort Rosebery, Fort Jameson, Kasama and Solwezi, gained some importance in the hierarchy of settlements. The district headquarters towns were small with some essential administrative establishments. Though these centres were connected by roads, they failed to attract any economic activity. They have a long history of evolution, desertion and rejuvenation. Some centres had changed their sites several times, while others failed in the competition with a better site near the line-of-rail or other economic viable points. The chiefs' headquarters appear to be more responsible in organising the settlements within the territorial framework. They clearly reflect the associated socio-political and territorial character. In due course, these settlements were able to add establishments, such as, schools, clinics and post offices. In the areas where missionaries were active, the above mentioned settlements faced competition from the nearby missions.

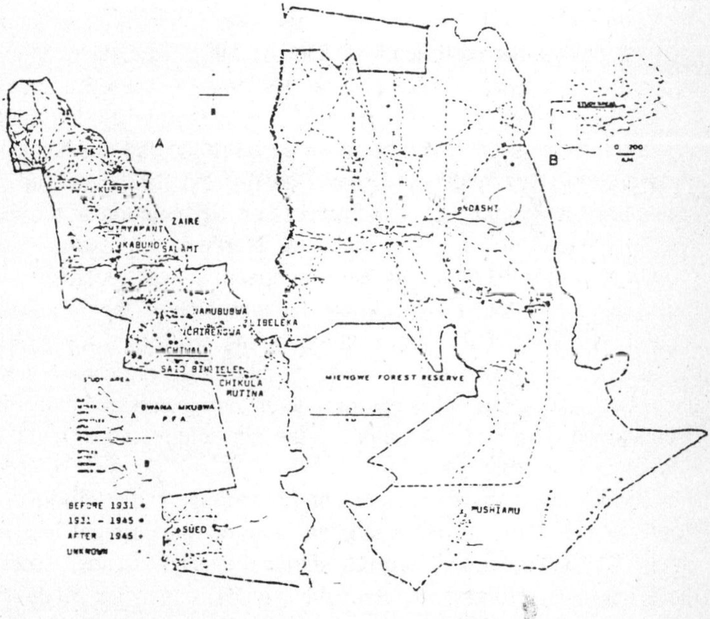

Fig. 2.2: Evolution of Settlements in Swahili Reserve Area

Missions developed as a centre of religious, social and transportational services in Reserves and Trust Lands. The neighbourhood or group of villages were the most common pattern of occupation of the areas other than Crown Lands. Such groupings of villages were not administratively recognized, but the 'neighbourhood centres' proved to be significant in the hierarchy of settlements, placing in between the chiefs' headquarters settlements and villages. The village, under a headman, was recognised as a population and settlement unit. Their sites were liable to change after the exhaustion of resources. Neither their boundaries were recognised nor the fields were demarcated. The large villages were divided into hamlets, homesteads and farmsteads.

Fifth Phase : After A.D. 1964

Independence brought certain changes in favour of Africans. Some of the measures have yet to show their effects as the legacy of the colonial period cannot disappear within the short span of the post-independence period. On one hand the colonial territorial structure is retained with some modifications. On the other hand, there is an attempt to the economic reorganise the settlements. Table 2.1 indicates the different order of chiefs' territories in the provinces of Zambia. Migration to the urban areas has been decontrolled and this has lead to mass-migration from the settlements away from the line-of-rail. The chiefs have less control over the process of depopulation of the settlements of their territories. In Luapula, Northern and North-western provinces, a negative growth-rate of population was recorded during the period 1963-69 (1969 census). Government of the Republic of Zambia is aware of the depopulation of the territories in the distant provinces. Attempts have been made to stabilise the population in these territories. Sufficient infrastructure, loan and technical advice have been extended in order to improve the agriculture in particular and rural areas in general.

Certain steps have been taken regarding land reforms. The Reserves and Native Trust Lands are merged and brought under the chiefs. The Crown Lands are redesignated as State Lands. However, the Europeans settlers still retain the paper occupancies of the farm settlements in the favoured areas of State Lands. Some farms are bought by the Africans. Settlement schemes have also been initiated on the reclaimed farms. The proliferation of squatter population and settlements in cities, towns and farms have become a notable feature along the line-of-rail. City, municipal and township councils are being appointed for the management and development of the urban settlements. At the national level, the Department of Town and Country Planning, National Housing Authority and consulting organisations are engaged in urban development. Urban territories are created to tackle the associated problems.

Table 2.1 : Type of Chiefs' Territories in Zambia

Provinces	*Paramount*	*Senior Chiefs*	*Chiefs*
Copperbelt	—	3	12
Central	—	4	26
Eastern	2	3	45
Luapula	—	8	30
Lusaka	—	2	5
Northern	1	8	39
North-Western	—	7	26
Southern	—	—	40
Western	Litunga (King)	—	11
Total	3+1	35	234

Source : General list of Chiefs, 1973

In the rural sphere, and additional territorial developmental infrastructure was impressed which is based on Provincial Development Committees, District Development Committees, Ward Development Committees and Villages Productivity Committees. "The purpose of these committees is to improve organisation for economic development at the people's level. Improved organisation will lead to the creation of decision-making centres in the rural areas, and therefore, provide further administrative decentralisation".[29] These committees had administrative, social, economic and political goals, maintaining family as a vital socio-economic unit. The chiefs' territories are reorganised into 'wards' (development units). In some cases two or three wards constitute a chief's territory. Further, the villages were reorganised into population and settlement groups by forming 'village productivity committees' (VPC). For example, in Mwinilunga district, 604 village in the 9 chiefs territories (also wards) were organised into 105 VPCs (Table 2.2). In the 7 districts of the Northern Provinces, the 48 chief's territories were reorganised into 158 wards, and 4,150 villages into

2,551 VPCs (estimated in 1972). In the districts where the ward boundaries have superimposed on the chiefs' territories, the territorial organisation of settlements in the new set-up is some what feasible; otherwise, there is a scope for confusion in the mind of the rural population about the advantages of the reorganisation of settlements. Ward centres and V.P.Cs centres are yet to compete with the existing chiefs' headquarters settlements, missions and agricultural camps.[30] The organisation of rural areas through V.P.Cs is no longer persued. However, the tribe as a politically and culturally autonomous unit has ceased to function, many of its members are "detraditionalised", but, tribal identity and a shared background may still form for appeals of support.[31]

Table 2.2 : Ward, VPC and Villages in Mwinilunga District

Ward	*Village Productivity Committees*	*Villages*
Senior Chief Sailunga	15	113
Chief Kanyama	9	64
Chief Ntambu	4	46
Chief Kakoma	9	84
Senior Chief Kanongesha	16	76
Chief Chibwika	12	65
Chief Mwinimilamba	8	47
Chief Nyakaseya	19	40
Chief Ikelenga	13	69
Total	105	604

Source : Rural Council, Mwinilunga District.

Recapitulation

The evolution of settlements and territories were not always combined into a single historical or cultural process. There are examples where settlements have evolved without any territorial significance. In due course, these settlements were incorporated within the territorial framework of other settlements. The former settlements are placed in the lower ranges in the hierarchy of settlements. Some of these settlements could retain their importance owning to social, economic and transportational services. The examples of these settlements are the missions, agricultural camps, (NAMBoard) depots and the like. On the other hand, the settlements of territorial importance appeared since the pre-colonial period. The hierarchy of territories and affiliated hierarchy of settlements, which appears today, were conclusive in the periods following to the one mentioned earlier. This arrangement was, however, disturbed when a new type of colonial economic activity started in this part of Africa. The existing territories were combined to form a district and a new arrangement of a territories and settlements was imposed. The settlements were reorganised in this arrangement. Some of the territories specialised in urban and mining activities, while other territories were left to the chiefs for administration and development. The present divorced nature of settlements has come out of this arrangement. The independent government has taken sincere steps to develop the territories away from the line-of-rail. Additional arrangement is being made by organising the settlements in the hierarchy of territorial committees. This attempt aims at the creation of decision-making centres at various levels. The people's participation in the new set-up was to improve the organisation of settlements at various levels.[32]

REFERENCES

1. Phillipson, D.W., *National Monuments of Zambia*, Zambia Information Services, Lusaka, 1972, pp. 9-16.
2. Nag, P., Asian Settlement in Zambia, *Africa Quarterly*, Indian Centre for Africa, Vol. XVIII, No. 4, April 1979, pp. 59-77.
3. Langworthy, H.W., *Zambia Before 1890*, Longmans, London, 1972, p. 21.
4. Nag, P., Basis of Zambian Settlements, *African Quarterly*, Indian Centre for Africa, Vol. XVII, No. 1, 1977, pp. 59-76.
5. Langworthy, *op. cit.*, pp. 38-40.
6. Roberts, Andrew, The Age of Tradition (A.D. 1500 to 1850), in Fagan, B.M. (ed.), *A Short History of Zambia*, Oxford.
7. Langworthy, *op. cit.*, p. 43.
8. Zambia Information Services, *History : About Zambia*, No. 6, Lusaka.
9. Nag, *op. cit.*, 1977, p. 61-2.
10. Mainga, Mutumba, *Bulozi Under the Luyana Kings : Political Evolution and State Formation in Pre-colonial Zambia*, Longman, London, 1973, p. 36.
11. Langworthy, *op. cit.*, p. 31.
12. Nag, *op. cit.*, 1977, p. 65.
13. Apthorpe, R. (ed.), *From Tribal Rule to Modern Government*, Rhodes Livingstone's Institute, 1966, p. vii.
14. Gluckman has characterised the Central Africa Village as a 'discrete group of people who reside in usually adjacent huts, who recognise allegiance to a headman and who have a corporate identity against similar groups', and 'are formed

crucially by common allegiance to the headman. The kinship links between the headman and his followers may vary from tribe to tribe, or within tribe, and within a single village there may be different kinds of kinsmen, but the headman is always regarded as the senior kinsman'. Quoted from Long, Norman, *Social Change and the Individual : A Study of the Social and Religious Responses to Innovation in a Zambian Rural Community*, Manchester University Press for the Institute for Social Research, 1968, p. 90. For changing settlement pattern, vide ch. v, 99-131.

15. Nag, p., Zambia : A Geographical Analysis of Settlement Planning, Ph.D. Thesis (unpublished), Banaras Hindu University, Varanasi, 1976, Chapter I.
16. Mainga, *op. cit.*, pp. 35-50
17. Omer-Copper, J., *The Mfecane*, workshop on the Teaching of Central and East African History, August 23-31, 1970, Lusaka (unpublished). Langworthy, *op. cit.*, pp. 92-93. For Ngoni settlements their history, political-structure land tenure, village structure and form and migrant labour vide Cowie, William James, Changing Settlement Systems and Economic Development, unpublished Ph.D.Thesis, University of London, 1982.
18. For the establishment of Estado da India see Haeriron, J.B., The Portuguese, in A.L. Basham (ed.), *A Cultural History of India*, Clarendon Press, Oxford, 1975, pp. 337-47.
19. Nag, *op. cit.* 1977, p. 63
20. "The Conference", June 9th, 1904, Argus Printing and Publishing Co.Ltd., 1904 (Reprinted from the Rhodesia Herald). See also Tordoff, Williams, Rural administration, in William Tordoff (Ed), *Administration in Zambia*, Manchester University Press, and University of Wisconsin Press, 1980, 185-212.
21. British South African Company (BSAC), Information as to the conditions on which land will be sold or leased to bona fide settlers in North-Western Rhodesia together with Notes on North-Western Rodhesia as a Farming Country, London, 1906, Raymer, A.C., *Should Chartered Administration be Abolished? - A Few Facts, Figures and Observations*, Bulawayo, March 2, 1914 (pamphlet, 16 p.).
22. Siddle, D.J., Colonial land rights, in Davies, D.H. (ed.), *Zambia in Maps*, University of London Press Ltd., 1971, p. 48.
23. Powdermaker, Hortense, *Copper Town : Changing Africa*, Greenwood Press, Publishers, West Point, Connecticut, 1962. (ch. 4 : The coming of first European, 52-65).
24. Kay, George, *A Social Geography of Zambia*, University of London Press Ltd., 1967, p. 29.
25. Rotberg, Robert I., *Black Heart : Gore-Browne and the Politics of Multi-racial Zambia*, University of California Press, Berkeleyl Los Angeles, London, 1977, 94-130 (ch. IV : The Creation of Shiwa Ngandu)
26. Jauhari, A.S. and P. Nag, Rural development in an underpopulated developing country of Africa : Zambia, in Singh, R.L. *et al.* (eds.), *Geographic Dimensions of Rural Settlements*, The National Geographical Society of India, Varanasi, 1976, pp. 1248-61.
27. Makintosh, I.M., *Some Pioneer Missions of Northern Rhodesia Nyasaland*, in The occasional papers of the Rhodesia - Livingstone's Museum No. 1—16, Manchester University Press for the Institute for African Studies, 1974, 249-96.

Also Hellen, J.A., *Rural Economic Development in Zambia 1890-1964*, Wilforum Verlag, Munchen, 1968.

28. Kay, G., Land apportionment in Northern Rhodesia. *The Northern Rhodesia Journal*, V. IV, 1959, p. 39.
29. Ministry of Development Planning and National Guidance, *Second National Development Plan*, Lusaka, December 1971, p. 34.
30. For similar study on Kasama District of Northern Province see Bratton, Michael, The social context of political penetration :village and ward committees in Kasama District, in Tordoff (ed.), *op. cit.*, 1980, 213-39.
31. Pettman, Jan, *Zambia - Security and Conflict*, Julian Friedmann Publishers Ltd . London, 1974, pp. 87-8.
32. Nag, P., Territorial Organisation of Zambian settlements, in T. Tanioka (ed.) *Historical Geography*, Konkon-Shoin Publishing Company, Tokyo, 1982, pp. 166-71

3

SPATIAL ANALYSIS OF POPULATION

FROM the previous chapter it is evident that different socio-economic and colonial factors have been responsible for the present distribution of population. In some places, their role can be noticed clearly in the population distribution pattern. For example, the colonial policy for development has been so prominent that the old line-of-rail still attracts population from all over the country. The new Tan-Zam rail-line has been effective in checking this pattern upto a certain extent. For the first time the population in urban centres of the Northern Province have recorded an annual growth rate of about 22 per cent.

Government Republic of Zambia has taken certain steps in order to redistribute population and to check excessive migration to urban centres.[1] After independence, the exodus has been even greater, which has not only overcrowded the large cities along the line, but has resulted in depopulation in scantily populated areas. The shifting of population to the Copperbelt and Lusaka has taken place in response to the expanding employment opportunities which exist there. In addition to this, a large number of families have joined the bread-earners in these urban centres due to improved housing conditions. The shifting of population to urban areas in this fashion, coupled with an unstable rural population has had undesirable consequences. In some of the cities like Lusaka and Kitwe, squatter population constitutes a sizable portion of the urban population. Simultaneously, rural areas have been deprived of educated and enterprising young people. In most of the projects for rural development, the government has not been able to find a sizable population base. In large areas, the government has provided the required infrastructure, which remains underused. Probably, redistribution of the urban population is the only answer to Zambia's problem of imbalance in rural and urban population distribution.

Growth and Distribution of Population

Zambia's population of 5,679,808 persons (1980) is distributed over 743,900 km² (290,586 sq. miles) having different densities of population and size of settlements. The average density of population is on 7.5 persons per km² (Table 3.1) The distribution must be planned to do away with the extremes in population densities. In 1969, the districts along the old line-of-rail have a population density of 13.6 persons per km². The spatial nature of Zambian population is evinced from Fig. 3.1. This line-of-rail which arranged the matrix of such nature has high density, positive growth rate and population change, high percentage of urban population, less population born in the same district, high potential for in-migration and inter-district migration. The areas elsewhere have reverse tendencies.

In the intercensal period of 1963-69, the average annual growth rate was 2.5 per cent which shot upto 3.1 per cent in the period 1969-80. During the latter period (11 years), there has been an addition of forty per cent population. Though the 1980 census data is not yet wholly available, it can be estimated that the sudden increase is not only due to natural increase, neither due to massive in-migration from neighbouring countries, but due to continuous decline in the death rate. If we consider the growth of population by province, we will find that the Copperbelt, Lusaka Central and Southern provinces contribute to about 55 per cent of the population, and the same provinces have high percentage increase during 1969-80 (Table 3.1).

It is apparent that the increase of population in urban centres in the province along the old line-of-rail is high but less than the other provinces, such as Eastern, Luapula, Northern, North-Western and Western (Fig. 3.2). This is due to the developmental activities in the urban centres in these provinces that has attracted the additional population which for various socio-economic reasons could not go to the urban centres along the old line-of-rail. The case of Northern province has been relatively more advantageous. Here, the new Tan-Zam railway line has been responsible for developmental activities in the successive national development plans. The increase in urban population is not mainly due to massive rural-urban migration, but for the identification of a large number of new towns in 1980 census as well. In the whole country, 33 new towns were identified which contributed to 4.57 per cent of the urban population. Only in Southern Province, the 13 new towns have added a population of 38,823 which about 21 per cent of the urban population of this province (Figs. 6.2&6.3).

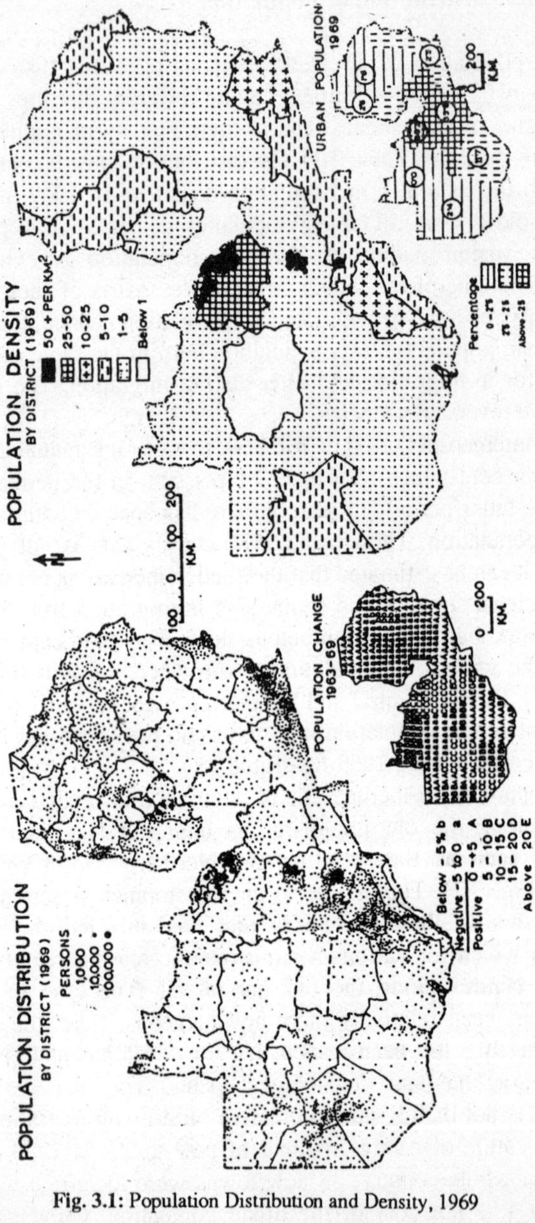

Fig. 3.1: Population Distribution and Density, 1969

Table 3.1 : Growth and Distribution of Zambian Population, 1963-80.

Province	*Percentage of Population*			*Average Annual Growth Rates %*		*Percentage Increase 1969-80*	*Density Persons sq km*	
	1963	*1969*	*1980*	*1963-69*	*1969-80*		*1969*	*1980*
Central	8.9	8.8	9.0	2.5	3.2	43.27	4.3	5.4
Copperbelt	15.6	20.1	22.1	7.0	3.8	52.99	26.1	39.9
Eastern	13.8	12.6	11.5	1.0	2.2	28.82	7.4	9.4
Luapula	10.2	8.3	7.4	–1.0	2.0	23.00	6.6	8.3
Lusaka	5.6	8.7	12.2	10.4	6.2	96.02	16.2	31.7
Northern	16.2	13.5	11.9	–0.6	1.9	24.36	1.8	2.4
North-western	6.0	5.7	5.4	1.6	2.4	30.18	3.7	4.6
Southern	13.3	12.2	11.9	1.0	2.7	38.39	5.8	7.9
Western	10.4	10.1	8.6	2.1	1.5	19.00	3.3	3.9
Zambia	100.0	100.0	100.0	2.6	3.0	40.00	5.1	7.5

Source : 1963, 1969 and 1980 Censuses.

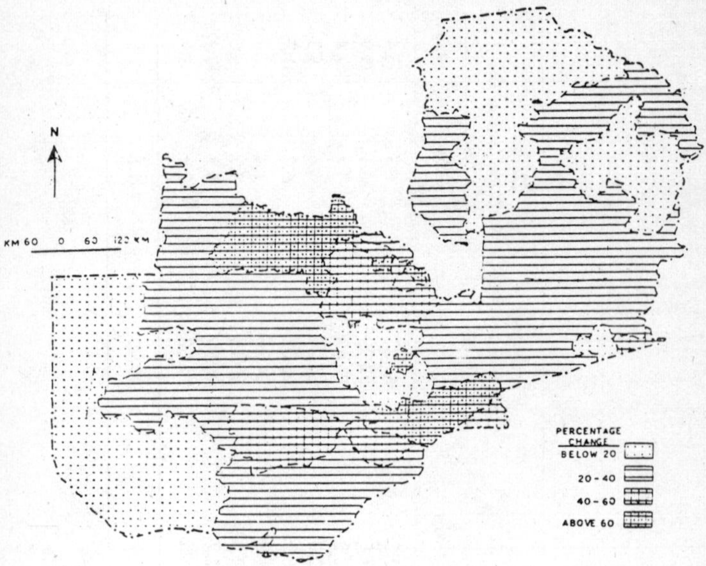

Fig. 3.2: Population Growth, 1969-80

In general the urban population had been increasing at a rate of 6.7 per cent per year, during the intercensal period of 1969-80. This is a reduction from the earlier intercensal period of 1963-69 when the figure was 8.9 per cent. On the other hand, the growth rate of rural population has shown a reverse trend. The rate has increased from 0.5 to 1.1 per cent in the successive intercensal period which indicates a tendency towards stabilizing of rural population. The percentage of urban population has increased from 20.5 in 1963, 29.4 in 1969 and 43.00 in 1980, thereby becoming one of the most urbanised country of Africa (Table 3.2).

Age and Sex Ratio

Zambia is an interesting case for the study of the role of women in the socio-economic setting of the country. Almost its entire African population is matrilineal. A rural household is considered to be a female institution in most of the regions. Women's control over land, property and lineage places them in an important position in the society. They play a crucial role among other things, in decision-making process relating to migration although it is men who migrate in a larger number. Another interesting point is that females are more numerous than males. There are 962 males per 1,000 females on an average. The migration of males to urban areas has resulted in numerical dominance of the females in rural areas and of males in urban areas. This imbalanced distribution of male and female populations has affected the household structure in particular and the Zambian social set-up in general.[2]

Zambian large urban areas (L U A) consist of the seven urban districts of the Copperbelt Province and the Kabwe, Livingstone and Lusaka urban district which are along the old line-of-rail. This urban corridor plays a significant role in male/female population distribution in Zambia (Fig. 3.3)

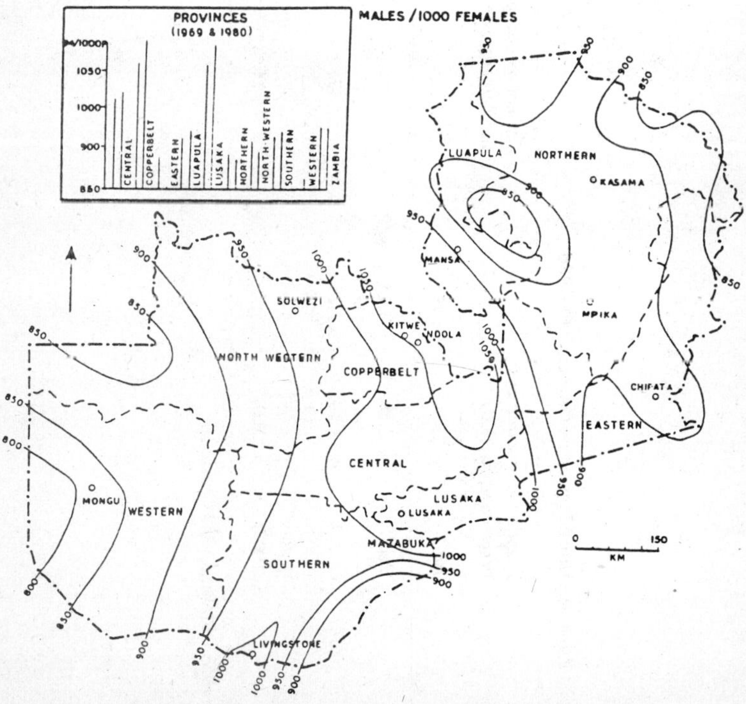

Fig. 3.3: Sex Ratio

Table 3.2 : Rural and Urban Population Growth, 1963-1980

Area	*Population absolute and percentage (in '000)*			*Population change Absolute and Percentage (in '000)*		*Average Annual Growth Rate*	
	1963	*1969*	*1980*	*1963-69*	*1969-80*	*1963-69*	*1969-80*
Rural	2,775	2,864	3,403	89	539	0.6	1.6
	79.5	70.6	60.1	3.24	17.17		
Urban	715	1,192	2,259	478	1,067	8.9	6.0
	20.5	29.4	39.9	66.67	89.45		
Total	3,490	4,057	5,662	567	1,605	2.5	3.1
	100.0	100.0	100.0	16.24	39.56		

Source : 1963, 1969 and 1980 Censuses.

Another most striking feature of Zambia's population is its youthfulness. During the period 1969-80 the ratio of youth (under 15 years) has increased and now about half of its population is young. Among males 50.7 per cent population is below 15 years. On the other hand, the ratio of population in the age group of 15-44 and 45-64 has decreased (Table 3.3). However, in the old age group (65 and above) the percentage has again increased. There can be several reasons for this pattern, such as understatement and overstatement of ages, out-migration of adults and high natural mortality. The provincial differences are due to fertility and migration patterns. For example, in Copperbelt and Lusaka provinces, the ratio of population over 65 years of age is minimum, indicating return migration to other provinces. The age structure implies that young population entering the labour market will increase continuously for atleast next two decades. On the other hand, the old population will also multiply faster. Both the trends will create certain socio-economic problems for which Zambian planners will have to be ready in order to meet the challenges.

Table 3.3 : Age Group and Sex, 1969 and 1980

Age group	*Total*		*Male*		*Female*	
	1969	*1980*	*1969*	*1980*	*1969*	*1980*
Under 15	46.4	49.8	47.5	50.7	45.6	48.7
15 - 44	40.5	38.3	37.9	36.3	42.9	40.0
45 - 64	10.8	9.1	12.1	9.6	9.5	8.7
65 and above	2.3	2.8	2.5	3.3	2.0	2.6

Source : 1969 and 1980 Censuses

In 1963, Zambia had 975 males for every 1,000 females. In towns and in European farming areas, there were 1,790 and 1,620 males per 1,000 females respectively, as compared with only 810 males to 1,000 females in African rural areas. It is clear that far more men than women migrate from rural areas.[3] In 1969, the overall sex ratio was 960 to 1,000 females while in urban areas there were only 895 males to 1,000 females. Thirty one out of forty-four district had more females than males and these districts were rural in nature. During the period 1963-69, there was a considerable improvement in this regard. Furthermore, it has been observed that "the fact that no great difference appears between the number of each sex who claimed to have migrated supports the trends towards normalisation of the sex ratio which appears in the study of total intercensal changes.[4] The situation has not changed much at the time of the 1980 census. There has been a decline in the number of males per 1,000 females in the Eastern, Northern and North-Western provinces. The sex ratio was still favourable to male along the old line-of-rail, where the male surplus was the result of sex selective immigration from other areas of the country (Census 1980). However, it is obvious from Table 3.4 that during the period 1969-80 the process of normalisation of the sex ratio has been effective in all sections of the Zambian society, especially in large urban areas. In Lusaka and Copperbelt provinces, there has been an increase of 100 and 55 per cent of females population respectively. However, the increase of female population during this period has been less than its counterpart

Literacy and Educational Levels

In Zambia persons aged 15 years and over who did not have any schooling are not considered as literate. The percentage of literates increased from 51.4 in 1969 to 63.8 per cent in 1980. During the same period, percentage of population having completed lower primary education increased from 26.2 to 53. The literacy is reasonably high in comparison to other developing countries. This achievement is due to Government's efforts in spreading education throughout the country.

Table 3.4 : Sex Ratio in Urban Areas, 1969 and 1980

Large Urban Districts	*Males per 1,000 females in*	
	1969	*1980*
Chilalbombwe	1,101	1,009
Chingola	1,091	1,008
Kabwe	1,098	1,042
Kalulushi	1,081	1,051
Kitwe	1,114	1,071
Livingstone	1,163	1,058
Luanshya	1,075	1,081
Lusaka	1,103	1,055
Mufulira	1,076	1,057
Ndola	1,120	1,057
Total Urban	1,113	1,061
Total Rural	895	916
Total Zambia	960	962

Source : Census of Zambia, 1969 and 1980.

Now secondary and primary schools are to be found even in deep interior area and they are well managed. During the period 1969-80 there was an increase of 54.3 per cent of population attending primary schools, but their percentage to population over 5 years actually reduced from 27.6 to 24.1 (Table 3.5). While in terms of percentage, there has been a substantial increase in secondary and higher education, particularly among the males. In actual numbers the attendance in secondary school rose from 56,284 to 107,961 (91.8%) and in higher institutions from 929 to 10,143 (over 10 times). The school attendance in the age group of 7-14 is over 60 per cent for both the sexes in Copperbelt and Lusaka provinces. But in the higher age groups this percentage has gone down sharply particularly in these two provinces.

Composition of Households

A household in Zambia is defined as a group of people who normally live and eat together. The average African household size was 4.7 persons in 1969 and 5.0 in 1980. In the provinces along the old line-or-rail, the size is either equal or more than this average; while, in the province which have been suffering from out-migration have less number of persons. In 1969 this average varied from 3.5 in Kabompo district in North-Western Province to 6.0 in Mufulira district in Copperbelt Province.

Table 3.5 : Educational Levels (5 years and Above), 1969 & 1980

(Percentage)

Educational Level	*Male*		*Female*		*Total*	
	1969	*1980*	*1969*	*1980*	*1969*	*1980*
No Schooling	41.2	35.4	59.2	48.8	50.4	42.3
Lower Primary	30.1	24.4	25.2	23.9	27.6	24.1
Upper Primary	19.6	24.6	10.2	19.4	14.7	22.0
Junior Secondary	4.2	9.3	1.6	5.1	2.9	7.1
Senior Secondary	2.2	4.3	1.0	1.4	1.6	2.8
Higher Education	0.4	0.3	0.2	0.1	0.3	0.2
Not stated	2.3	1.7	2.8	1.3	2.5	1.5
Total	100.0	100.0	100.0	100.0	100.0	100.0
	1,619,698	2,262,213	1,686,249	2,379,561	3,305,947	4,641,774

Source : C.S.O., Lusaka.

According to the 1969 Census, in the households with male heads, there was on an average 0.88 wife, 2.10 sons and/or daughters, 0.03 parents, 0.79 other relatives and 0.13 unrelated persons. On the other hand, households with female head have 1.49 sons and/or daughters, 0.03 parents, 0.78 other relatives and 0.12 unrelated persons. In 1969 about one quarter (23.84%) of the Zambian households were with female heads. The size of these households were small (3.6 persons) in comparison to the households headed by males. This is also apparent from the number of persons staying in both the types of households. One of the reason of less number of persons in female headed household is the absence of the male counterpart, who is likely to be employed along the line-of-rail. However, there is a reasonable number of males (8.58%) having an average of 2.65 persons per household but without wives (Table 3.6). The household size multiplies with the

Table 3.6 : African Households Classified by Sex Head, No. of Wife Present (Male Heads) and Size

Male Head	*Total No. of persons*	*Total No. of households*	*Household size*
No wife	342,867	129,307	2.65
1 wife	2,554,746	481,832	5.30
2 wives	304,091	35,763	8.50
3 wives	50,838	4,127	12.32
4 wives	11,856	727	16.32
5 wives	4,468	202	22.12
Total	3,269,042	6,51,994	5.01
Female head	727,955	204,118	3.57
Grand Total	3,996,997	856,112	4.67

Source : Census of Population and Housing, 1969, First Report

increasing number of wives, for example, a household with 3 or 5 wives will have an average of 12.32 or 22.12 persons, respectively. From Table 3.7 it can be observed that on one hand the household size has increased, while on the other hand, the ratio of male household heads has decreased everywhere except Northern Province. In Western Province the decrease of households with males as head is substantial. All the four provinces lying along the old line-of-rail have larger size of households. The comparison of 1969 and 1980 data reveals that there has been an overall increase of large size households (more than

4 persons) headed either by males or females. The percentage of households having 2-3 persons have reduced substantially during this period (Table 3.8). Further, in a society such as Zambia, with a pronounced tendency towards monogamy, the different propensities of men and women to take part in internal migration means that the actual number of family units are fewer than potential number.[5] The 1980 census has not yet brought out the data related to the socio-economic conditions. From the improved sex ratio especially in urban areas it is apparent that the urban households are becoming more complete and larger in size. The migration of males and females has contributed in shaping the Zambian households, which has been discussed here in detail.

Marital Status

The Zambian censuses of 1969 and 1980 provide data for both the sexes about marital status : (a) never married, (b) married, (c) divorced/separated, and (d) widowed. This information is available for different age groups starting from 15 years. In 1969 about 69.5 per cent

Table 3.7 : Average Size of and Sex of Household Head, 1969 and 1980

Province	1969 Household Size	1969 Household head % Male	1969 Household head % Female	1980 Household Size	1980 Household head % Male	1980 Household head % Female
Central	4.7	80.2	19.8	5.7	78.4	21.6
Copperbelt	5.6	90.4	9.6	5.7	85.8	14.2
Eastern	4.3	6.4	36.0	4.3	62.4	37.6
Luapula	4.0	66.0	34.0	4.2	64.2	35.8
Lusaka	4.7	88.2	11.8	5.1	79.2	20.8
Northern	4.5	61.4	38.6	4.8	63.1	36.9
North-Western	4.1	75.7	24.3	4.6	69.0	31.0
Southern	5.3	82.9	17.1	5.8	74.9	25.1
Western	4.4	73.9	26.1	4.3	64.0	36.0
Zambia	4.7	76.2	23.8	5.0	72.3	27.7

Source : C.S.O. Lusaka.

males and 86 per cent females; and in 1980 about 63.5 males and 79.4 per cent females were married. The ratio of married males and females have declined in the age group below 30 years (Table 3.9). While the proportion of 'never married' has increased in all the age groups and in both the sexes. The ratio of 'divorced' or 'separated' is higher regarding female population however this ratio is also decreasing in all the age groups. In the age group of about 40 years the ratio of widowed females is high. Table 3.9 also indicates that most of the females marry before attaining the age of 25 years. The proportion widowed and divorced increase for both sexes with age. If the figures for both the sexes and for divorced and widowed are compared, particularly when females are more in number, we will find that there is a tendency of remarriage of males in all the age groups, but only in reproductive age group for females.

Table 3.8 : Percentage Distribution, Household Size by Sex, 1969-80

Number of household Members	*1969*		*1980*	
	Male	*Female*	*Male*	*Female*
1	9.2	21.7	10.9	20.4
2–3	27.2	36.1	22.9	28.7
4–6	36.8	31.1	33.4	32.7
7 and above	26.8	11.1	32.8	18.2

Source : C.S.O., Lusaka

The proportion of unmarried males and females are higher in urban areas. There has been some influence of schooling on the marriage patterns. School attendance may account for the relatively low proportions of never married among the rural youngsters. Among the females the proportions of currently married in each age group except 15-19 age group are higher in the urban areas than in the country side.[6] The ratio of divorced or widowed is higher in rural areas than in urban areas where marriage is more stable. However, as mentioned earlier males remarry more rapidly than their counterparts.

The mean age of marriage and age at first child birth are important indicators of the socio-economic condition and traditional customs. The average age for first marriage is 18.3 years. In Central, Copperbelt, Luapula and Northern provinces this age is even less. But in general in the urban areas the age of marriage is less than rural areas and a similar pattern has been observed regarding the age at the first child birth. In the Western Province the age of marriage and first birth are higher than the other parts of Zambia (Table 3.10).

Table 3.9 : Marital Status of Adult Population, 1969-1980

Age group	*Year*	*Never Married*		*Married*		*Divorced/Separated*		*Widowed*	
		m	*f*	*m*	*f*	*m*	*f*	*m*	*f*
15-19	1969	97.3	58.4	2.3	37.7	0.3	3.7	1.0	0.2
	1980	98.0	68.3	1.9	29.5	0.1	2.0	—	0.2
20-24	1969	63.8	9.4	33.7	81.4	2.3	8.5	0.2	0.7
	1980	69.2	19.6	29.8	73.4	1.0	6.5	0.1	0.6
25-29	1969	21.6	3.6	73.5	86.8	4.3	8.5	0.6	1.1
	1980	27.1	7.9	70.2	82.5	2.5	8.5	0.2	1.1
30-34	1969	8.4	2.1	85.7	86.9	5.3	8.9	0.6	2.1
	1980	10.3	4.4	86.1	85.0	3.3	8.6	0.3	2.0
35-39	1969	5.2	1.8	88.8	85.3	5.3	9.3	0.8	3.6
	1980	6.1	3.3	90.1	84.6	3.5	8.8	0.5	3.3
40-44	1969	3.6	1.9	90.2	80.7	5.2	10.6	1.0	6.8
	1980	4.5	3.2	91.4	81.6	3.6	9.5	0.6	3.7
45-49	1969	2.9	2.1	90.6	74.3	5.1	11.9	1.4	1.7
	1980	3.5	3.3	92.2	77.4	3.6	10.7	0.8	8.7
50-54	1969	2.4	2.7	89.7	61.6	5.6	14.5	2.3	21.2
	1980	2.9	3.7	92.2	69.4	3.8	11.1	1.1	14.7
55 and above	1969	2.8	4.4	86.4	38.6	6.1	16.5	4.7	40.5
	1980	3.3	6.3	88.5	46.5	4.9	14.7	3.3	32.56

Note: Data for 1969 is for Zambian population, while for 1980 is for African population (99.3% of total)
Source : C.S.O., Lusaka

Fertility and Mortality

Fertility and mortality are two important factors for studying different aspects of a population. These factors are relatively more significant for Zambia, because it has matrilineal society and there is a numerical dominance of females over males. 'Total fertility', 'complete family size' and 'gross reproduction rate' are some of the important parameters for studying the fertility pattern in this country. There has been an increase in infertility from 1969 to 1980 (Table 3.11). But, this is due to improved data collection techniques. Nevertheless, the discrepancy between the total fertility rate of 5.7 and completed family size of 6.5 in 1980 is a strong indication of under-reporting of the former though the latter may not be completely free from omission errors.[7] The fertility level in Zambia is not less than 6 children per woman who has passed through the child bearing period (15-49 years). Thus figures vary from 7.6 in Luapula Province to 4.7 in North-Western Province. The 'gross reproduction rate' or the average number of female children a women would have if survived to the end of the child bearing years is more than three for Zambia (exact figure is 3.4). This implies that each fertile woman will be replaced by about three daughters in next generation. It appears that the fertility level in Zambia is considerably high and this pattern was same over last few years. The mean age of fertility is 293 years, while reproductive survival ratio is 0.75.[8] According to certain estimation, the fertility in urban areas is reported to be higher than the rural areas. This is due to (a) improved medical facilities resulting decrease in pregnancy wastes, (b) reduction of breast feeding period and post-portum abstinence, and (c) little use of contraceptives. Owing to the traditional customs which prevails in urban areas as well and urban facilities the fertility level has become higher. There has been a lot changes in the fertility pattern during the period 1969-80. At the provincial level, the low fertility can be linked with the proportion of childless or single woman aged 30 years and above. In North-Western and Western provinces this factor has been atleast partially responsible for low fertility rates.

Table 3.10 : Age at First Marriage and First Birth, 1980

Provinces	*Age at marriage*			*Age at Birth*		
	Total	*Rural*	*Urban*	*Total*	*Rural*	*Urban*
Central	18.1	18.3	17.8	18.7	18.9	18.1
Copperbelt	17.8	17.9	17.8	18.2	18.6	18.1
Eastern	18.7	18.7	18.5	19.6	19.7	18.8
Luapula	17.8	17.9	17.5	18.6	18.7	18.1
Lusaka	18.3	18.5	18.2	18.4	18.7	18.3
Northern	18.0	18.0	17.7	18.7	18.8	18.1
North-Western	18.6	18.5	18.3	19.4	19.6	18.4
Southern	18.8	18.8	18.6	18.8	18.9	18.6
Western	19.1	19.1	18.9	19.9	20.1	19.1
Zambia	18.3	18.5	18.0	18.9	19.2	18.2

Source : C.S.O., Lusaka.

The crude death rate has been estimated to be between 19 and 20 per thousand in 1960's. According to 1980 census this rate has been reduced to 16.7. Similarly infant mortality has declined from 141 to 97 per thousand live births during the same period.

The pattern of life expectancy in different provinces of Zambia with rural and urban variation for both the sexes is apparent from Table 3.12. The average is 43.1 years for males and 46.2 for females in 1969,

Table 3.11 : Reported Total Fertility Rates and Completed Family Size

Province	*1969*		*1980*	
	TF	*CFS*	*TF*	*CFS*
Central	4.8*	5.0	6.9	6.8
Copperbelt	5.4	4.7	6.2	6.6
Eastern	3.2	5.7	5.0	6.6
Luapula	5.2	5.3	5.8	7.6
Lusaka		5.3	5.7	7.0
Northern	6.1	6.3	6.0	7.2
North-Western	3.0	3.3	4.7	4.7
Southern	4.2	4.2	5.4	7.0
Western	1.9	3.5	4.1	4.9
Zambia	4.0	4.9	5.7	6.5

* Central and Lusaka provinces, T.F. — Total fertility,
CFS — Completed family size.
Source : C.S.O., Lusaka

which increased to 53.3 and 56.0 years in 1980 respectively. In the provinces along the old line-of-rail, the life expectancy at birth is higher which is due to improved medical facilities. However, there is a marked improvement in life expectancy at birth from 1969-80, all over the country.

Similarly, infant and child mortality rates have improved at a rate of 0.64 years per year. This rate is lower in urban areas. However, owing to under-reporting, the above estimates should be used with caution. On one hand, it is possible to establish a relationship between medical facilities and mortality rates; on the other hand, there is no clear relationship between the educational attainments of the months with child mortality rates.

Migration and Movement

The study of human movement in southern Africa has drawn the attention of sociologists like Gugler[9], Hutton[10], Mictchell[11], Watson[12] and Mwanza.[13] They have studied the movement of population as a part of rural urban migration, stabilisation, deportation, detribalisation and urbanisation. In such studies, emphasis is laid on claim, lineage, village or rural affix of migrants to urban areas. The movement of population is mostly studied on an individual basis rather than as waves or flow of people. The present study on Zambia throws light on some of the above mentioned aspects of population movement.

Table 3.12 : Estimated Life Expectancy at Birth, 1980

Province	*Male*			*Females*		
	Total	*Rural*	*Urban*	*Total*	*Rural*	*Urban*
Central	52.5	52.6	52.5	56.6	56.6	56.1
Copperbelt	55.0	51.8	56.4	58.0	55.0	58.7
Eastern	44.3	43.4	48.7	45.5	45.1	51.6
Luapula	44.6	43.8	48.5	45.2	44.0	50.6
Lusaka	53.4	56.9	50.1	55.3	58.2	54.6
Northern	48.1	46.5	48.7	52.7	52.4	55.0
North-Western	51.8	50.4	57.8	53.8	53.3	57.3
Southern	49.7	49.6	52.0	53.9	53.0	55.9
Western	46.2	45.8	47.6	48.0	47.1	51.8
Zambia	53.3	48.6	53.9	56.0	50.3	56.3

Source : C.S.O., Lusaka.

In the beginning of the present century, Zambian labour force was employed in the mines of South Africa, Rhodesia (Zimbabwe) and Katanga (in Zaire). Around 1908, the Zambian Copperbelt developed, thereby creating ample employment opportunities for the labour force. There was also a demand for labour in the farms and towns along the old line-of-rail. With this, the movement towards the Copperbelt and the line-of-rail became a part of the Sub-Saharan labour circulation. Kay has elucidated the internal and international labour migration during the colonial days.[14] However, after independence, this situation changed considerably. Depopulation in rural areas during 1963-69 reached an alarming rate (Fig. 3.4). In some districts the rate of decrease in population was 5 per cent per year. During the same period, Northern and Luapula provinces recorded a decline of 5.9 and 3.4 per cent respectively in their population. In fact, the 24 districts away from the line-of-rail had a population density which is even less than the then country's average of 5.5 persons to a km^2. On the other hand, in the urban centres along the old line-of-rail there was a great influx of population. In 1970, squatter population accounted for 40 per cent of the total population in Lusaka, 59 per cent in Kabwe and 22 per cent in Ndola. If one considers a belt of 36 km, on the either side of the old line-of-rail, the population of such belt was found to be approximately 1.6 million or 40 per cent of the total population of the country (1969). The 16 urban centres along this belt contain 28.48 per cent of the country's population. During the period 1963-69, the population of the urban centres north of Kafue town increased by more than 75 per cent.

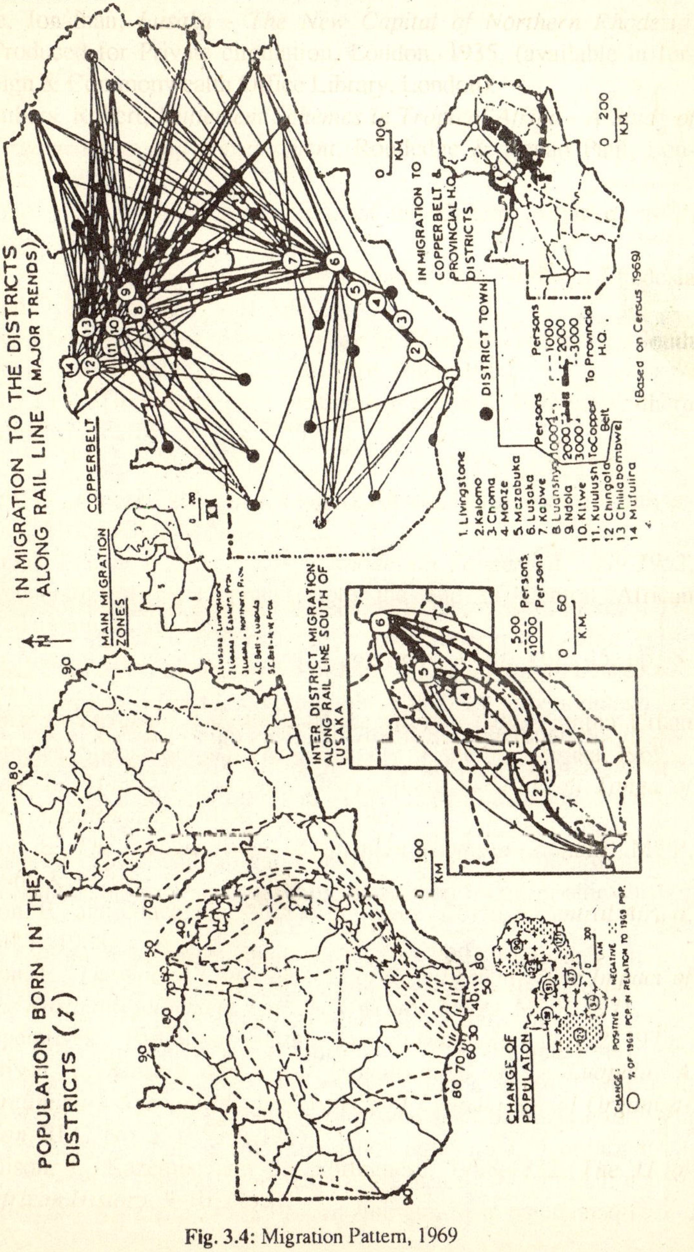

Fig. 3.4: Migration Pattern, 1969

Table 3.13 : Net-Migrants, 1968-69 and 1979-80

Province	*1968-69*		*1979-80*	
	Number	*%*	*Number*	*%*
Central	6,059	0.97	1,714	0.35
Copperbelt	1,845	0.25	5,596	0.47
Eastern	3,976	0.84	5,774	0.93
Luapula	2,723	0.90	413	0.10
Lusaka	—	—	9,882	1.53
Northern	7,186	1.49	8,089	1.26
North-Western	3,495	1.75	2,937	1.02
Southern	6,408	1.65	2,612	0.41
Western	2,378	0.61	2,591	0.56

Note : 1. Percentage of 1969 and 1980 population of each province born in Zambia, i. e. excluding those for whom birth place was not stated or outside Zambia.

2. Lusaka province was included in Central province in 1969.

Source : C.S.O. Lusaka.

The pattern of movement of population can be estimated by an analysis of the number of persons born in the districts in which they have been enumerated during the census of 1969. The ratio of the population born and enumerated in the district along the line-of-rail is as low as 40 per cent of the population of the district. This ratio increases in any direction away from the old line-of-rail. In the districts at the eastern and western boundaries of the territory this ratio is as high as 90 per cent. This clearly indicates that the districts away from this line have the least in-migration while the districts along the line have experienced a considerable influx of population from other parts of the country. (Fig. 3.4)

The Census of 1969 reveals the high degree of mobility of the Zambian population. A year before the census was compiled, 875,821 (21.6%) persons were living in districts other than the ones in which they were enumerated. If we consider inter-province migration during the period 1968-69, about 200 thousand persons or 5.53 per cent of the population changed their place of residence (Table 3.13). The volume of migration is reasonable considering the period involved. Central (which then included Lusaka), Copperbelt and Southern provinces had a high percentage of in-migrants as well as out-migrants. The outlying provinces like Eastern, Northern, North-western and Western lost population during this period. The net migration in the provinces along the old line-of-rail was positive.

The floating population along the old line-of-rail is an indication of particularly high degree of mobility in urban areas lying along this line. About 37 per cent of the squatter population of Kitwe City previously lived in official residential areas; 41.86 per cent in Greater Kitwe (including its numerous squatter settlements), and 13.45 per cent in other places along the old line-of-rail. However, there is substantial migration within the squatter settlements. The unstable nature of the population also becomes apparent from a study of the migration trends during 1968-69. The Census of 1969 reveals that 36 per cent of the out-migration from Kitwe City was to the other adjoining cities of the Copperbelt and 31 per cent of the total in-migration to Kitwe City were from the same region (Kitwe Development Plan I). Only 33 per cent of Kitwe's population is born in the district.

The migration pattern provided the major trends over a larger time period. In order to understand the human movement over the Zambian space, information regarding the vehicular traffic, and passenger traffic by the country's most popular mode of transport, i.e. bus service, was collected. Information from both the sources indicates the circulatory organisation of space.

A traffic Census in 1973 was conducted at 53 points in the country. This census also provides the percentage of heavy vehicles which is significant in a landlocked country having a heavy export based economy (Fig. 3.5). Frequent closer of the southern border has created additional burden, however, the new Tan-Zam railway line has shared the burden to some extent.

Out of the 53 points surveyed, two-third are located along the old line-of-rail of which the largest concentration is in the Copperbelt and around the capital city of Lusaka. The volume of traffic along the Great North Road and Great East Road have been stable throughout their length. Roads emerging out of them to old Mukushi or Sesheke also have considerable traffic. The relatively new tarred road to Mongu in the west has steep decline in the traffic with increase in distance from Lusaka. The largest percentage of heavy vehicles to the total traffic is on the Great North Road (50%). This percentage increases away from the old line-of-rail as this road is one of country's major outlet to the rest of the world. From Figure 3.5, it can be observed that vehicles other than the heavy ones are more along the old line-of-rail, par ticularly in Corpperbelt and around Lusaka. Obviously, the other vehicles consist of private cars and buses which have been the major means human movement in Zambia.

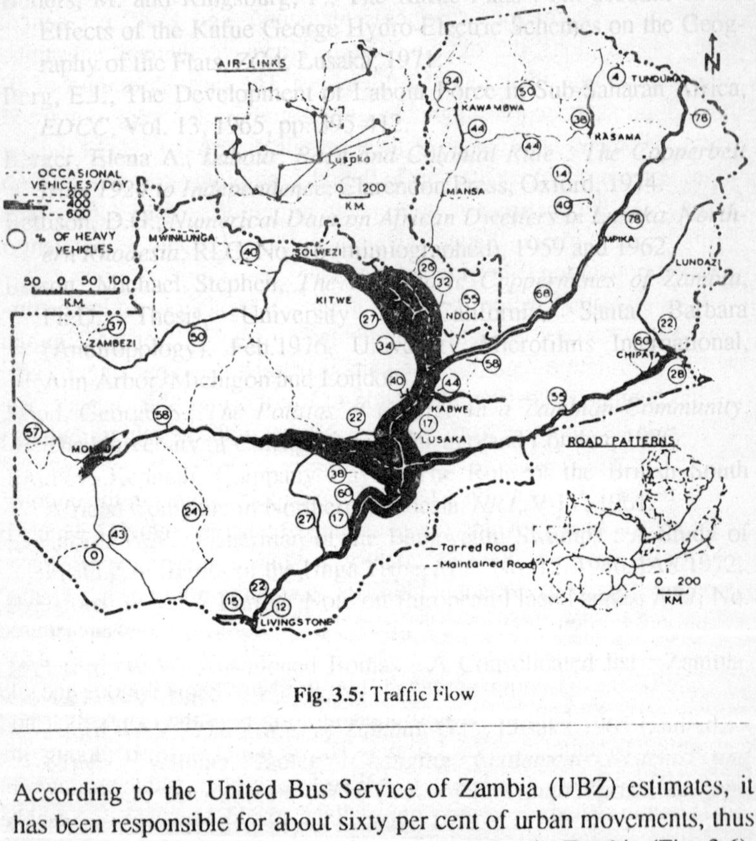

Fig. 3.5: Traffic Flow

According to the United Bus Service of Zambia (UBZ) estimates, it has been responsible for about sixty per cent of urban movements, thus becoming a major agency for human circulation in Zambia (Fig. 3.6). The U.B.Z. with its local and long distance services has three division : (a) Ndola-Luanshya, (b) Kitwe, and (c) Lusaka. These three urban areas act as focii for human circulation. The long distance service is of much interest for the present study. The data provide only number of tickets sold on a particular route, hence, the direction of the movement cannot be estimated though popularity can be observed. Mass movement by this service was recorded along the following routes: (a) Kitwe-Lusaka-Chipata, (b) Kitwe-Mpika, (c) Kitwe-Kasempa-Kaoma, (d) Lusaka-Mpulnug, (e) Lusaka-Kitwe, and (f) Lusaka-Chinsali. All these are inter-provincial connections. Nearly all the *Boma* towns are linked with Kitwe or Lusaka urban centres.

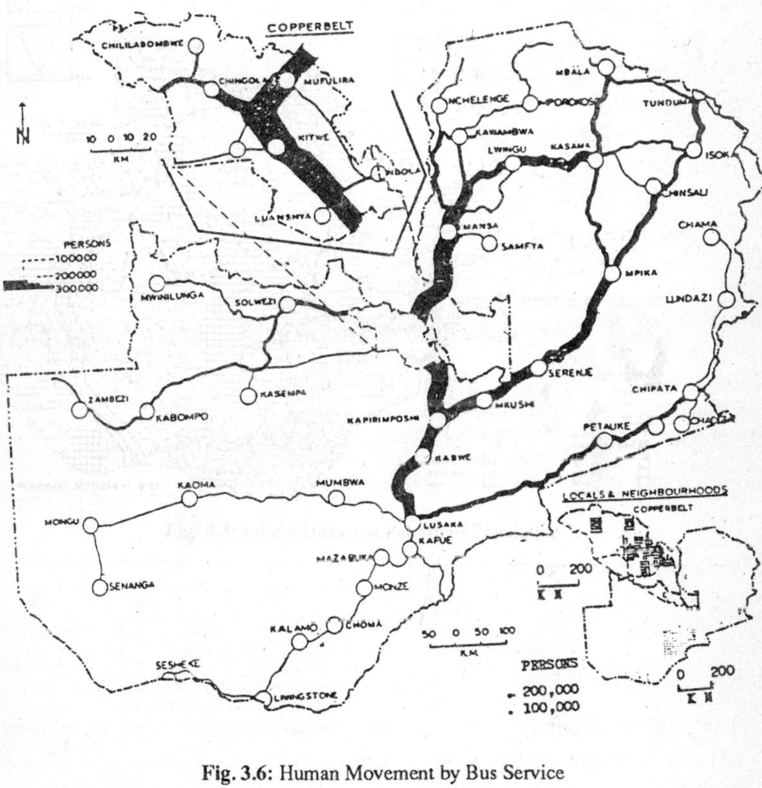

Fig. 3.6: Human Movement by Bus Service

The human movement can also be estimated by knowing the number of tickets sold per km. Frequency of 15 tickets per 100 km was observed in most of the long distance service. The frequency reduced with (a) longer distance and (b) less density of population in the area served by the bus service. The shorter routes, such as Petauke-Mawando School or Petauke-Missolo School or Chipata-Mwami have 116,93 and 91 tickets sale per 100 km. All these routes lie in the densely populated Eastern Province. Further, higher frequency was observed in local and neighbourhood services. Lusaka-Chillanga-Kafue route has 118 while Matero-Lilanda route in Lusaka city has 556 tickets sale per 100 km. However, the bus service in local areas are concentrated in the Copperbelt and around Lusaka and Livingstone cities.

The pattern of migration during 1979-80 was not much different from that of 1968-69. The net migration in the old line-of-rail provinces continued to be positive. Though the number of migrant increased by about 50 thousand, their ratio to total population decreased to 4.68 per cent (Table 3.14).

Table 3.14 : Place of Birth, 1980

In Percentage

Province	*Born in District of Enumeration*	*Born in other Districts of Province of Enumeration*	*Born elsewhere in Zambia*	*Born outside Zambia*	*Not stated*
Central	58.40	7.30	30.10	4.20	0.00
Copperbelt	49.50	11.26	34.44	5.02	0.00
Eastern	83.96	5.99	7.05	2.60	0.39
Luapula	79.67	7.37	11.20	1.51	0.25
Lusaka	44.79	4.55	43.22	6.78	0.67
Northern	81.60	6.95	9.82	1.47	0.17
North-Western	77.77	9.07	7.50	4.95	0.73
Southern	70.63	13.21	13.27	2.40	0.46
Western	79.70	10.76	5.18	4.00	0.35

Source : Census, 1980.

The pattern of migration can also be assessed by analysing the data of place of birth during the 1980 Census enumeration (Table 3.14). In the outlying provinces, the ratio of persons born in the district of enumeration is high. But, in the provinces along the old line-of-rail, the population born in other districts of the province of enumeration and born elsewhere is high indicating (a) high mobility within the district of the province, and (b) high in-migration to these provinces. Though Copperbelt Province had 34.44 per cent population born elsewhere in Zambia, the migration of this province has been redirected to Lusaka. The economic prospects of this province has been effected by recession due to falling copper price in the world market. During 1979-80, this province recorded heavy out-migration (4.71%) indicating return migration to Northern and Luapula provinces or elsewhere. However, in most cases the traditional migration flow is either increased or remained similar, e.g. migration from Western Province to Southern Province or Eastern Province to Lusaka and Central Provinces.

Female Migration

Considering the greater role of women in Zambian society, and the normalisation process of sex ratio, migration trend of females have been studied in details. It is difficult to estimate the exact volume of female migration in Zambia. If we compare the number females born in a particular district to the number of females enumerated in the same district, the difference will indicate the internal migration pattern to certain extent.

Female migration in the Southern and Western provinces was negligible. In Luapula, Northern and North-Western provinces, there has been a reasonable amount of out-migration of the female population, while the remaining provinces along the old line-of-rail have been receiving female from other provinces. Nearly a half of the female population of Lusaka province was born elsewhere. In general, 6.8 per cent of Zambian females were enumerated in districts other than those they were born (Table 3.15).

Although detailed migration figures for the 1980 Census are not available, an estimate of female migration can still be made. The number of females increased from 2,070 thousand in 1969 to 2,894 thousand in 1980; however, the sex ratio improved marginally. In urban districts, there has been overall decrease in the number of males per 1,000 females. Since male population in these areas has increased at a higher rate during this period, the normalisation process of the sex ratio was due to the inmigration of females.

If we consider female population growth during 1969-80, we find that some districts of Lusaka and Southern provinces, whose population doubled, were definitely characterised by female in-migration. A similar increase was also recorded in the Kabwe Urban district. The districts around the Copperbelt urban complex and Namwala district in Southern Province demonstrated substantial female population growth,

Table 3.15 : Place of Birth and Enumeration, 1969

Province		*Place of birth*	*Place of enumeration*	*Difference in percentage*
Central	M	1,49,250	1,81,231	17.65
	F	1,56,219	1,77,424	11.95
Copperbelt	M	2,15,402	4,25,612	49.39
	F	2,17,985	3,90,697	44.20
Eastern	M	2,99,761	2,39,115	28.04
	F	3,25,790	2,75,400	18.30
Luapula	M	1,84,955	1,61,075	14.83
	F	1,94,742	1,74,509	11.59
Lusaka	M	83,756	1,84,313	54.56
	F	87,471	1,69,662	48.44
Northern	M	3,23,090	2,55,850	26.28
	F	3,40,320	2,89,246	17.67
North-Western	M	1,33,418	1,09,589	21.74
	F	1,38,564	1,22,114	13.47
Southern	M	2,30,465	2,44,791	5.85
	F	2,46,256	2,51,250	1.98
Western	M	2,09,954	1,90,435	10.25
	F	2,21,863	2,19,652	1.01
Zambia	M	18,31,578	19,87,011	7.82
	F	19,29,269	20,69,984	6.80

Source : Census 1969.

however, in Copperbelt urban and mining districts (except Kalulushi and Kitwe), the increase was close to the national average (39.8%). Furthermore, a similar pattern was found in vast areas where female out-migration has been consistent. Growth was below average in outlying areas that had suffered heavy female out-migration (Table 3.16). This was the case of the Zambezi district in the North-Western Province where there has been a reduction in the number of females. Table 3.16 gives an aggregate picture of females population growth in Zambia's nine provinces.

Working Population

In 1969 census economic activity of population over 15 years was recorded but in 1980 census this age was lowered down to 12 years. There are other differences in the collection of data regarding working population in both the censuses which do not always allow comparisons of the results of 1969 and 1980 censuses.

Table 3.16 : Zambia : Growth of Female Population 1969-80

Province	*No. of females in*		*Increase in %*
	1969	*1980*	
Central	1,77,424	2,25,062	26.85
Copperbelt	3,90,607	6,06,221	55.17
Eastern	2,75,400	3,47,663	26.24
Luapula	1,74,509	2,15,797	23.66
Lusaka	1,69,662	3,38,872	99.73
Northern	2,89,246	3,58,521	23.95
North-Western	1,22,144	1,57,721	29.13
Southern	2,51,250	3,48,876	38.86
Western	2,19,652	2,65,606	20.92
Total Female	2,069,984	2,894,339	39.82
Total Male	1,987,011	2,785,469	40.18
Total Zambia	4,056,995	5,679,808	40.00

Source : 1969 and 1980, Censuses.

In 1969 the African population over the age of 15 years was more than 2 million, out of which 33.82 per cent were working, 17.70 per cent were seeking work, 0.91 per cent were not seeking work, while 42.89 per cent were students, housewives, aged and sick persons, the remaining population (4.68%) fall in the category of 'others and Not Stated'. There has been a reasonable variations from this average picture if the data of provinces or sexes are analysed separately.

In 1980 only 0.5 per cent of population over 12 years of age were employers, while 61 per cent were employees (49.8% in rural and 80.6% in urban areas), and 32.1 per cent were self-employed. The ratio of unpaid family workers were 32.1 per cent. This ratio is as low as 0.3 per cent among the urban males (Table 3.17). The spatial pattern of working population can be estimated by the activity rates in different provinces. There is less variation in rural and urban areas within a province, while in some provinces there is much variation in male and female activity rates. In Copperbelt Province, 73.9 per cent males and 29.3 per cent females over the age of 12 years were economically active (Table 3.18). In general the male activity rate is almost the double than the female (72.1% and 37.3% respectively).

Table 3.17 : Employment Status of Working Population (12 + Years), 1980 (%)

Employment status	*Total*	*Male*	*Female*
Employer	0.5	0.6	0.3
Employee	61.0	66.2	49.8
Self-employed	32.1	30.4	36.0
Unpaid family worker	32.1	30.4	36.0
Not stated	1.3	0.7	2.7

Source : C.S.O., Lusaka.

In 1980, about 72.5 per cent of the labour force was employed which is higher than 1969 census figures of 66.2 per cent. The labour force constitutes of 69.7 per cent males and 30.3 per cent females. The census of 1980 records that 51.2 per cent of the labour force was engaged in primary activities, i.e. agriculture, forestry, hunting and fishing, followed by 16.3 per cent in production related activities. As mentioned earlier, agriculture which is basically subsistence in nature is dominated by females. There is 68.5 per cent of the female against 43.7 per cent of the male working force engaged in this activity. If the occupation of the household heads is considered, almost same pattern is found for this category 'Agricultural, Animal Husbandry etc.' (Table 3.19). The percentage of female household heads engaged in this category is higher (77.64%) in rural areas. The other major

Table 3.18 : Refined Activity Rate of Working Population (12 + Years), 1980 (%)

Province	*Refined Activity Rate*		
	Total	*Male*	*Female*
Central	54.1	74.0	33.8
Copperbelt	52.8	73.9	29.3
Eastern	53.6	72.7	38.4
Luapula	57.4	79.8	46.8
Lusaka	58.2	76.9	37.9
Northern	48.6	66.3	33.9
North-Western	54.9	70.5	41.5
Southern	51.9	68.5	36.1
Western	59.4	72.1	49.7
Zambia	54.1	72.1	37.3

Source : C.S.O., Lusaka.

Table 3.19 : Occupation of Household Heads, 1980

(In Percentage)

Occupation of Head		*Total*	*Rural*	*Urban*
Professional Technical and	M	8.84	7.06	11.28
Related Workers	F	8.35	6.06	15.44
Administrative and Managerial	M	1.82	0.85	3.16
Workers	F	0.52	0.21	1.48
Clerical and Related Workers	M	4.43	2.56	7.02
	F	5.42	2.28	15.13
Sales Workers	M	5.50	3.23	8.63
	F	14.00	6.35	37.64
Services Workers	M	12.04	7.25	18.65
	F	4.64	2.37	11.65
Agricultural, Animal Husbandry,	M	38.96	62.70	6.22
Forestry, Fishery and Hounting	F	60.96	77.64	9.40
Production, Transport and Related	M	26.09	14.80	41.66
Workers	F	5.17	4.41	7.51
Workers not classified elsewhere	M	2.32	1.55	3.38
	F	0.94	0.68	1.75

Source : C.S.O., Lusaka and S.N.D.P., p. 52.

source of occupation for males is 'Production and Transport' which is 41.66 per cent in urban areas. The percentage of household heads in 'Professional, Technical and related workers' is reasonable. In urban areas the percentage of females is more than the percentage of their counterparts. However, in 'services' the percentage of males household heads is high. Details of 1980 census would have allowed such analysis at provincial or district levels as well. However, the economic activities of urban population based on 1969 census has been studied in chapter 6.

Recent Population Trends

If the present growth rate of 3.1 per cent persists, Zambia will be doubling its population in less than 23 years. Incidentally, the 1980 census results are about 4 per cent less than the I.L.O. estimates for the same year. Nevertheless, the population is not only growing fast, but the growth rate is accelerating as well. The provinces along the old line-of-rail have recorded largest increase in population during 1969-80. The other states have also increased their population marginally, whereas in the earlier intercensal period 1963-69, in many of the districts of these states have recorded negative growth.

During 1969-80, the percentage of Zambia's urban population increased from 29.4 to 43.0. This was due to (a) natural increase in population in urban areas, (b) rural urban migration, and (c) inclusion of new town/townships during the concerned period. But, 78 per cent of the urban population was residing in ten Large Urban Areas, which fall in the old line-of-rail zone. These towns are now growing less rapidly. This is due to the governments commitment for dispersal of industries in the successive development plans. Further, the larger urban population base of 1969 allows to have lower urbanisation rates in the future. The last factor is owning to the stagnation in the industrial development of the country's economy during the later half of the seventies.

The shift of population to urban areas was associated not only with the unemployed males but also with the movement of their families who joined them in towns. This process was further facilitated by the liberal post-independence housing policies. In addition, young educated females could also find jobs in offices and shops. Schuster and Glaser, in their recent study on women of Lusaka, describe the urban way of life in Zambia today. They observe that success in school and training programmes has given young women confidence, pride and a sense of their own worth. This is a solid basis for such high self-esteem for such educated women to enter the urban scene ready to achieve both financial independence and high social status.[15] There is a tendency among the educated and enterprising female and male population to move to urban areas. The rural areas left with the elders and infants, the less productive section of the Zambian population. The urban growth rate measures, among other things, the disparities between rural and urban living standards, perceived opportunities and aspiration.[16]

The recent change in Zambia's population is likely to alter the situation of 1969 when regions of male and female numerical dominance could be identified. Urban centres would however still dominate in vast rural areas. Under these circumstances, a socio-economic transitional stage could be traced. Single male household is likely to be replaced by a matured household. The size of household has also increased. In rural areas, the situation is likely to change as well but at a slower rate. There would be a decrease in the number of female household heads and absenteeism of males and females which affect the land ownership pattern and agricultural output. As a consequence, the matrilineal rural society would have to adjust to the changing situation. The Government of the Republic of Zambia will sooner or later have to take notice of the situation in the light of its commitments to rural development. Zambia is promising African country where some aspects of the population and migration should not be ignored so as not to allow them to hinder the development processes.[17]

REFERENCES

1. Nag, P., Population redistribution : Aspects of Zambian national development plans and projects, *Geographical Review of India,* 1981, 43 (1), pp. 41-9.
2. Nag, P., The role of women in internal migration in Zambia, *Population Geography*, 1983 5(1 & 2), pp. 60-9.
3. Kay, G., Age structure, sex ratio and migration, in D.Hywel Davis (ed), *Zambia in Maps*, University of London Press, London, 1972, pp. 46-7.
4. Jackman, M.E., *Recent Population Movement in Zambia : Some Aspects of the 1969 Census,* Zambia papers No. 8, Institute of African Studies, Lusaka, 1973, pp. 47.
5. Heisler, H., *Urbanisation and Migration : The Inter-relation of Urban and Rural Life in Zambia,* C. Hurst & Company, London, 1974, pp. 63.
6. Central Statistical Office, *Demographic Situation in Zambia,* paper presented to the National Seminar on Dissemination and Utilisation of the 1980 population and Housing Census Data, 25-29th November, 1985, Lusaka, p. 8, (mimio).
7. C.S.O., *op. cit.*, p. 95.
8. C.S.O., *op. cit.*, p. 45.
9. Gugler, J., On the theory of rural-urban migration, the case of Sub-Saharan Africa, in J.A. Jackson (ed) *Migration*, Sociological Studies 2, Cambridge University Press, Cambridge, 1969, pp. 134-55.
10. Hutton, C.R., *The Causes of Labour Migration*, Institute of Social Research, Working Paper 17, Kampala, 1966.
11. Mictchell, J.C., *Social Network in Urban Situation : An Analysis of Personal Relationships in Central African Towns,* Manchester University Press and Institute for the Social Research, Lusaka, 1969.
12. Watson, W., *Tribal Cohesion in a Money Economy : A Study of Mambwe People of Northern Rhodesia,* Manchester, 1958.
13. Mwanza, J.M., Rural - urban migration and urban employment in Zambia, in B. Tmok (ed), *Development in Zambia : A Reader*, Zed Press, London, 1979, pp. 26-34.
14. Kay, G., *A Social Geography of Zambia*, London, 1967, pp. 41-86.
15. Schuster, I. & M. Glaser, *New Women of Lusaka*, Mayfield Publishing Company, California, 1979, p. 66.
16. Simons, H.J., Zambia's urban situation, in Turok (ed), *op. cit.*, p.15.
17. Nag, P., *op. cit.*, 1983.

4

RURAL SETTLEMENTS

In Zambia, the traditional village system, as in most part of Africa, was influenced by a particular clan or tribe, which took over a certain territory (mostly nebulous) out of seven major tribal regions and emerged as the power elite which then had clean domination over a chief's area.[1] Zambian society was never segregated in social classes though 'tribute labour' existed, rather it developed a social homogeneity homogeneity in a tribal area which had in the past naturalised foreign elements through marriage. The ruling tribe or clan was the only corporate political group in the territory and other were non-significant. The dominant tribe or the chief's tribe dominated the political authority over the tribal area and the population and settlements falling within it. In most cases members of the royal clans were made the headmen of the village.[2]

Tribo-Territorial Basis of Settlements

In the process of settling in Zambia, most probably on virgin lands, the clans had their separate territories or areas, but later, owing to the increasing pressure of population on land and limited natural resources, they were forced to diffuse. Meanwhile the territories of the weaker tribes shrunk and inter mixture of population took place. This ultimately resulted in the fading away of the territorial character of the clans.

The territorial, political, administrative and social set-up of the tribal settlements are arranged through (a) paramount chiefs, (b) senior chiefs, and (c) chiefs. These traditional rulers still hold the land and exercise political authority over it, though they may not always be treated as the 'lords of land'. Lewanika, the kingship of Barotseland, had a different pattern of administration through appointed officials, while the political control over people, land and settlements was approximately the same. The nature of such tribal authorities in political, social and administrative set-up of Zambia has largely been retained even after the independence.

Moreover, Zambia consists of varied geopolitical orders. It varies from acephalous societies such as Tonga (Bantu). Futwe or Luvale to highly politically organised societies such as Lozis or Bambas. The manipulations of the chiefs' prestige directly depends on the size of the capital, the dimensions of the area ruled and the number of people under them, the latter being the most important factor. "Africa as a whole, consists of centralised political organisations of the Lozi or Bemba types or inter-lacustrine examples which are deviation from the norm. The models we should have of the norm of indigenous political organisation are non-centralised systems such as we find in Northern Rhodesia among the Plateau Tonga and the Luvale.[3]

The fugitive kingdoms have always recognised their superiors and paid tributes in the form of moral and military support. The tribute paid were not only the political necessity but a sign of respect. The demonstration of political power depends on (a) such tribute collection, (b) receiving tribute labour, and (c) raiding territories. The traditional-tribal hierarchy of settlements could clearly be seen by the flow of tributes. This created a traditional arrangements in the organisation of settlements. Such hierarchy of settlements contributed to organising the area of a tribal region. Further, the subject tribes also attached themselves to this arrangements and hence developed a number of traditional hierarchical arrangements of settlements of the past and even in present day Zambia.

Though the polity varied from highly centralised administration to indirect rule, yet at village level the headman, who might be head of an extended family system or a man or woman highly placed in society, was recognised throughout Zambia. Zambian history clearly reveals that the external agencies connected with the trade of slave or ivory or cattle had little to do with the holding of land. Whenever the village shifted or diffused there was no change in the village administration of headman who continued to hold their rights over land and people. Any change in the policy at the top hardly affected the village administration or constitution and the village always remained as a basic unit.

The Europeans were largely responsible for developing the present territorial structure. Tribal wars were common and vague boundaries were put in a state of coma which still persist.[4] It should be noted that indirect rule in Africa as in India, was an easy apparatus for foreign administration though the people were against it. After independence the whole framework was dissolved in India, whilst in the African countries the system was neutralised. The chiefs of Zambia were the backbones of African Local Government which looked after tribal affairs and the administration of rural areas, although the nature of the local governments were different to that of other African countries under the Crown.[5]

Rural Settlement System

There are 32,472 villages in Zambia which supports nearly 60 per cent of the country's population. These villages are termed here as rural settlements. However, there are sizable rural areas which have virtually no population or very thinly settled. Large tracts of rural areas are covered by forest and game reserves. The settled area is under the control of chiefs. Today only tribes have territorial character. The rural settlements in a chief's territory can be classified hierarchically as follows:

Chief s Headquarters

The chief's headquarters have created centripetal force in the tribal set-up and influence on the arrangement of social institutions. These settlements have establishments such as primary schools, rural health centre (RHC), agriculture camps, depot of National Agricultural Marketing Boards (NAMBoard), bus service, welfare hall, rest house, water supply, shops, community development centre, depot of agriculture mechanisation schemes, post office, police station, consumer's shop (C.B.C.), tea room, a small market, churches, air strips, and Indian shop. In colonial days, primary schools were attached almost to every centre of administrative importance. In ordinary rural settlement system, the chief's headquarters are the highest in the hierarchy, but are smaller than the *boma* settlements. These settlements had political importance in the past. Limilunga (Western Province) has schools, rural council, king's residence and number of villages around it. Chief Kazembe's headquarters contain a post office, police station, schools and chief's residence and it is considered to be largest village of Zambia. Chief Mukeni's headquarters, near Livingstone, has school, R.H.C, agricultural camp, court, veterinary clinic, police station, bus service, grocer's shops, bars and a population of about 1,500. These settlements are located at the headwaters of a river or a stream, overlooking the down flow or its valley. Such settlements are also linked with the *boma* settlements. Hence, they become significant and pivot element in the settlement fabric, synthesising tribal and modern settlement organizations.

Neighbourhood Units and Neighbourhood Centre

Rural settlements in Zambia have developed in pockets consisting of 5-10 headmen and their villages. Such a grouping is developed from a single village, i.e., the mother village and the rest of the villages are its offsprings. In less settled areas such units are far apart. The arrangements of such neighbourhoods determines the pattern of rural settlements in Zambia. They have a socio-territorial character through which the Zambian rural society is vividly expressed. As every village has fields, a neighbourhood unit has certain area under its influence though this is not recognised by the administration. Colson recognised this pattern of rural settlements in the Tonga (Bantu) tribal area, which is known as Cisi.[6]

In a neighbourhood two establishments denoted by a single name may be within a walking distance.[7] In Northern Province, Mulanga Mission (10° 59′ S : 32° 10′ E) and Mulanga village (10° 33′ S : 31 11′ E) lie at a considerable distance. Similarly, in the Western Province there are 18 villages in a small area (14° 14′ S to 17° 14′ S and 22° 20′ E to 24° 51′ E) names as Mubita.[8]

Neighbourhood centres generally are located at the nuclei which may have a few of the establishments that are found in chief's headquarters. A single institution, such as school or R.H.C. or court successfully makes centres potential. They are the end points of functional network and lowest but most significant points to diffuse development impulses. These settlements are scattered in remote areas, hence they have a clear area of influence. In such centres as well as within the neighbourhoods, social functions are more dominating. However, with the introduction of money economy, selling of goods, such as fish, potato, onion, dried caterpillar, basket, corn and beer are breaking through such isolated social systems.

Villages

Villages are basically residential units, recognised by the government. The headman has political control over the land and the members of the village are generally related to him. Thus a village primarily is a social unit. In short, a village is a physical separation of a few members of the same lineage or clan. Each village area extends to the fields of its members under the same headman.

The shape of a village is roughly circular or oval depending on the members of the village. In general, village can be demarcated in two zones within the village territorial unit. One zone is the settled area with huts and small gardens. This determines the form of the village. The second zone is covered by fields with crops. The density of fields decreases away from the settled area and on the fringes there are scattered round fields under *chitemene* system of cultivation.[9] This area is likely to shift with the growth of population in the village or exhaustion of soil. A third zone also exists which is outside the village limits and which is for hunting and other robber economies. Fish, game and caterpillars are exploited from this zone. The zones continuously shift outwards and when the soil of the second zone and the fauna of the third zone are exhausted the village is likely to change its site.

Some villages are compact units while others consist of a number of hamlets or homesteads. The village is named after the headman, e.g., Ndongo's village (Mwinilunga district). The villages may change their sites but the socio-political structure remains the same.

Hamlets and Homesteads

The hamlet is socially a more integrated unit than a village, and it is also a territorial unit. It can easily change its location since it is not a recognised administrative unit. When a hamlet grows bigger it is treated as a separate village under a new headman if recognised by the administration.

The homestead is a smallest, close kinshiped residential unit and hence more well knitted than the village or the hamlet. The number of huts in such settlements depend on the social customs and traditions. A homestead may enlarge itself to become a hamlet. Colson remarks that 'the homestead is the basic subsistence unit. Its members share the work in the fields, the care of cattle and other livestock and the domestic work. The homestead is also a ritual unit under the charge of the married man who heads it.[10] In brief, the pattern of growth of rural settlements in Zambia is from homestead to hamlet, then a village and finally to a neighbourhood.

Rural Settlement Pattern and Related Economy

The environment and its related economy has shaped the neighbourhood units which ultimately contributed to the areal patterns of rural settlements. In the underpopulated developing country like Zambia, the environment, resource and the settlement patterns have close association in the different provinces and districts. The districts of Northern Province and eastern part of Luapula Province, have low and undulating topography; poor soil; and limited resources. The villages are more scattered with an average distance of 2.75 km. It seems that a village in these provinces needs a sizable area surrounding the rural settlement. The villages are along the tracks, near the water sources. In the district of Mporokoso and Mbala, semi-compact patterns are observed. Another exceptional pattern of compact villages between the marshes is noticed in Mbala. The neighbourhoods are reduced in size owing to topographical conditions and water bodies (Fig. 4.1)

In Mongu-Lealui district of Western Province similar pattern is also observed, where water bodies like lakes, dams, marshes, dambos and rivers provide comparatively limited area for population and settlements. The neighbourhood takes the form of a semi-compact settlement pattern (Fig. 4.2-4). In the same area, linear settlements along the flood plain of Zambezi (Fig. 4.2-1) and its tributaries, have multiple economy based on fish, cattle and agriculture. the neighbourhood in the above area takes a linear form and villages are very compact and are located on the edges of the flood plain. One can have an aerial view of these regular villages arranged along the east of the Zambezi river and north and south of Mongu town (Fig. 4.8, Nakonga Village). Similar linear arrangement of settlements is also observed along both the banks of the Kafue river flats (Fig. 4.2-2)

In the flood plain of Zambezi, there are regularly scattered round villages on artificially raised platforms which suffer seasonal migration during the rainy season. This settlement pattern is most regular. The plain, apart from fisheries, is used for cultivation and for grazing. This area, known as Bulozi, is the richest in resources and therefore it supported the Lozi kingdom in the past. The canals developed earlier for communication have functional as well as administrative importance. It has been observed that apart from the above pattern, isolated settlements forming a single neighbourhood is connected with some water bodies (Fig. 4.2-1). In the district of Sesheke, the settlements are

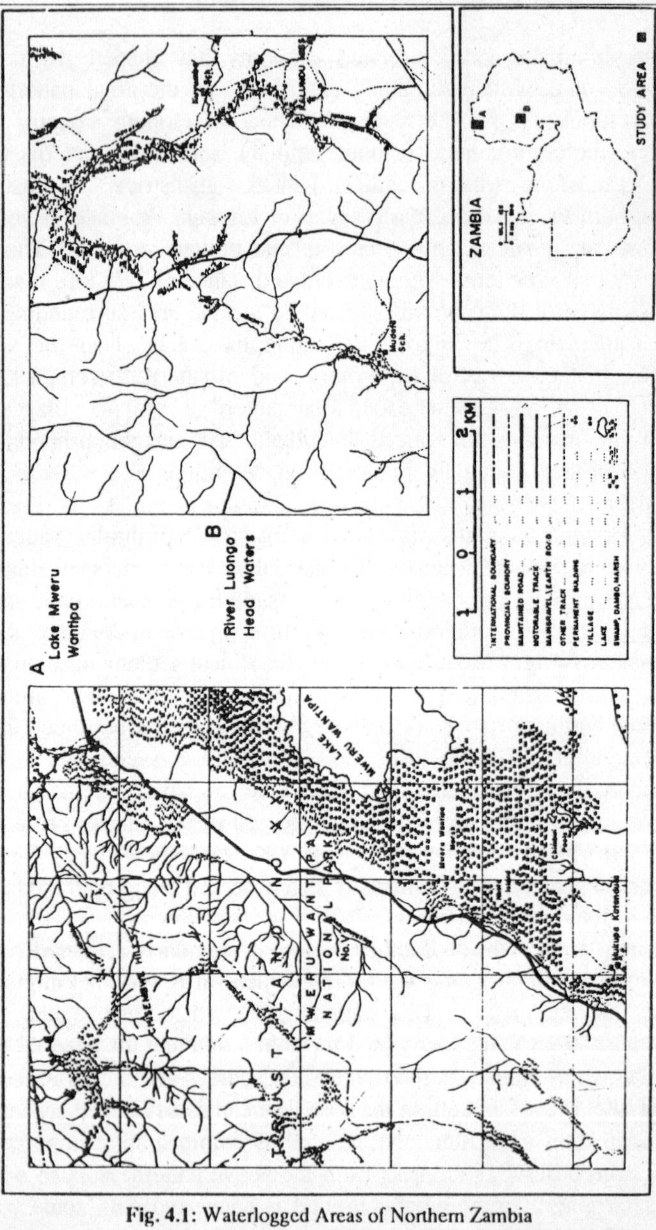

Fig. 4.1: Waterlogged Areas of Northern Zambia

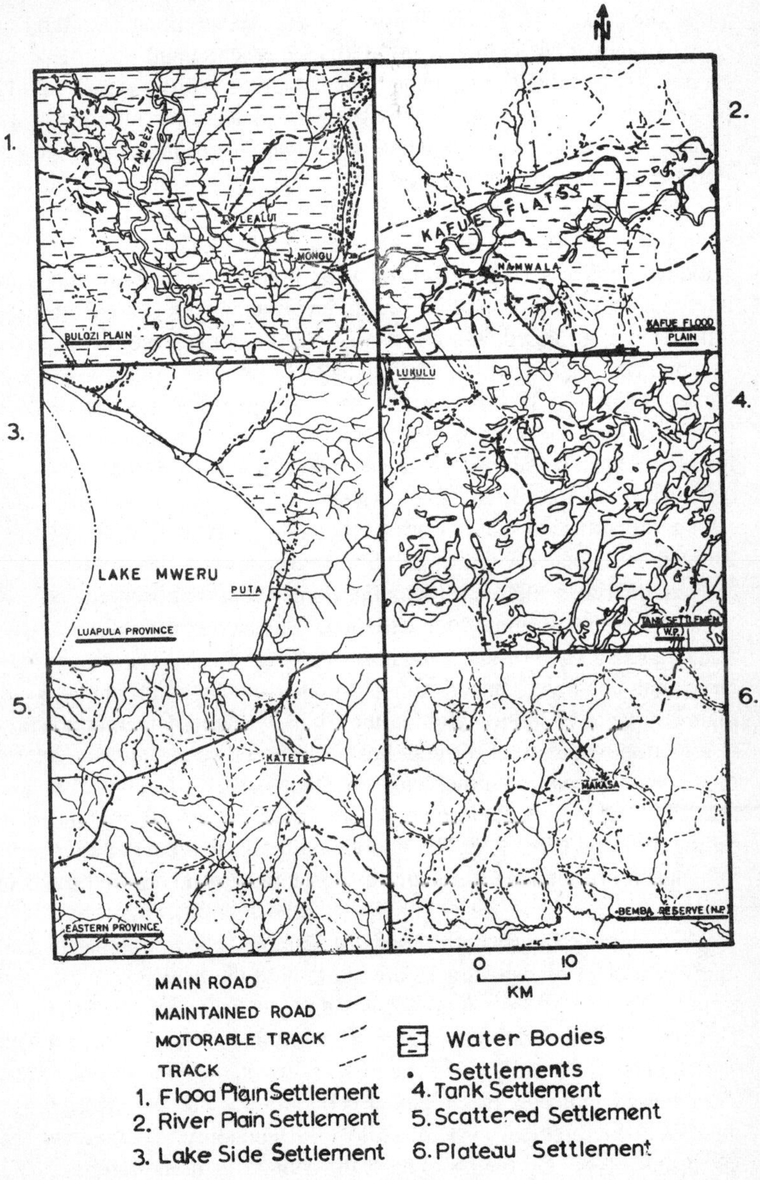

Fig. 4.2: Settlement Types

exceptionally very loosely distributed though they are permanent along the roads. There are almost no settlements along the Zambezi river. However, in Namibia, a Bulozi type settlement pattern is observed between the Zambezi and the Chobe rivers. Since rice is gaining popularity, one can notice oblong fields penetrating into the water bodies. All the above settlements which were once under the King of Barotseland had no complications in the land rights.

The other examples or rural settlements associated with water bodies are around the Lake Bangweulu and the Lukanga swamp. The settlements have surrounded these water bodies and they are very well interconnected. The Lake Bangweulu has islands with settlements. The villages are arranged along the roads approaching the lake or the swamp. The road encircling the Lukanga swamp lies at distances varying from 1 km to 10 km from the shore. Temporary huts are built for fishing. Along the Lumpa river (Kaoma district), semi-compact and linear villages lie along the tracks while the river is not always a dominating factor. Small size swamps are without any settlements. Along the artificial Lake Kariba, there are only a few widely distributed settlements while to its north semi-compact, and further north in Fiera district, scattered settlements along rivers are observed.

The last, but an important settlement pattern based on water bodies is along Lake Mweru and Luapula river (Fig. 4.2.3). The villages are large and lineally arranged and are connected by roads. Fish is the main source of economy while in the Chief Mushoto's area, agriculture is important occupation. Kaputa has a linear and semi-compact pattern of settlements while further east on the plateau villages are located sparsely. The area is overcrowded and population growth was negative during 1963-69 (Fig. 3.1). The population has grown beyond the carrying capacity of the area and hence a substantial out-migration has taken place.

As mentioned earlier, the roads of Zambia follow watersheds and inter-settlement roads or tracks are along both the banks of rivers. The former are of regional importance while the latter are of local significance. Further, one can visualise negligible influence of road on settlements as virtually on settlement exists at the junction of roads. This pattern indicates that regional economy has not yet matured and attained a hierarchical system while local economy is largely of the subsistence type. On the other hand the flying functions[11] do not effect settlement pattern.

Moreover, the general model of settlement pattern in Zambia is scattered – varying from sprinkled to the semi-compact. The districts which have not advanced in agriculture and depend largely on natural environmental conditions have sprinkled settlements, as in Serenje, Mpika, Namwala, Isoka and Kabompo districts (Fig. 4.2-6). The districts with comparatively sound agriculture, specialising in some cash crops like tobacco, groundnuts and maize, need less area surrounding the settlements and they are densely settled. These are districts like Chipata, Kabwe, Petauke, Monze and Katete (Fig. 4.2-5).

In the North-Western province the villages are concentrated around social institutions such as chief's headquarters, schools, missions and *bomas*. In Mwinilunga and Solwezi districts the settlements are concentrated around Ikelenga-Kalene complex (Ikelenga is Chief's headquarters and Kalene is a mission with a hospital, school and airstrip), Ntambu, Chibwe and St. Frances. In the eastern part of Lundazi district an exceptional pattern has been observed, having permanent settlements connected with roads and lying near the water sources. The Ndola Rural District is least influenced by the network of the railway line of Copperbelt and it is also loosely settled. In the same district, in the Swahili reserve areas, the villages are concentrated on the watersheds while fields are on the slopes (Fig. 4.2)

Further, there are large tracts of unsettled areas, which are lowlying and suffer from diseases such as sleeping sickness (Fig. 4.2). National parks, game reserves or forest reserves (Fig. 4.3) are other unsettled areas.

Finally, a general model of Zambian settlement can be developed based on such an empirical study. The capacity to contain settlements depend largely on environmental resources and multiplicity of economies, which in turn are closely associated with topographic variations. For example at the junction of two topographic systems, lies the potential points for settlements. Water bodies provide a special featrue in this regard. The cultural and social institutions provide centripetal force to settlements which are economically or socially related to it.

Quantitative Analysis of Rural Settlements

For a better explanation of Zambian rural settlements, a new index is introduced here. The unsettled gaps in between the fringes of settlements are calculated by observing the difference between the hypothetical spacing 'D' (= 1.074569 $\sqrt{A/N}$) and the hypothetical distance from fringe to the centre, considering area under agriculture only

(D_A). The average area under agriculture of a village in a district is thought to be a hexagon, and like D, D_A is calculated. Where D is equal to D_A ($D = D_A$), a perfect mosaic of settlements, arranged in accordance with Christraller's hypothesis is expected, $D-D_A$ gives the required gap in between the fringes of settlements, which is noted here as D_F. The latter is found to be an important variable to explain the settlement distribution pattern like that of Zambia.

In the past, several attempts have been made to quantify the distributional pattern of settlements. Clark and Evans studies the distribution of plant communities, mathematically representing by R_N-Values, ranging from 'O' for aggregated to 2,1491 for regular patterns.[12] This method has been widely used by geographers to study the distributional patterns of settlements, both rural and urban. The R_N-Value is the ratio of observed intersettlement distance (r_O) and expected inter-settlement distance (r_E)

$$R_N = r_O/r_E$$

In an attempt to find out an alternative approach for the identification of randomness in settlement pattern, some changes can be introduced to the above formula. It has been found that the hypothetical spacing (D) explains similar distributional notion as

$$r_E = \frac{1}{2}\frac{\sqrt{N}}{A}$$

The difference between r_E and D is based on the presumed conditions considered to be ideal for the distribution patterns. Both the indices are comparable and inter-changeable. For any distributional pattern, the relation $r_E = 0.4653028$ D (or $D = 2.149138\ r_E$) holds good. The above relation points out the possibility of a new equation for the identification of randomness, which is as follows:

$$R_X = r_O/D$$

By replacing r_E by D, we get a new set of values lying exactly between 'O' and '1'.[13] Table 4.1 indicates the ranges of R_X and R_N values for each distributional pattern of settlements. These patterns are also observed in Zambia (Fig. 4.2).

Apart from the indices mentioned above, a few other indices are also taken into consideration in analysing the Zambian rural settlements. These indices are (a) area under each village, (b) dwellings in each village, (c) area under agriculture in each village, and (d) number of persons in each village.

Table 4.1 : Distribution Pattern and Random Values

	Distribution	*Range of R_X Values*	*Ranges of R_N Values*
(a)	Highly clustered	Less than 0.2	less than 0.43
(b)	Loosely clustered	0.2 - 0.4	0.43 - 0.86
(c)	Random	0.4 - 0.6	0.86 - 1.29
(d)	Loosely regular	0.6 - 0.8	1.29 - 1.72
(e)	Highly regular	above 0.8	above 1.72
	Total Range	0.0 - 1.0	0.0 - 2.15

Highly Clustered (less than R_X 0.2 R_N 0.43)

This pattern covers 169,996 km^2 or 22.85 per cent of the country's area. It is observed in the districts having a large number of water bodics, as Mansa (R_X = 0.16). Zambczi (0.09), Kabompo (0.17), Mumbwa (0.11), Kalabo (0.18) and Senanga (0.17). The size of village varies from Mumbwa (80.5 km^2) to Mansa (24.2) and have no particular pattern. Again the villages in Mumbwa district have the largest area (1.23 km^2) under agriculture in each village, while the rest of the districts have either around 105 or 55 persons. The average number of dwellings in each village varies considerably from 52 (Mumbwa) to 9 (Sesheke). The districts have high spacing, r_E-value, D_A-value and D_F-value. The average actual inter-settlement distance, r_O, is 0.87 km.

Loosely Clustered (R_X : 0.2-0.4, R_N : 0.43-0.86)

This pattern is found in 14 districts, comprising 310,392,27 km^2 (41.73%). Kawambwa (R_X-0.27). Samfya (0.30). Kabwe Rural (0.37), Lusaka Rural (0.33) and Mongu (0.22) do have water bodies but the rest of the districts are relatively at a higher level. The average area under each village varies widely from 74 km^2 in Mongu to 60.9 km^2 in

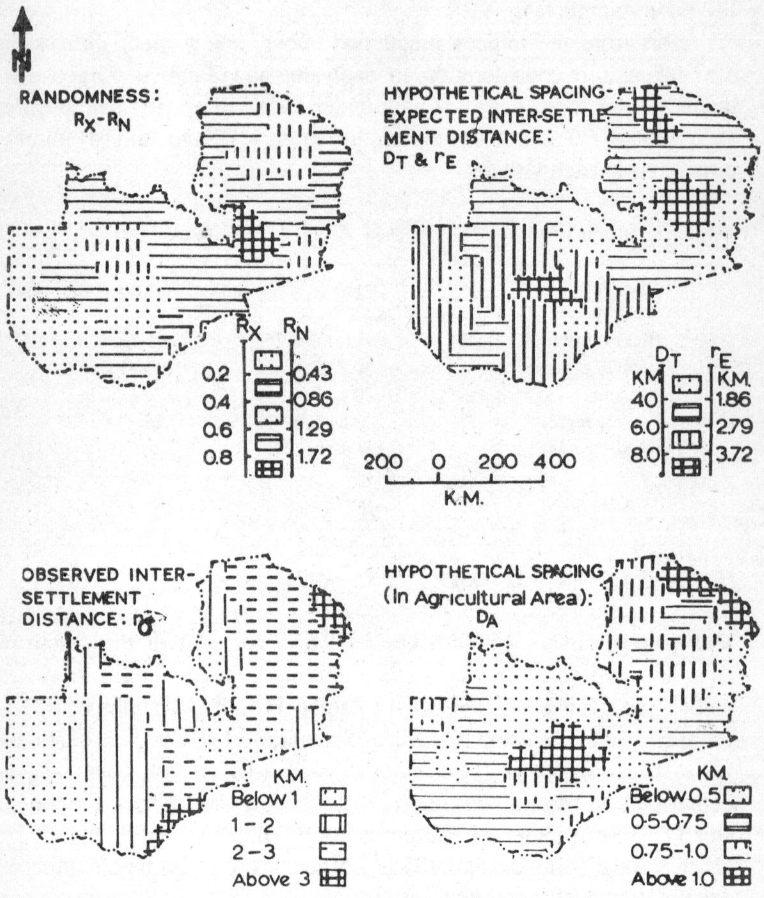

Fig. 4.3: Distribution of Rural Settlements

Mpika. Relatively densely settled districts, though away from the old line-of-rail such as Mongu, Mukushi and Mwinilinga have less area under each village. Except Kabwe Rural (1.02 km²), the villages in the rest of the districts have less than 0.65 km² under agriculture, while in five districts it is even less than 0.20 km². The villages of the districts along the main roads Lusaka Rural (281 persons), Choma (158),

Kabwe Rural (213), Kalamo (117) and Mpika (89) have big villages; while the other districts, away from the line-of-rail, have small villages. The number of dwellings, more-so-ever, following the same pattern. The D, D_A, D_F and r_E values are relatively high. The average r_O value is 1.67 km.

Random (R_X : 0.4-0.6 , R_N : 0.86-1.29)

Random pattern is found in Northern and Eastern provinces, and in Solwezi district (North-Western province) and in the old Gwembe district (Southern Province). It covers an area of 199,844.04 km² (26.86%). Large areas under each village and large areas under agriculture in village in the concerned districts of the Northern Province indicate the loose occupation of land; while in Eastern Province, owing to converse reasons, it is densely occupied. Except Solwezi (34 persons and 9.4 dwellings), the villages have a population around 120 persons 30 dwellings; and with the exception of Chipata District, the D and r_E values are about 5 km and 2.25 km, respectively. The D_A value is low, indicating larger occupation of land especially in Eastern Province. The average r_O value is 2.33 km.

Loosely Regular (R_X : 0.6-0.8, R_N : 1.29-1.72)

The pattern is found only in the districts of Lundazi (R_X-0.64), Mazabuka/Monze (0.63) and Isoka (0.62), covering an area of 55,974.40 km² (7.53%). This category is associated with small villages with relatively large population (except Lundazi). The number of dwellings does not have specific pattern. The D value is high in Isoka (5.90 km.), while in other two districts it is 3.75 km. The D_A, r_E and D_F values follow the same pattern. These areas have some degree of regularity and as well as randomness in the settlement distribution pattern. The average r_O value is 2.83, which is the maximum.

Highly Regular (R_X : above 0.8, R_N : above 1.72)

Highly regular pattern is an exceptional for this region of Africa. It is found in the Serenje District covering 68,439.04 km² (3.1%). This district has small villages with less number of persons. D, D_A, r_E and D_F values are one of the lowest for Zambia. The fragmentation of settlements in the form of very small villages scattered throughout the dis trict is responsible for such a regular pattern. The average r_0 value is 2.80 km.

There are certain relationships between the quantitative indices describing the salient features of the distribution pattern of rural settlements. It is easy to understand some relationships because there are some mathematical equations explaining the relationship. For example, the density of rural settlements is inversely related to their spacing; or the expected intersettlement distance has a linear relationships with spacing r_E = 0.465 D). There are other relationship in between the quantitative indices which are similar to other parts of the world, such as, if clustering increases in a spatial distribution, then density should have increased; or the pattern should become increasingly orderly time assuming that most land remains in farms. There are third type of relationship between quantitative indices which are most peculiar to Zambia. These relationships are owing to the unique distributional pattern of Zambian rural settlements. Large unsettled areas, unstable settlements, hunting and gathering based rural economy and the like have contributed to the peculiar relationships. Districts with clustered settlements, low density and small size of villages have such characteristics.

Zambian Villages

Zambia is a vast country having diversified physical, social, economic and environmental conditions. These factors have been responsible for shaping Zambian villages. Can we develop a model of Zambian village at all? How are the social factors being transformed by economic realities? What is influence of the nearby town or important settlement in terms of village economy, housing and socio-economic amenities? How are the fields being changed? In short, what is the process of transformation of Zambian villages? Anthropologists, sociologists, historians and geographers have been looking into the related issues within the social structure of the Zambian society.

A typical Zambian village should consist of members of not only same tribe or class but even of the one extended family. As mentioned earlier, the headmen are the senior members of such social group. He is recognised by the administration and the local chief and commands respect in the village. The villages are generally named after their headmen. The case of Sandaliya village 5 km northeast of Mansa town in Luapula valley is an example of such village (Fig. 4.4). The population in this village of Ushi tribe which fall in the broad tribal and linguistic group of Bemba, Lala and Lamba. The neighbourhood, relationship largely depends on clan relationship, instead of tribe. Richardson observes that the members of the same clan consider themselves to be a kin even though they cannot trace direct relationship.[14] Similarly Mubila village located about 18 km southeast of Livingstone town and north of Zambia - Zimbabine international border consists of population of Tonga (Leya) tribe only (Fig. 4.5). It is very close to the Chief Mukune's headquarters in Kalamo district. This village was settled in 1954 with fugitives from the chiefs village which became overcrowded. Though the villages have been shifting, their social structure remains mostly unchanged. The Pemba village in Chipata district was shifted to the Kalichero Intensive Development Zone (Chapter 5). Its population consists of Chewa tribe of Nyanja and Chewa tribal and linguistic group.[15]

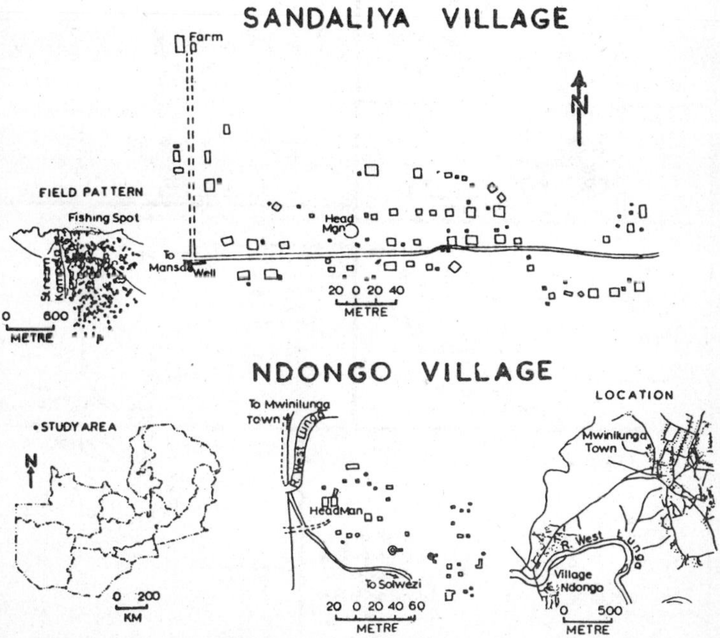

Fig. 4.4: Sandalya and Ndongo Villages

As the village become bigger in size, members of the other tribes are likely to be included. In Ndongo village consisting of only 8 households and located at a distance of 2 km from Mwinilunga town (Fig. 4.4), the headman is of Luvale tribe.[16] But, there are households of other tribes as well, such as Lunda, Bunda and Kaonde. Similarly, the chief Chiwala's village, located 15 km east of Ndola city has over 350 persons (Fig. 4.6). In this village of social importance of Muslim population, there are households of Christians and even pagans.[17] The Mutamino village located north of Lusaka International Airport and 37 km northeast of Lusaka City and 10 km away from Chongwe Mission consists of Soli tribe.[18] But, people of Ndebele tribe of Zimbabwe who migrated to Zambia in 1960 owing to severe droughts have also settled

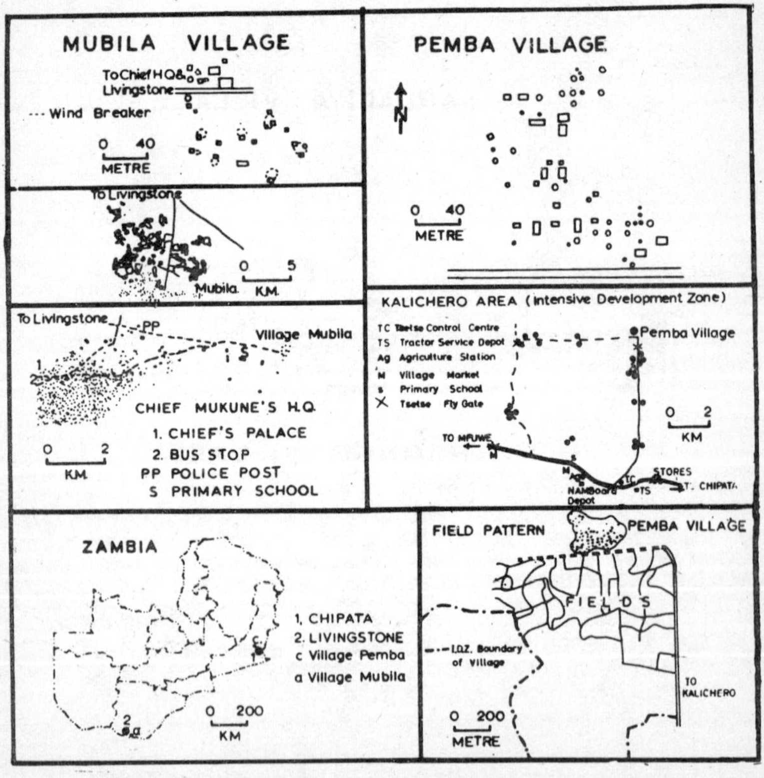

Fig. 4.5: Mubila and Pemba Villages

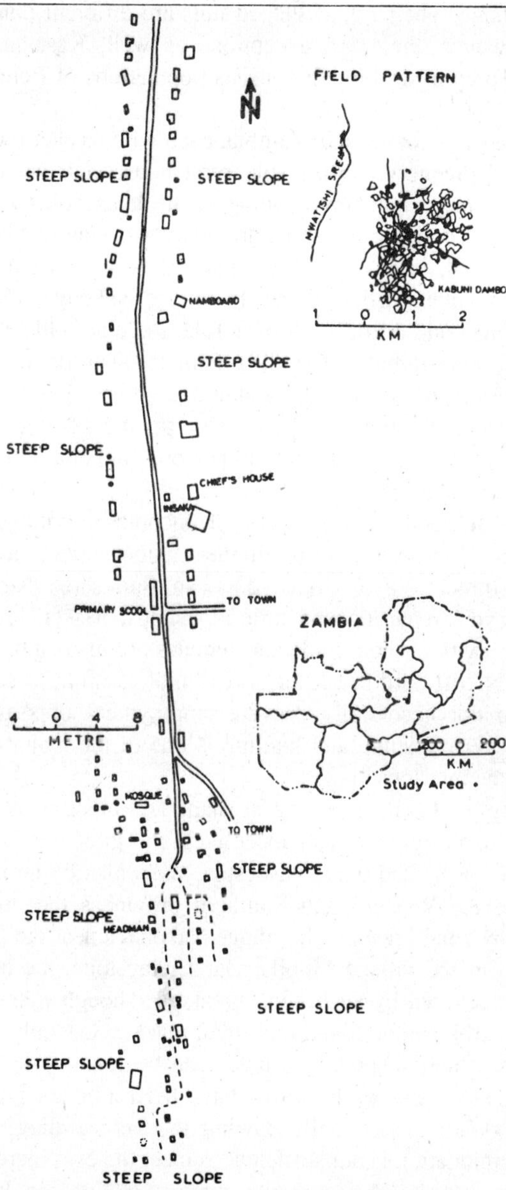

Fig. 4.6: Chief Chiwala's Village

in this village. Their round shaped huts are different than that of Soli tribe. However, there are exceptions as well. Kasama village near Kasama Town is sizable but consists populations of Bemba tribe (Fig. 4.7).[19]

Polygamy is common in Zambia, each wife has her own household, garden and greenery. As a result, rural households are dominated by females. In large number of villages, the households are incomplete (Table 4.2). The male members are either working in towns along the old line-or-rail, or divorced or separated or have been just deserted their other halves in the village. In village Nakonga, 15 km south of Mongu Town and 3 km north of Sefula, there are only 17 adult males against 37 adult females (Fig. 4.8). Females also dominate in agriculture. However, in general, the young age group 15.35 prefers to move to urban centres. As a result the enterprising population is missing from the villages. One can find old persons, and children in good numbers in the rural areas.

There are additional sources of income in villages other than agriculture. The persons in the highest income group are working for the Government. In a village one can find shop, bars, butcheries, poultry, cycle repairing and tailoring shops, basket, brick and curio making activities where male and females are also employed. In some villages, NAMBoard centre or agricultural camp has been established which do not necessarily provide employment opportunities to the local villagers. Fishing and hunting is one of the major occupation of males in the interior villages.

Mostly the huts are oblong in shape and made of pole and dagga. But, due to the government incentives, the grass roofs are being replaced by corrugated iron or asbestos, and walks by burnt or kimberly bricks. In the Western and Southern provinces the houses are surrounded by wind breakers. In village Nakoanga near the Zambezi flood plain and in the village Mubila near Livingstone, the huts and cattle sheds are covered by such wind breakers. Though round huts are not common but it can be found in several places. Generally the granary or toilets are round shaped. The latter can be found over an ant hill as well. Villages close to the towns have been used for providing cheap accommodation occasionally. Owing to overcrowding, the provision for accommodation is not sufficient to meet the ever increasing number of persons employed in urban centres of all orders. In large urban areas, the solutions to this problem are site and service schemes or even shanty towns. But, in the case of small town like Mwinibunga, the

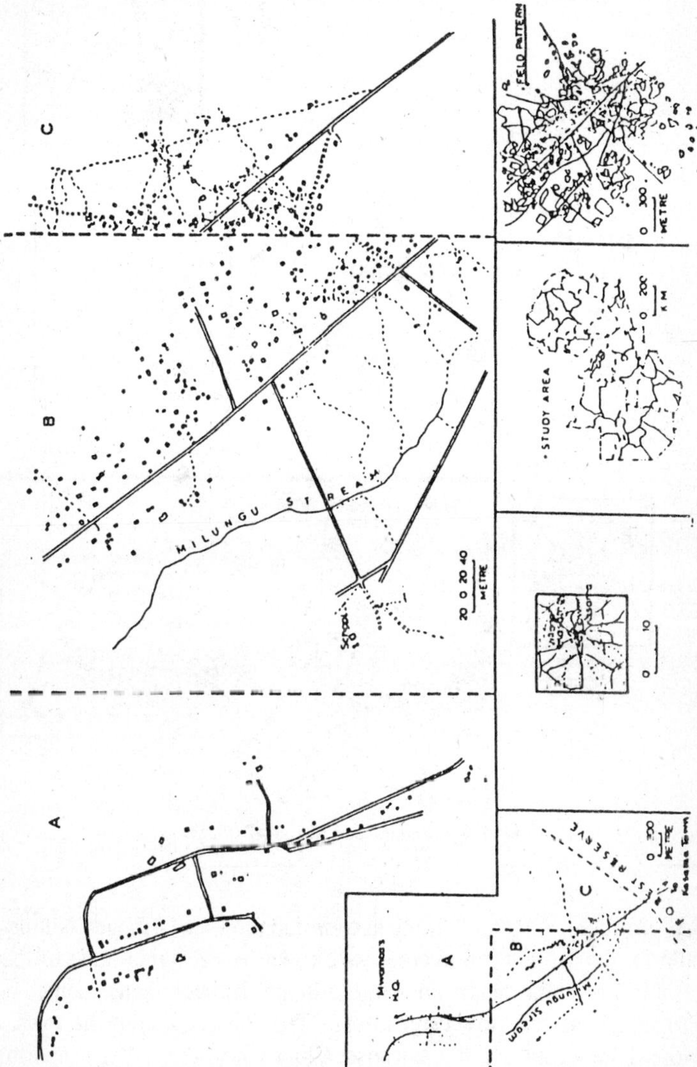

Fig. 4.7: Kasama Village

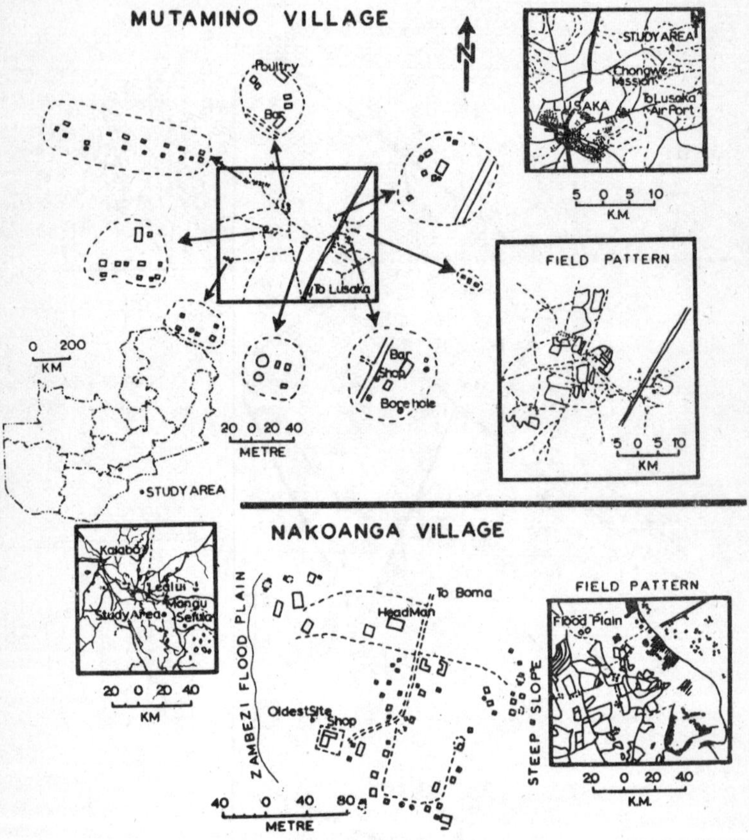

Fig. 4.8: Mutamino and Nakonga Villages

urban workers have to find accommodation in village Ndongo. Similarly, the workers in average size town like Kasama have to look for their accommodation in large village by the same name but separated from the town by forest. The distance from the town is obviously important for this purpose. Chief Chiwala's village in Ndola Rural district and Mubila village in Kalamo district are connected by regular bus service, but due to the distance from urban centres these villages are rarely used for providing cheap accommodation. People visit town for several reasons including medical purposes.

Table 4.2 : Characteristics of Sample of Villages

Sl. No.	*Village (Tribe)*	*Nearest Town (Province)*	*Distance from Nearest Town (km,*	*Popula-tion %*	*Adult Male (15+) %*	*Adult Female (15+) %*	*Children (below 15 years)*	*Occupational Structure*
1.	Sandaliya (Vshi)	Mansa (Laupula)	5	126	20	23	57	Unemployed, Agriculture
2.	Ndongo (Mixed)	Mwinilunga (North-Western)	2	82	16	20	54	Govt. service in town; Agriculture, Fishing
3.	Chiwala (Swahili)	Ndola (Copperbelt)	15	359	19	30	58	Government Serive, Business Labourers
4.	Mubila (Tonga)	Livingstone (Southern)	18	40	30	23	47	Agriculture, Curio-making
5.	Pemba (Chewa)	Chipata (Eastern)	25	94	17	27	53	Agriculture; Government Service
6.	Mutamino (Soli)	Lusaka (Lusaka)	37	117	14	20	66	Agriculture, Household Industry
7.	Nakonga (Lozi)	Mongu (Western)	15	93	18	40	42	Agriculture
8.	Kasama (Bemba)	Kasama (Northern)	5	971	12	19	69	Agriculture, Government Service, Business.

Source : Fieldwork by the author.

In most cases the agricultural output of a village is below subsistence level. Due to government's efforts for improved agricultural practices and marketing, there has been marked changes though such efforts are effective locally. In village Pemba which lies in the intensive development zone, the production of main crops, such as cassava, maize, groundnuts, cotton and banana is much above subsistence level. In this village fields are of rectangular in shape and used for several years. In Nakonga and Mutamino villages most of the fields are of this shape. On the other hand, the shape of fields in general are either irregular or circular and unsystematically distributed around the cluster of huts. If one studies Zambian villages with the help of air photos, he will find such patches, some currently under cultivation while other deserted.

The total shape of the village consists of the huts and the fields. In villages like Sandalya near Mansa, or of Chief Chiwala it is easy to trace the older or new parts of the village. In the former village the huts of the new generation are behind that of the older generation; while in latter case, the older huts have clustered in the southern part and the new development has taken place in the north of the mosque. The space in between the huts are being utilised for kitchen gardens. Particularly in a bigger village, like Mutamino near Lusaka, the merging hamlets and homestead can be noticed. Agglomeration of huts or their cluster under the same headmanship gives the shape and morphology of a Zambian village. As a result there cannot be a definite shape of the village even in any region of the country. Identical shape can be found in a very localised area, such as in the case of villages along the Zambezi flood plain where village Nakoanga is located. Further, due to shifting of village after the exhaustion of environmental resources, the village shape and morphology is likely to change with such events. In some districts the density of population is below 2 persons per km^2 and such a low density will continue to permit shifting of villages in the year to come.

REFERENCES

1. The seven major tribes are Nyanja, Bemba, Lozi, Tonga (Bantu), Luanda, Luvale, and Kaonde. It may be noted here that philologists have used the word Bantu to describe these linguistic groups.
2. Watson, W., *Tribal Cohesion in a Money Economy*, Manchester University Press, 1971, pp. 18-19. Kalolo also instituted one Makalolo family in each village of the Lozi country (Bulozi), vide Fagan, B.M. (ed.), *A Short History of*

Zambia, Oxford University Press, 1970, pp. 126-7.

3. Apthorpe, R. (ed.), *From Tribal Rule to Modern Government*, Rhodes-Livingstone Institute, Lusaka, 1966, p. VII.
4. For example in Mwinilunga district (in 1930) of Ndembu people, 'formerly the sub-chiefdoms seemed to have quite firmly established, but today the political boundaries have been greatly altered and in the interest of centralized recognition has been withdrawn from "redundant" chiefs and several areas have been amalgamated', vide Turner, V.W., *Schism and Continuity in an African Society*, Manchester University Press, 1972, p. 12. Conversely in Mbala district of Mambwe people Watson records, 'There are sixteen traditional chieftancies, thirteen of whom have chiefs of the royal clan, but the British recognized only three chiefs, all of them royal', Vide Watson, W., *Op. cit.*, p. 18.
5. Apthorpe, *op. cit*, p. V.
6. Colson, E., Plateau Tonga, in Schneider, D.M. and Gough, K. (eds.), *Matrilineal Kinship*, A.H. Wheeler & Co., Allahabad, 1972, p. 42.
7. *Gazetteer of Geographical Names in the Republic of Zambia*, Government Printers, Lusaka, 1966, p. 42.
8. *Idem*, pp. 34-35.
9. The local name for shifting cultivation is known as *chitemene system* in Zambia.
10. Colson, E., *Marriage and the Family Among the Plateau Tonga*, Manchester University Press, 1958, pp. 55-62.
11. The flying functions, especially related to distribution or administration, operated by roads, are point to point basis. It hardly affects the settlements lying nearby the roads. Such aloof functions are terms here as flying functions.
12. Clark, P.J. & Evans, F.C., Distance to nearest neighbour as a measure of relationship in population, *Ecology*, 1954, Vol. 35, pp. 445-53.
13. Nag, P., Alternative Approach for the Identification of Randomness in point patterns, *Geographical Review of India*, 1978, vol. 39, No. 2 pp. 193-4.
14. Richardson, E.M., *Aushi Village Structure in the Fort Rosebery District of Northern Rhodesia*, Rhodes — Livingstone Communication No. 10, Institute for African Studies, 1959, see also Cunnion, I., *History of Luapula : An Essay on the Historical Nations of a Central African Tribe*, Rhodes—Livingstone Paper No. 21, 1969, pp. 50-3; and Cunnion, I., *The Luapula Peoples of Northern Rhodesia*, Manchester University Press, 1967.
15. The Chewas are matrilineal tribe under Paramount Chief Undi. "In the traditional Chewa society, the major occupation of the men was hunting, deliberating on tribal affairs and fighting as member of their tribes". see Tuthill, D.F., John A. Williams and P.W. Foster, *The Structure of Shifting, Agriculture in Two Chewa Villages*, University of Maryland, Miscellaneous Publication 629, 1968, p. 13.
16. White, observes that "the Luvale regard them as maximal matrilineages and if two individuals belong to the same clan they do not doubt common unilinear descent". They are able to trace their genealogies, through matrilineages upto 20 generations, an exception among Zambian Tribes. Further White mentions : "......the (social or tribal) structure is essentially based upon lineage although it is expressed in terms of clanship. Clanship as a concept in Luvale society conceals a true lineage structure of society rather than highlights it". See White,

C.M.N., North Rhodesia : Luvale political organisation and the Luvale lineage, in Apthorpe, R. (ed.), *From Tribal Rule to Modern Government*, Rhodes-Livingstone Conference Proceedings, 1960.

17. See chapter II for Swalili population and relocation of villages in Chief Chiwala's area.
18. This village falls in the area of Chieftainess Nkomesha of Tonga-II a major tribal and linguistic group. This is the third generation residing in the village. Since the colonial administration, Soli has been known as a tribe. Earlier it was only a linguistic and cultural group and hence did not have a centralized political system in the past. Argyle studying the Soli political organisation of Mapanshya and Unda. Unda Chiefs noticed that even the headquarters of the chiefs did not contain more than 50 huts, including those of their relatives, dependents and slaves. He further observed that lineages form the foci of social identity for Soli institutional organisation. The clans of Solis are derived from other tribes and it is difficult to find any genuine Soli at all. See Argyle, W.G., *Northern Rhodesia : Soli chieftainships and political adaptation*, in Apthorpe (ed.), *Op. cit.*, pp. 103-11.
19. This village was shifted from the present town area by Europeans because the villagers disturbed them. The present site was chosen during the early years of this century. This village now comes under senior chief Mwambwa of Bemba, Lala, Lamba major linguistic and tribal group.

5

RURAL DEVELOPMENT AND POPULATION REDISTRIBUTION

ZAMBIA poses problems very different from the well populated or overpopulated countries both in nature and dimension, more especially regarding development in the rural sphere. This problem gets accentuated due to the high aspirations of a nation freed from the bonds of slavery only a little more than two decades back. Physical environmental hazards limiting the base for productive farming have caused varied type of obstructions to the extension of rural settlement fabric. Swampy and vast tsetse fly infested areas, low population base and very weak transport system have all combined to retard economic activity over the greater part of the country. Under these handicaps, the achievement of freedom has not yet markedly accelerated rural development, particularly when the harmful features of the minority rule are boldly perceptible on the face of the country. The transformation of the rural settlement fabric is a necessary prelude to a sound economic development of the country which has witnessed different political systems and has passed through several phases of cultural development.

Rural Development during Colonial Period

This era of 75 years can be clearly divided into two periods: (a) The early colonial rule–1889-1947, and (b) Late colonial rule–1947-1964. Both these periods have their specific nature and pattern of rural development.

In Zambia as a whole, since most of the native population was forced to settle in thirty-nine reserves (54,250 sq. miles) or hardly 19.2 per cent of the total area, the rural settlement fabric was largely confined to this very limited area. The importance of various policies adopted by the early colonising power on rural settlements becomes evident from the fact that the area along the old line-of-rail (built in 1905-1909) was considered to be an area to be saved for 'a great coming influx of European settlers', which as in Chipata and Mbala, never in fact materialised. Along the line-of-rail some 23 million acres of land were cleared off Africans to make room for European expansion. By 1960 only 2 million acres had been taken up, and of these only 70 thousand acres were under cultivation. The number of active white farmers in the area was 260. The native reserves totalled 24.9 million acres for an African population of 268 thousand giving 92.8 acres per head. In all, some 26 thousand Africans were moved.[1]

'The reserves, however, got so densely populated that sometimes the densities reached over 39 km^2, twelve times greater than the safe ecological limit'. Thus the policies pursued by the political power had adverse effects on the rural settlement fabric of the country which brought about concentration in some areas and vast empty spaces with almost no population and settlements, though environmental factors were not largely unfavourable for their development. It is this legacy of the past which has made the settling process of the country so very problematic today. There was an acute problem of land in Eastern Province. Almost whole of the state land was owned by European farmers and located in the most favoured zone of the province. The nearby reserves were then getting over-crowded. Because of the population pressures in the reserves, the Colonial Office and the North Charterland Concession Company (NCEC) eventually reached a financial agreement whereby the government bought the substantial remains of the concession for resettlement purposes. Resettlement began in 1941 and by 1946 some 28 thousand people had been moved from Fort Jameson Reserves and 17 thousand from Petauke Reserves.[2]

The late colonial period i.e., the period when other territories under the Crown were becoming independent or agitating for it, the administrators laid some emphasis on African rural development. Permanent and compact settlements were encouraged more because of administrative expediency than providing benefits to the native population. However, to release the pressure on African reserves new settlement schemes were pushed forward. The African farmers within European agricultural lands improved their agricultural techniques. Their fields which had no regular geometrical shape before, became either oblong or square. Extension service for the Africans was introduced. Co-operatives were also encouraged in African farming techniques, and agricultural growth poles were created. But the agricultural sector continued to be dominated by the Europeans. The net effect on African rural development was only in pockets. The country side continued to practice the 'Chitemene system' (shifting cultivation). In 1941 a resettlement programme was started to relieve pressure on the reserves and to introduce soil conservation.

A ten years development plan was prepared in 1947. The objectives of this plan were for more food and dwellings and better roads.[3] However, there was no particular emphasis on rural development. Increased mechanisation was proposed, both in agricultural and industry, in order to meet the labour shortage. Then African labour was not readily available. Obviously, the concern was for European farming only. For example, there was much emphasis in this plan for agricultural marketing and development of secondary industries. In 1948, this plan was reviewed for the first time. The programme of rural development for 1948-49 was so-called radically altered so as to increase the tempo of development basically by increasing food production, while at the same time increasing soil fertility and checking soil erosion. The second review of this plan was made in 1951 in which social implication of revòlution in African agriculture was also emphasised. It was suggested that the pattern of agricultural settlement must be so as to encourage progress in other directions but within the framework of a progressive African social order. The ideal pattern of agricultural settlement and progress was yet to be discovered. However, Improved Farmers and Peasants Farmers schemes expanded rapidly especially in Mazabuka District. Peasant Farming Scheme was an attempt to use the same incentives as are provided to improved farmers, but, to present them in a somewhat different form while at the same time integrating the farmers into the social structure of their tribe.[4]

Shortly after Second World War, the Peasant Farming Schemes were begun to move the cultivators from overcrowded areas to replace shifting cultivation with a prescribed 4 to 5 years rotation and to develop a commercial cash crop farm economy. A survey of 1000 established farms in 1961 revealed 75 per cent of peasant farmers were located in the Eastern Province, some of which were within few miles of the Katuwa and Chikumbe villages. Some more examples have been chosen to throw light on the pattern of rural development. The Chief Chiwala's village is an example of a traditional service centre while Mungwi settlement scheme is representative of the governmental efforts to improve rural settlements of the country, though without much success.

Mungwi Scheme

Mungwi is a story of failure of an area with high investment, mechanised agriculture and a neatly planned settlement. The scheme lies about 23 km east of Kasama town. It covers approximately 20 thousand acres (8,100 ha) and has 200 thousand acres on the adjacent minor watersheds (Fig.5.1). The scheme designed as a Tractor Mechanisation Unit with agriculture station, training centre, grazing area and electricity. It is also well connected with Mungwi township, which is close to the scheme, having rural council, secondary school, a post office, bus service and stores. The scheme failed mainly because of human factors as the loans which the government had given to the settlers were not repaid.

The scheme, however, has brought about changes in its environs. While the participants have moved near to the Mungwi streams, the inhabitants of nearby areas have created squatters in the scheme area. It is of interest to note that the large and some of the rectangular fields along the stream are due either to the deserted farmers or due to those villagers who have adopted the farming system of the scheme more especially the shape and size of the farms. However, such schemes 'aimed at land conservation as much as improving African farming'. In most cases the schemes were based on a single node or growth pole. Outside these single centre schemes, progress was much slower, consisting of a rather sparse distribution of mission, schools and hospitals and the retail stores of superannuated urban employers.[5]

Inspite of all these efforts, "during the period of colonial rule the main preoccupations affecting rural development were administrative expediency and religious conversion and most of the centres which developed are a direct product of these circumstances, district and chiefs' headquarters, or mission schools and hospitals".[6]

Rural Development in the Post Independence Period

In the present day Zambia there are two basic approaches to rural development.

(a) First involves the extension of services (shops, clinics, schools, roads, agricultural advisory services, cooperative and community projects) throughout the country; and

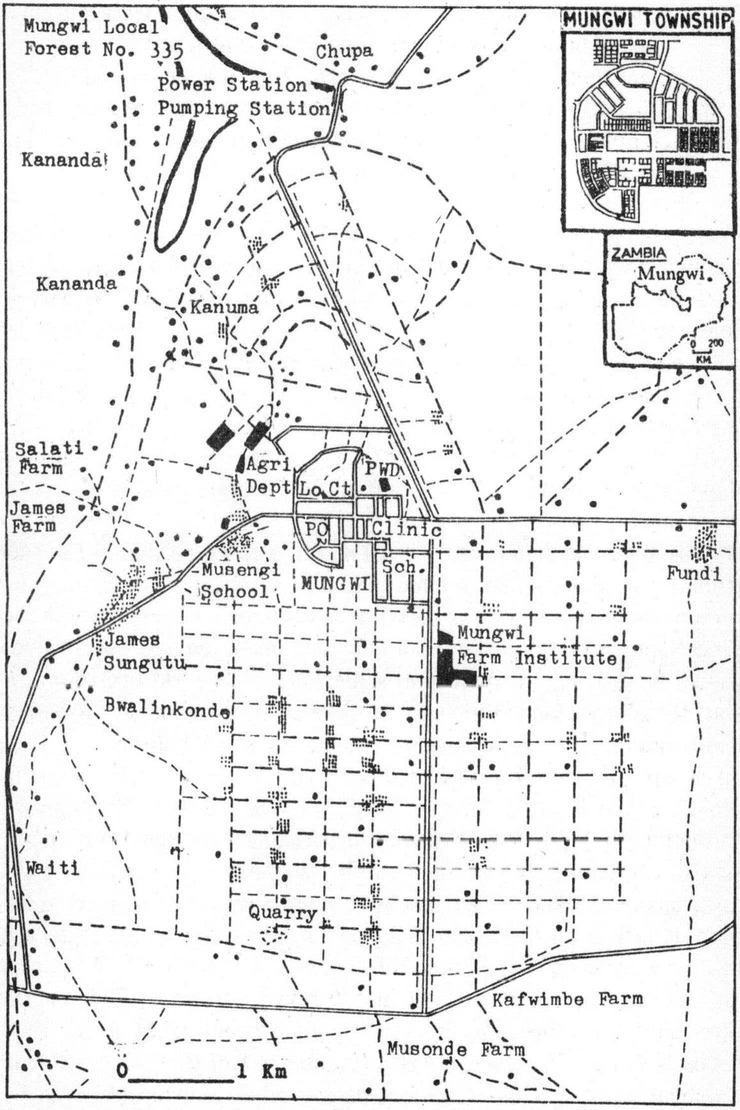

Fig. 5.1: Mungwi Scheme

(b) The second type of growth aims at concentrating funds and energies of limited staff in specific 'nodol' development schemes for which sites are chosen in relation to broad national aims. These comprises (i) State farms and ranches, (ii) settlement and production units, and (iii) tractor mechanisation scheme. Of these, the aims of settlement schemes are quite complex as they aim at an increase in production and also resettlement of people from overcrowded reserves.

It may be pointed out that towards the end of its rule, the British colonial government promoted the idea of regional plans. One of the main aims of the Catchment and Conservation Plans (CCPs) was to conserve good soils. People were not allowed to move on to these areas until such time as they were properly planned and the basic requirements, such as roads and water supply provided. After independence the Regional Planning Office continued and expanded the policy of CCPs, since the Government of Zambia fully realised the value and importance of these plans within an overall policy of rural development.[7]

The scattered pattern of villages and houses in the rural areas particularly in districts like Serenje is quite widespread. Throughout the rural areas the population is very thinly scattered and very early in the First National Development Plan the government realised that services cannot be provided to such rural settlements off the old line-of-rail. It was, therefore, planned to regroup these scattered villages into larger communities. The group housing scheme for better housing at Nalubi taken up in 1965 by the Department of Community Development proved to be a great success. Therefore, the District Development Committee in April 1967 resolved that adequate propaganda be made so that regrouping be accepted by the people. At the same time the government was keen to see that not only regrouping is encouraged but there is proper and adequate planning of regrouping scheme.[8] Such a task was, however, not without difficulties and failures. The Mapepela Village Regrouping Scheme in Chief Kafindas area nearly 72 km north of Serenji township in a poor and depressed area taken up in 1968 ended in failure. However, it was taken up again in 1970 when only six Zambian settled on the scheme whose number went up to seven by 1972. Though these, short term aims may have been achieved, yet the planning of the infrastructure for the scheme may present problems in the near future.

Miengewe Village Regrouping Scheme

This scheme is located about 55 km south of Ndola in between Ndola-Kabwe road and the railway line (Fig.5.2). It was planned taking into confidence the Ndola Rural Council and the concerned chief, and its implementation started in 1970. It incorporates the grouping of twenty-four villages, though till February 1974 only four villages were registered for shifting. The entire scheme comprises the resettlement of 200 families but till February, 1974 only 142 farmers were recorded in the scheme area. Each family has been given 15 acres (6 ha) of land which is considered to be sufficient for small commercial farming. In order to supplement agriculture, a piggery is being developed. The amenities provided in the scheme include two shops, a primary school and a health centre. However, transport is a problem as it lies 16 km away from the main road.

Kafubu Block : Israeli Settlement Scheme

Some of the rural settlement patterns of Israel have been incorporated in the villages with the assistance of Israeli government. They are based on collective and a communal mode of life and observe the principles of complete social equality, mutual responsibility and direct democracy.

The Kafubu Block is located in the Ndola Rural District off the Kitwe-Kipari Mposhi road in the south. The scheme comprises three villages fully planned with 406 members (Fig. 5.3). Though land for a fourth village has been reserved, yet its planning has not been done so far. The administrative block under the scheme comprising twenty families and has a rural health centre, a primary school, two stores, a workshop and one bar. It is connected through a bus service with Luanshya town. The scheme is administered by the managing committee of the board of directors. The management supplies all the requisites for farming and the produce is marketed through the cooperatives.

By now about 420 families have been settled in the four villages. Each house in such villages has a residential plot of 0.8 ha, within which livestock buildings can be built and rain-fed crops grown. Co-operative unions have been involved in every stage, such as selling livestock feeds, buying eggs, credits, equipments and the like.[9]

Since rural development in the post-independence period is confronted with several problems which are the legacies of the colonial rule, it would be in the fitness of things to have an overall view of the nature and dimension of the entire problem. Firstly, it is to be noted that the distribution between rural and urban population is not clear cut as many people live in between. From time to time peri-urban areas are brought under municipal administration. Since social and economic imbalances exist between the rural and urban areas of one province and another, the information is given provincewise. It is clear that whereas North-Western Province is entirely rural and Western almost rural, the Copperbelt Province is highly urban closely followed by the Lusaka Province.

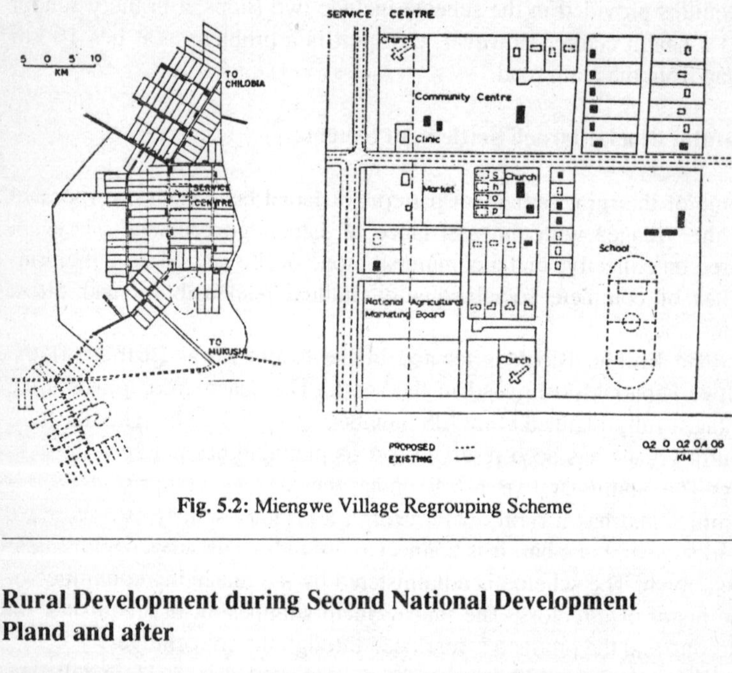

Fig. 5.2: Miengwe Village Regrouping Scheme

Rural Development during Second National Development Pland and after

Realising the vastness of the country's development problems the Second National Development Plan (1972-76) had kept as first priority objective the speeding up of the economic and social development in the rural areas so as to reduce the income gap between the rural and urban sectors of the economy, and to this end an increasing share of total resources available to the nation which was supposed to be directed

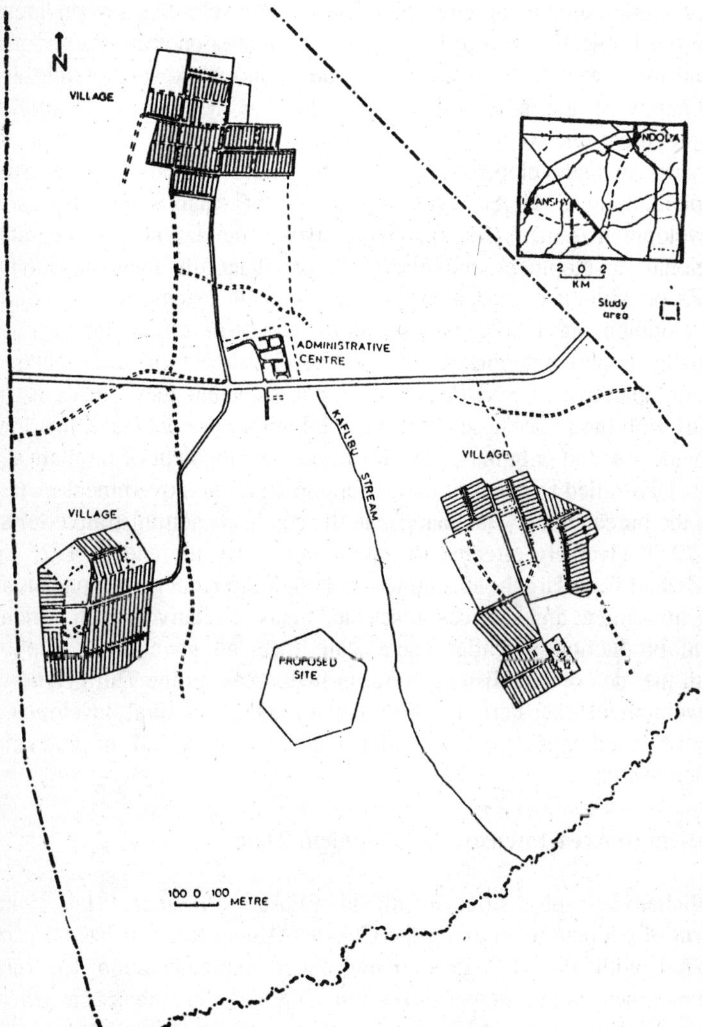

Fig. 5.3: Kafubu Block

towards rural areas. Another objective of the plan was to give increased assistance to small to medium sized family farms in transforming their farming methods into more productive and market oriented ones, agriculture being the chief lever for developing several areas. The third objective was to increase employment opportunities and personal income of the masses in rural areas and wherever possible, exploitation of the natural resources will be encouraged to provide employment and to create centres of cumulative economic and social services in undeveloped areas. Another major objective was to start implementing a larger term programme of establishing 'Intensive Development Zones' (IDZs) so as to lay the foundations for integrated regional development and also to assist villager in areas out side the IDZs or without development projects, through extension, community development and other services with the aim of improving the farming, nutritional and hygienic levels. The establishment of IDZs being a major objective of SNDP, it was emphasized that they must start in areas with the greatest inherent potential within provinces, so that they provide a sound pragmatic base for future development of rural areas.[10] But IDZs failed to get continuous support from the government including the bureaucracy. The changes in the country's administrative set-up in 1973 adversely effected this programme. By the end of 1975 the IDZs had been largely abandoned, although the strategy of concentrating investment and services in selected areas of relatively high agricultural production potential once again received government support with the idea of establishing 'rural growth areas' in the Third National Development Plan Period.[11] Alternative methods of rural development were by then considered to be advantageous than the IDZ in producing quick results.

Kalichero Area-Intensive Development Zone

Kalichero is a sub-district of Chipata in Eastern Province. It lies 35 km north of Chipata town along the Chipata-Mfume Road. It has been included with the IDZ programme under implementation for rural development of comprehensive nature (Fig. 5.4). The object has ben to improve the rural economy as a whole through an increased and more diversified agricultural production and the establishment of supporting rural industries for the sake of creating more employment opportunities there. The programme has been financed by a heavy investment of the Zambian Government and foreign aid. The villages were brought closer together from the nearby areas. The IDZ area which has agglomerated 42 villages in groups ranging from 2 to 5 villages raising the population to 300 or so from the average size of about 55 persons at the present.

This is the first programme in Zambia dealing with (a) regional development without creating foreign and strange environment, and (b) it deals with secondary and tertiary activities in planning a rural areas as well. It is expected to bridge the gap between the standards of rural and urban population.

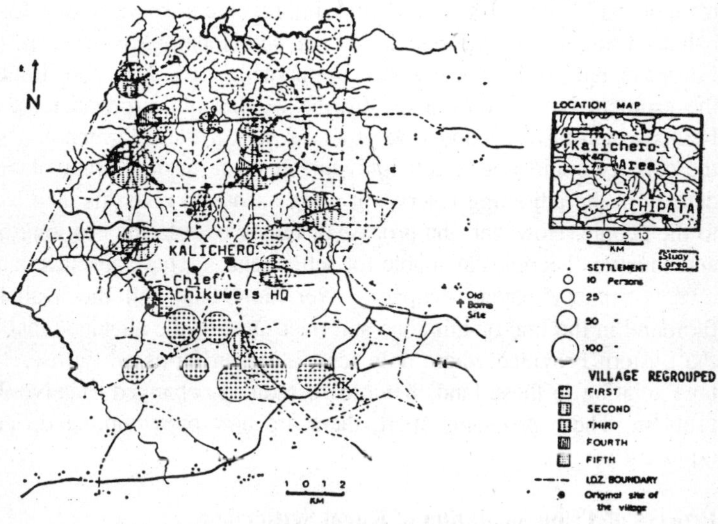

Fig. 5.4: Kalichero Area

hifwile Scheme

hifwile is a mixed farming scheme located about 65 km southeast of vingu town and about 145 km from Kasama town (Fig. 5.5). It is out 8 thousand acres (3,238 ha) in size with plenty of space for exision. The objective of the scheme was to settle farmers in this tential area having integrated farming system based on cattle and iculture.

Though it is a good example of a well operated settlement scheme, yet it is isolation and an absence of settlements around it neither predicts the effects of it in the regional settlement synthesis, nor it becomes a model for development for extra-scheme population. If the ultimate aim is to create a well organised rural service centre, its socio-economic effects on the environs have to be properly evaluated. It is also to be assessed as to what will be the return from such capital investment and, that in a democratic set-up how many people are going to be benefited by it.

The process of rural development is faced with other problems as well. Government is conscious about the "indeterminate nature of traditional land rights (under customary law) which clearly inhibit permanent settlement and agricultural improvement so necesary for a balanced growth of rural population and settlements. Moreover, as the European land rights have been safeguarded in the new constitution, the problem has become acute by the exodus of European farmers. Farms which have become vacant as a result of these farmers leaving the country could not be left idle, and in much desired areas of high density in the adjoining reserves it makes sense to give this land back to the people. However, the process of taking over farms is a long one and squatters becomes available for settlements.[12] These absentee landowners retain a paper occupancy over more than half the available farmland in the line-or-rail zone and over most of the alienated land in the Eastern Province where only few European farms are in use. The laws relating to these lands have to be radically changed to solve this problem. These problems apart, there are new ones coming up at a rapid rate.

Process of Transformation of Rural Settlement

The habitation in rural areas covers about twenty-five per cent of the country's areas; however, as mentioned earlier, government controlled transformation is effective upto forty-six per cent. The rural habitat is of the form of chief's headquarters, neighbourhood centres, villages, hamlets, homesteads, farms and settlement schemes. They can be classified in two broad divisions, *viz*, (a) unplanned habitat or villages; and (b) planned habitat or rural settlement schemes.

The agricultural camps[13] and rural settlement schemes[14] are meant to transform the Zambian rural habitat. Both the agents have different patterns of transformation. Agricultural campus provide agricultural requirements, technical knowhow and marketing of products to rural settlements. They are responsible for the effective transformation in Central, Southern and Eastern provinces. The infrastructure provided by these camps has encouraged the production even before the independence. In these areas the agriculture has developed from subsistence cultivation to semi-commercial farming. The settlements and the fields are permanent in nature. Geometrical shape of fields, use of fertilizers and production of cash crops are few of the significant changes from the traditional subsistence cultivation. However, this process of transformation suffers from inaccessibility caused by the lop-sided distribution of roads and railways. The rural areas away from the transportation lines and agricultural camps, await for similar impulses. The process of transformation depends on the nature, organisation, and the most significant, on the spacing of the camps.

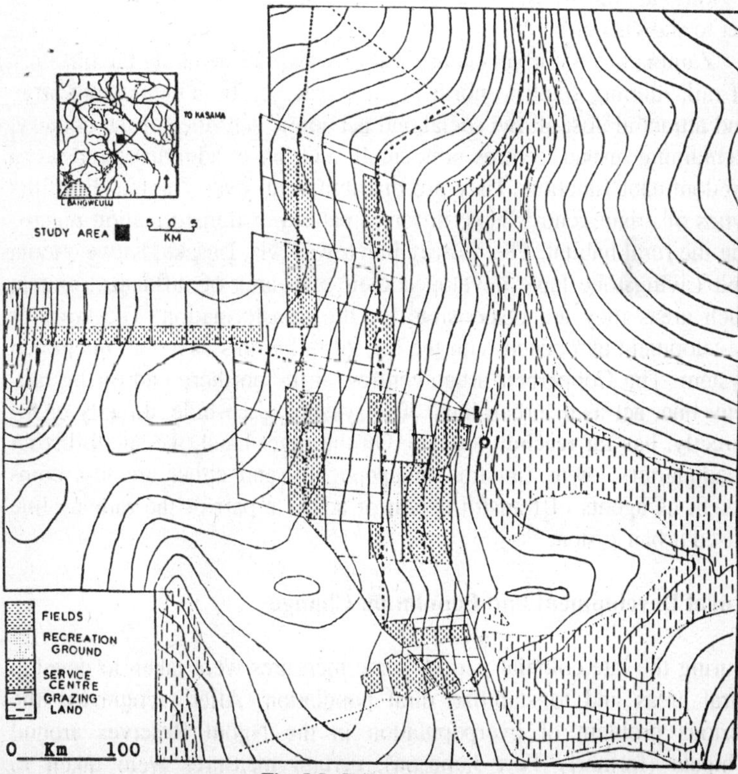

Fig. 5.5: Chifwile Scheme

Since the colonial period, the rural settlement schemes were thought to be models to trigger-off growth impulses in rural areas.[15] Funds and energies were concentrated at a point of development to (a) boost agricultural production, (b) open new areas for agriculture, and (c) cultivate settlements in rural areas. Such schemes have mixed effects. Kalichero Intensive Development Zone[16] and Chifwile Mixed Farming Scheme[17] are somewhat successful while Mungwi Scheme[18] is a case of failure. The role of such agricultural growth centres in transforming the nearby areas is indeed a matter of interest for the present study. Mungwi scheme has transformed the surrounding areas in terms of the size and shape of the fields and technique of agricultural farming. The Kalichero Intensive Development Zone has uplifted the rural infrastructure and transformed the growth process in a desirable direction. However, Chifwile Scheme is located in an underpopulated region and transformatory process transmitted through this scheme is yet to show its effect.[19]

Zambia has 85 urban centres out of which 25 lie along the old line-of-rail, running south to north in the territory. These centres are large and attract almost all the social and economic activities of the country. Remaining urban centres are small and have administration as a predominant function. They are distributed all over Zambia. Both the types of urban centres have different pattern of transformation regarding the rural habitat. The railway line towns, viz. Lusaka, Kitwe, Ndola and Livingstone have developed their own area of influence; and in such areas they are responsible for the transformation. The corridor development associated with the line-of-rail works as a well integrated system. The Copperbelt urban centres, at the northern end of the railway line, act as a 'urban hub'. The system as a whole, directly or indirectly, has far reaching effects. On the other hand, the small district headquarters towns function independently and either are less competent as agents of transformation or act as a part of the railway line based urban system.[20]

Rural Development and Population Change

During the late colonial period, some measures were taken to develop rural areas and to stabilize rural population. After recognizing the serious problem of overpopulation in the Ngoni Reserves around Chipata (formerly Fort Jameson), certain measures were taken to reduce this rural overcrowding. The purchase of a part of North Charterland Concession in 1941 and of certain unoccupied European freehold lands and other measures failed to bring about a permanent solution. In 1952, a rehabilitation plan was started with the progressive resettlement of some Ngoni villages in the unoccupied land to the north of the two existing Ngoni reserves.[21] Chipangali in 1951 and Rukuzie in 1957 were regionally planned as reception areas for the resettlement of population from overcrowded reserves of south and of the North Chawa. In 1957 the development of the infrastructure for Chipangali resettlement scheme began. It was expected that response to the scheme would be slow at first, but that the transfer of people would gather momentum within two or three years. By July 1958 five villages and eighteen farming families had been settled, but, contrary to expectation, this scheme then failed to accelerate and at the end of 1962 only twelve villages and fifty-nine farmers (a total population of about 2,000) had moved into the area. This failure can be attributed to a variety of reasons, such as tsetse fly infestation. It was felt that there is a need for legally recognized and socially acceptable system of land tenure which is compatible with capitalised commercial farming.[22] With renewed efforts for the development, 400 farmers in eleven villages settled in this scheme by 1972. Similarly in Rukuzie, about 2,000 farmers moved in twenty-six villages of this scheme. Moreover, the redistribution of population improved the farming practices and gave rise to a new class of rural population–the peasant farmers. As mentioned earlier, as early as 1957, Mungwi was planned for intensive rural development. The aim of the scheme was to set-up a model for the development of modern agricultural community with arable land and by farming in family farms. Extensive measures were undertaken for soil conservation, water management, development of infrastructure, provision of loan and the like. A few villages from the surrounding areas were resettled in this scheme.[23]

After independence, the problems of urban and rural overcrowding were tackled simultaneously. An attempt was made at the regional level to find a solution to these problems. The resettlement of population was undertaken owing to several reasons, apart from reducing pressure in the erstwhile reserves. The major objectives of agricultural and land settlement during the First National Development Plan period were to provide infrastructure for the redistribution of people in areas of overpopulation, wherever possible as part of tsetse consolidation measures, and to assist in the aggregation of population in overpopulated areas of the outlying provinces.[24]

The Government of Zambia fully realised the importance of rural growth centres and agricultural growth poles. Around 1970, various types of development schemes were implemented to harmonise with the broad national aims and objectives of the country. The Department of Cooperatives, Land Use Services, Tobacco Board of Zambia (TBZ), Project Division, Department of Community Development, Credit Organisation of Zambia (COZ)[25] and Zambia National Service are involved in these schemes. Besides these organisations, such schemes are also managed and/or financed by other agencies, such as, Israeli Government, F.A.O., Gossner Service Team (GST), United Church of Zambia, Barclays Bank and Family Farms Limited. (Table 5.1)

The diverse nature of the organisations involved indicates the nature of these schemes. Some of the schemes are aimed at the stabilising of rural population; while in other schemes, the settlement of population is the main aim. However, there are several schemes for rural development which do not take into account a population base, such as, ranches and grazing schemes. On the other hand, the Kafubu and Kafulafuta schemes, near the urban centres of Copperbelt are aimed at the resettlement of villages. The Department of Cooperatives, the Israeli Government and the Land Use Services are involved in these dry farming-semi-commercial schemes. By 1974, three villages of 406 farmers were settled under the Kafubu Scheme. The irrigation schemes, such as Ipafu and Chapula are highly sophisticated, depending on a centralised irrigation lay-out and complicated marketing arrangements. These schemes have brought about the resettlement of a sizable population. Schemes of Tobacco Board of Zambia, Family Settlements Schemes, Development Schemes, Vegetable Schemes and the like have contributed to considerable redistribution of population at the local level.

Apart from these schemes, Tractors Mechanisation Centres, NAM-Board depots and agricultural camps are some of the new foci in rural Zambia. These units alongwith the schemes mentioned above have not always produced desirable results with regard to stabilisation and redistribution of population.[26] In some schemes the operational size of the population could not be attained. Participants in these schemes are migratory in nature. The psychological attachment and tendency towards permanent settlement is lacking among the participants. The infrastructure created by such attempts remains underused. The old line-of-rail is still considered to be more promising, while in the urban areas the site and service schemes are replacing the squatter settlements. Among the larger cities, like Lusaka, Kitwe and Ndola, new areas have been developed as planned residential areas. However, the squatter population is continuously increasing in spite of above

Table 5.1: Nature of Some Plans and Projects

	Name of Plan/ Project	District	Year	Managing/Financing Agencies	No. of farm Households	Av. H.H. Size	Density of pop. (p/km²)	Type
	1	2	3	4	5	6	7	8
1.	Mabaya Musuma	Mazabuka	1970	UCZ/B/OF/MRD (LUS).	64	5.8	95	DFSC
2.	Upper Kaleya	Mazabuka	1971	MRD(LUS)/OF/B/FEL	13	5.8	95	DFMC
3.	Ngweri (Ext. 3)	Mazabuka	1971	MRD(LUS)	22	5.8	95	DFSC
4.	Muchila	Namwala	1968	MRD(LUS)	22	4.4	10	DFSC
5.	Katete	Katete	1971	MRD(LUS)	54	3.9	95	DFSC
6.	Jimoli	Chipata	1970	MRD(LUS)/B	7	3.9	95	—
7.	Kafubu	Ndola R.	1966	DC/IG	380	4.2	228	DF-S6
8.	Kafulafuta	Ndola R.	1969	DC/IG	250	4.2	228	DF-SC
9.	Kangwelema	Katete	1965	DA	18	3.9	95	MFS-S6
10.	Kalimeta	Katete	1955	DA	14	3.9	95	DMFS-S6
11.	Mpangwe	Katete	1957	DA	4	3.9	95	DF-S6
12.	Masumba	Chipata	1958	DA	80	3.9	95	DF-S6
13.	Mailo	Serenje	1970	MRD(LUS)	92	4.5	15	D-SP
14.	Chipangali	Chipata	1951	DA	(11*)400	3.9	95	D-SP
15.	Rukuzie	Chipata	1957	DA	(26*)2000	3.9	95	D-SP
16.	Chadzombe	Chandiza	1965	DA	130	3.9	95	D-SP
17.	Milambo	Mansa	1969	DA	15	4.1	33	D-SP
18.	Chipungu	Nchelenge	1969	DA	20	4.0	26	D-SP
19.	Mulumbi	Mansa	1969	DA	30	4.1	33	D-SP
20.	Chapula	Ndola R.	1971	FAO/PD/MRD(LUS)	80	4.2	228	IS
21.	Nakungwa	Chipata	1969	MRD(LUS)	20	3.9	95	IS
22.	Kavuu	Lundezi	1969	DA/LUS	17	4.3	26	IS

Table 5.1 (*Contd.*)

	1	*2*	*3*	*4*	*5*	*6*	*7*	*8*
23.	Ngosa Muchishi	Ndola R.	1972	PD/LUS	40	4.2	95	TR
24.	Zemba	Katete/ Chandiza	1972	TBZ/MRD	1600	3.9	95	TS
25.	Vubwe & Chikoma	Katete/ Chandiza	1971	TBZ/MRD	200	3.9	95	TS
26.	Sindi Misale	Chipata	1973?	TBZ/MRD	150	3.9	95	??
27.	Lumezi	Lundazi	1971	TBZ/MRD	400	4.3	26	??
28.	Kaoma	Kaoma	1972	TBZ/MRD	400	3.9	15	??
29.	Mkushi	Mkushi	1973	TBZ/MRD	—	4.1	18	??
30.	Kapiri Mposhi	Kabwe	1973	TBZ/MRD	—	4.6	26	??
31.	Serenje	Serenje	1971	TBZ/MRD	240	4.5	15	??
32.	Kakwelesa	Kabwe	1973	TBZ/MRD	-	4.6	26	??
33.	Kabile	Kabwe	1972	TBZ/MRD	70	4.6	26	??
34.	Kapara	Chipata	1967	TBZ/MRD	400	3.9	95	TS
35.	Chibwe	Kabwe	1969	TBZ/MRD/World Bank	50	4.6	26	TS
36.	Mukwela	Kalomo	1970	TBZ/MRD/World Bank	30	4.9	15	TS
37.	Npima	Kabwe	1971	TBZ/MRD/World Bank	10	4.6	26	TS
38.	Tara	Choma	1972	TBZ/MRD/World Bank	14	6.2	34	TS

DFSC : Dry Farming Scheme Commercial; DFMC: Dry Farming Mixed Commercial: DF-S6: Dry Farming—Semi Commericial; MFS-SC: Mixed Farming Scheme—Semi Commercial: DMFS-SC: Dry Mixed Farming Scheme—Semi Commercial; D-SP: Dryland-Subsistence Plus; IS: Irrigation Scheme; TR: Tenant Scheme; Ranching; TS: Tabacco Scheme; FFL; Family Farms Ltd.; TBZ: Tabacco Board of Zambia; OF: Oxfarm; DC: Department of Cooperatives; IG: Israel Government; BB: Barclays Bank; PD: Project Division; UCZ: United Church of Zambia;

* Number of Villages

It is evident from the present study that the efforts of the Government of Republic of Zambia to redistribute and stabilise the population have yet to produce significant results. The inherited colonial structure cannot be changed within period of about 20 years, which is the span of post-independence period. The measures incorporated in the national development plans and implemented through various projects have to create a suitable alternative to counteract the considerable attraction of the old line-of-rail based urban system. An integrated population policy is required for the balanced distribution and absorption of the increasing labour force. Social, economic and transportation facilities have to be co-ordinated to make the rural areas more promising. A judicious population policy will not only curb the growing unemployment in the favoured zone, but will also be helpful in the exploitation and management of the vast resources of Zambia. There is certainly much scope for a suitable population policy in this under-populated country. The problems of Zambia can be atleast partially solved by the redistribution of its population.

REFERENCES

1. Robin, Palmer (ed.) *Zambian Land and Labour Studies*, National Archives Occasional Paper No. 2, Vol. 1, Lusaka, 1973, p. 7.
2. Priestly, J.R., The transfer of agricultural land in the Eastern Province of Zambia, *The Journal of Tropical Geography*, 1978, Vol. 46, pp. 47-60.
3. *Ten Years Development Plan*, Government Printers, Lusaka, 1947.
4. *Second Review of the Ten-Year Development Plan Northern Rhodesia*, Government Printer, Lusaka, 1951.
5. Siddle, David, J., "Rural Development in Zambia : A Spatial Analysis". *The Journal of Modern African Studies*, Vol. 8, No. 2, 1970, p. 274. See also Chamber, Roberts, *Settlement Schemes in Tropical Africa : A Study of Organisation and Development*, Routledge & Kegan Paul, London, 1969, (ch. 2 : The background and origins of settlement schemes in Africa, 15-39; Ch II : Types of settlement schemes, 227-39). This book also refers to Mungwi scheme.
6. Siddle, *Ibid*, pp. 271-84. Also Hellen, J.A., *Rural Economic Development in Zambia 1890-1964*, Wilforum Verlag, Muchen, 1968.
7. *Case Studies in Development, Research Project on Administration for Rural Development*, National Institute of Public Administration, Lusaka, March, 1972, p. 1.
8. Dixon, Carole L., *The Development of Agricultural Policy in Zambia, 1964-71*, O'Dell Memorial Monograph 5, Department of Geography, University of Aberden, 1977.
9. Pudrey, D.M., Farming Co-operatives in the Copperbelt Province, *Zambia Geographical Association*, Handbook Series, 1979.

10. *Second National Development Plan,* Jan. 1972 to Dec. 1976, Ministry of Development Planning and National Guidance; Lusaka, (Dec., 1971), pp. 175-77.
11. Gertzel, Cherry, Two case studies in rural development, in Tordoff, William (ed.), *Administration in Zambia*, Manchester University Press, University of Wisconsin Press, 1980, 257. Also Government Republic of Zambia, *Third National Development Plan,* 1979-83, Lusaka, 1979; and Gertzel, Cherry (ed.). *The Political Process in Zambia : Documents and Readings,* Vol. 1, Revised Edition, University of Zambia, Lusaka, May 1974 (mimeo).
12. McDonnel, Gerry, *Settlement Schemes and their People in Southern Province,* Zambian Geographical Association Handbook, 1974, 155-9.
13. Godel, G.L., *An Analysis of Zambian Agricultural Camps*, Ministry of Rural Development, Lusaka, July 1972. Idem, *An Analysis of Zambian Agriculture,* Planning Unit, Ministry of Rural Development, Lusaka, 1972.
14. Beaumont, A.N., *Settlement Schemes and Policy Guidelines,* Landuse Services, Ministry of Rural Development, Lusaka. Also *Case Studies in Development,* Research Project on Administration for Rural Development, National Institute for Public Administration, Lusaka.
15. Coster, R.N., Peasant Farming, *Agricultural Bulletin* No. 15, Government Printers, Lusaka, 1958.
16. Harvey, R.H., *Some Determinants of the Agricultural Productivity of Rural Households : Report of a Survey in Kalichero District, Eastern Province,* Msekera Regional Research Station, Ministry of Rural Development, Chipata, April 1973.
17. *Policy Matters for Discussion and Approval : Chifwife and Kapatu Settlement Schemes,* Ministry of Rural Development, Lusaka.
18. Verboom, W.C., *Planned Rural Development in the Northern Province of Northern Rhodesia,* I.T.C. Delft, The Netherlands, 1961.
19. Jauhari, A.S. and P. Nag, Rural Development in an Under Populated development country of Africa, Zambia, in Singh, R.L. et al. (eds.), *Geographical Dimensions of Rural Settlements,* National Geographical Society of India Publication, Varanasi, 1976, pp. 298-61.
20. Kay, G., *A Social Geography of Zambia*, University of London Press Ltd., 1967.
21. Hellen, Anthony (1969) Some aspects of land use and over population in the Ngoni Reserves of Northern Rhodesia. *Erdkunde*, Vol. XVI, pp. 180-205. See also Priestley, M.J.S.W. and Greening, P., *Ngoni Land Utilisation Survey 1945-1955*, Government Printers, Lusaka, 1956.
22. Kay, George, Resettlement and land use planning in Zambia : The Chipangali scheme, *Scottish Geographical Magazine*, Vol. 81, 1965, pp. 163-77. Also published as chapter 21 in Prothero, R. Mansell (ed.), *People and Land in Africa South of the Sahara-Readings in Social Geography*, Oxford University Press, 1972, 284-97. For Ngoni settlements, their history, political structure, land tenure, village structure and migrant workers see Cowie, William James, *Changing Settlement Systems and Economic Development : The Case of Kanyanja Parish, Zambia*, Ph.D. Dissertation (unpublished), University of London, 1982.
23. Verboom, *op. cit.*, 1961.

24. *First National Development Plan*, Ministry of National Development and Planning, Government Printers, Lusaka, 1966.
25. Harvey, Charles, Rural Credit in Zambia : Access and Exit, *Development and Change*, 1975, Vol. 6 (2), pp. 89-107.
26. For example in Chama District in Eastern Provinces having all the desired infrastructure did expected results. See Spengen, W.Van, Rurale ontwikkleing en perificvic het Chama District in de Eastern Province, van Zambia, *Geografisch Tijdscebrift* (Amsterdam) Vol. 10, 1976, pp. 279-94. Also Spengen, W. Von, Rural Development in Northern Luangwa Valley: A micro-regional synthesis, *Zambia Geographical Journal*, vol. 31-32, 1976-7, pp. 11-32. Regarding Kasempa District in North-Western Province, the resettlement plans contained implicit assumptions which were not tested but still regarded by the technical planners as almost established facts. See Jaeger, Dirk, *Settlement Patterns and Rural Development — A Human Geographical Study of the Kaonde, Kesempa District, Zambia*, Royal Tropical Institute, Amsterdam, 1981, pp. 110-11.

6

URBAN SETTLEMENT, URBANISATION AND URBAN DEVELOPMENT

CITIES, towns, missions and farms and the gifts of the colonial period. Although most of towns evolved by the turn of twentieth century, they could only attain form and develop their economy in the thirties. These urban settlements even acquired a par excellence position in the tribal network of settlements. Farm settlements have a similar history as that of the towns which are largely planned. Urban centres like Lusaka, Livingstone and Chipata developed due to their geographical position as service centres, while Copperbelt towns grew alongwith the mining activities in their surroundings. There are other settlements along the old line-of-rail, such as Kipari Mposhi and Choma, which developed from railway sidings to sizable urban settlements. The mission settlements similar to urban settlements evolved with the arrival of European population in the north of River Zambezi. During the 1980 Census, several erstwhile siding along the old line-of-rail have been included as towns.

Origin of Urban Settlements

The history of urban development in Zambia indicates that the process of cultivating the seeds of towns and cities has not been a smooth one. In some cases several sites were chosen before finding out a viable location which may be connected either with mining activities or for administrative convenience. As a result, when such activities were no longer attached to these settlements, such sites were abandoned. Brelsford has traced eighty-three abandoned *Bomas* (administrative posts) in Zambia.[1] Such settlements have a long history of debacle, rejuvenation and redevelopment. Some of them are still surviving as sizable settlements, such as Mongoya in Southern Province and Chilanga in Lusaka Province. However, a few settlements like Fort Monze, Chienji,[2] Koka[3] and Katumbi[4] remained as villages. Kakulwani was the first boma in Sengana district. It was build in 1907 on the eastern bank of the River Zambezi, but its building collapsed in the floods of 1913 and a new boma was built in Namalai and then in Nalolo.[5] There are several example which can be added here, however, the causes for desertion are varied. The choice of a better site has largely been responsible for this process. However, for number of *bomas*, the reasons of abandonment is not known. Perhaps, their survival would have changed the present urban scene of Zambia.

Some settlements did survive at the cost of the abandoned bomas and they are responsible in shaping the present urban scene in a large way. A few of the surviving bomas are the towns of present day Zambia. Ndola was shifted to the present site near the railway siding in 1911.[6] Mukushi was abandoned thrice during the period 1900-1954 before the selection of the present site.[7] Some of the bomas could not survive owing to the concentration of activities in nearby growing town along the old line-of-rail. Mwomboshi was the headquarters of West Loangwa district from 1902 to 1906. Chipawa (Chipapa), Chasonga and Feira were its subordinate stations. Mwomboshi was closed down in 1906 when the railway line reached Broken Hill (now Kabwe) and the boma was shifted there.[8] Chilanga (1905-31), 15 km south Lusaka, could not complete with the capital city. Senkobo a railway siding now in Kalamo District, could survive as a sub-boma of Livingstone from 1904-7. This was the time when railway was being introduced in the territory. Other bomas close to the old line-of-rail met with similar fate during the colonial period. On the other hand, the pre colonial town Cheinge, developed with slave trading activities in Central Africa, is now a village in Luapula Province having Swahili population.[9] Mongu, another pre-colonial settlement developed with the concentration of colonial and missionary activities in and around this town.[10]

Bomas had close association with missions in the early colonial period. Missions, however, continued to survive independently, and where they were located within a settlement, such settlements became important, for example Fort Rosebery (now Mansa) in Luapula Province.[11] Some of the settlements having missions developed as urban centres in the later period. Survival capacity of missions was certainly more than that of the *bomas*. Mpongwe (13° 31′ S, 28° 10′ E),

Ibune Mynygama (16° 6′ S 28° 30′ E) and Johnston Falls (10° 31′ S, 28° 38′ E) are surviving mission settlements, which once had administrative functions. In Chilanga and Chirunda, police station still exists. These settlements were located over looking a vast area on high healthy and scenic spots. However, by 1916, the European population of about 2,000 was concentrated in three places. They are Lusaka, Livingstone and Fort Jameson (Chipata).[12]

Early Town Plans

The early town plans were based on grid iron pattern. Such pattern was used for planning most of the urban settlements along the old line-of-rail. These settlements have expanded enormously since their initial layouts were prepared. As a result, the planned grid pattern became focus for the development of these settlements. In almost all the towns along the line-of-rail have this pattern of town/city centre. Such layout had been common during early twentieth century in England and other colonies under the Crown (Fig. 6.1).

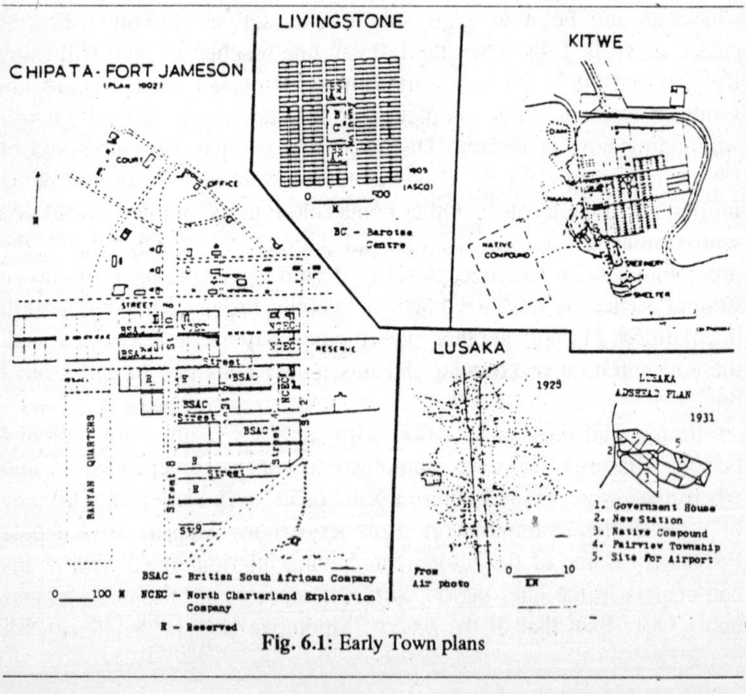

Fig. 6.1: Early Town plans

The plan for Livingstone town is an ideal example of grid pattern.[13] Its plan was meant only for the European use (Fig. 6.1). Chipata (Fort Jameson) was first planned in 1902 on similar pattern. It had provision for the Indian population. Banyan Quarters[14] was meant for this purpose (Fig. 6.1). Around 1930, Kitwe had made provision for African population their plan (Fig. 6.1). The city centre of Ndola, near the railway station, was planned on grid basis. The sketch map of Fort Rosebery (now Mansa) of 1913 A.D. demonstrated the early character of this boma town. The development of the town appears to be an extension of sectors based on the features shown in the sketch map.[15]

The case of Lusaka was different. Lusaka developed from a small African village at the railway halt (1904) on the way to the largest urban centre of Zambia.[16] It became a multi-functional settlement by adding agricultural, transportation, administrative, industrial and commercial functions, with the multiplicity of these functions a proper planning became necessary. In 1905, a grid iron plan was prepared for this settlement near the railway station. This area, as in the case of other cities, forms the city centre of Lusaka. In 1928 this planned area was still underdeveloped and there were four subdivided farms known as Emmasdale, Villa Elisabetta, Fairview and part of Farm 90a.[17] During this period the territorial capital was at Livingstone. The colonial government engaged S.D. Adshead and later P.J. Bowling to select a new site to plan this capital city. The settlement developing slowly on this grid-iron pattern was finally selected for a generous and gracious and garden city making the full use of the ridge (now known as Ridgeway) lying east of the line-of-rail. Collins refer to the 'non-statutory development plan' which started in 1938.[18] This was replaced by the first statutory development plan in 1952, which was the year when settlement was raised to a municipal council which permitted it to have its own planning authority.

The implementation of the Bowling Plan brought it two other nuclei, *viz.* Ridgeway and Government House (now State House), both lying east of the old town. Plot size and land values were planned to create the best residences (Fig. 6.2).[19] This ultimately developed into a linearly arranged multi-nuclei settlement. At the time of independence, this settlement added many legacies and problems to town planning. The myth of a garden city was not in tune with the growing need for housing and urbanisation.

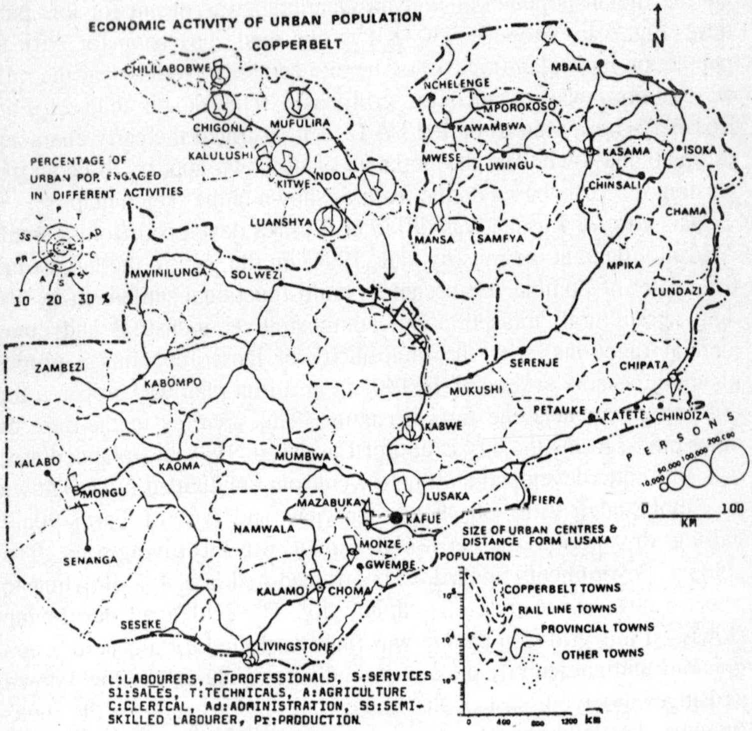

Fig. 6.2: Distribution of Urban Centres, 1969

African Urbanisation and Colonial Policies

The development of towns in Northern Rhodesia was the imposition of a new socio-economic structure. They derived their origin from administrative camps, mining camps and marketing centres and many of the settlements founded before 1900.[20] Railway sidings and halts developed at regular intervals after 1905. At many of these points small communities began to develop, and initially consisted solely of railway workers' hut; but as farms, producing maize and cattle, were established in the areas adjacent to the railways, shops and stores came into being around the sidings.[21] Small European population was then added to such centres along the old line-of-rail upto Copperbelt, and in administrative posts. These centres alongwith nine townships became the focuses of African urbanisation. People migrated to these places from interior villages in search for work, cash and to find a better way of life. Zambian labour force also found employment in the mines of South Africa, Zimbabwe and Katanga, with this the movement towards minging centres and farms became a part of sub-Saharan labour circulation. The government was then allowing a circulatory system of labour migration. Africans with jobs were only permitted to stay in the towns. In the 1930s the African workers had to return to their villages after two years of stay in urban areas.[22] With the passage of time, Africans working in towns became permanent urban dwellers and their contacts with their tribal areas slowly faded away.[23] During the 1930s and 1940s there was a continuing debate on the desirability of stabilising the urban population, in other words allowing the men to bring their families to the towns with them. Private employers were also expected to provide married accommodation.[24] After retirement from active job, they continued to stay in their owned house in location if they have any, or in the squatter settlements in the peri-urban areas. These compounds were on European owned lands as well, and provided several advantages then the well administered locations, the African housing areas.[25]

Towns exercised a strong attraction for African. Staying in towns meant relief from (a) inter tribal conflicts, (b) administration of chiefs, (c) social obligations, and (d) capital gain in order to provide poll tax for the other members of the extended family.[26] Around 1940s, substantial member of Africans were not willing to return to their village. Some employers considered it to be a welcome change. This meant stabilising of the labour force. Families were growing up with practically no roots in their respective native villages. Mitchell developed an index of stabilisation for the study of African population in Ndola and Luanshya. Most highly stabilised group of population was found among the migrants from peri-Copperbelt areas. This was followed by those who migrated from Central Province. Then it was possible to correlate between the proximity of the area of origin to the Copperbelt and the degree of stabilisation.[27] The African urban community was thus becoming detribalised.[28] In his classical work on the economies of detribalisation, Godfrey Wilson describes the changes in the African community during this period in Broken Hill (now Kabwe) in particular, and Northern Rhodesia in general. This work includes the study of wages, clothes, food habits, goods, social customs and relationship with the fellow tribesmen.[29] In 1948, Urban African Housing Ordinance was passed which permitted to keep aside an area within a municipality or township exclusively for the housing of Africans residing there. Kabwe also drew the attention of Kapferer. In his survey of 1964, he found that many people in this town have moved into their second, and in some cases third generation of urban residence. Some consider it as home and have developed extensive kinship network. However, owing to less opportunities for employment and low wages, the youths have had the tendency to look for better opportunities elsewhere.[30] This town had been considered as a base from where the Africans having well knit social network preferred to travel to other urban centres along the old line-of-rail. African population from other parts of Zambia initially came to this town and later moved to a place which was considered better. It appears that in urban African communities in general the concept of western civilization or the European way of life provides a scale along which African townsmen are able to measure prestige and so to ascribe social status to the many and diverse individuals with whom they are thrown into association.[31]

Urban Development after Independence

At the time of independence two predominant problems faced the urban planner : (a) The colonial pattern of towns, and (b) increasing housing problems. In First National Development Plan (FNDP) the colonial segregation of townships from the higher income housing, industrial and commercial areas was no longer acceptable. During the first year of the National Development Plan each of the major local authorities[32] were to produce plans for the progressive integration of housing areas for workers with low density housing and other areas of the town.[33]

The density and cost basis of housing areas were discouraged. The government and the councils raised multi-storied flats which do not fit into the conventional density pattern of urban planning. In the new Kafue town a landmark of the early days of independence, which was planned in 1967 by Doxiadis Associates[34], much use is being made of higher density housing types--flats, terraced housing, two and three storied units--all features comparatively rare in Zambian urban settlements.[35] During the same year, quinquennial reviews of development plans were prepared for major towns and cities of Zambia. Since then, the two divisions of Town and Country Planning, based at Lusaka and Ndola were engaged in preparing and reviewing the physical plans for the urban settlements. But most of the *boma* towns were still developing on the basis of the pre-independence development plans. The National Housing Authority which was established in the FNDP at Lusaka, has a group of experts for housing and urban and town planning. At the beginning of the Second National Development Plan (SNDP) the problem of unauthorised settlements became acuate and this plan was more concerned with the upgradation of these settlements. Wherever physical planning in urban areas was done, it was in order to provide better housing for squatter population. The existing urban settlements added a planned or pseudo planned housing sector to their infrastructure and no new urban settlements were planted. However, after independence several development plans of existing urban settlements and proposed urban settlements (such as missions, sub-*bomas* or place of tourist interests) were prepared by different planning bodies.

Housing, which was an important feature in urban planning in F.N.D.P., became more significant in S.N.D.P. In the former case the policy changed from making a few number of high standard houses to greater number of less expensive houses. The site and service schemes were considered as an alternative to the rising number of unauthorised urban settlements. In practice, two types of housing programmes were established in the F.N.D.P. period : (a) civil service housing ; and (b) low-cost housing for the general population. Funds were allotted for the construction of 19,000 houses and 8,000 serviced plots in the site and service self-help programme.[36] In S.N.D.P, the urban planning as well as housing programme hinged on : (a) service-plots for self-help developers ; and (b) the upgrading of squatter settlements. As a result, the proportion of conventional council houses was reduced from 70 per cent in 1965 to nil in 1971. In practice the burden has been shifted on to the people on the assumption that a serviced site was their main priority.[37] The method of urban housing is not only solving the housing problem of this developing country, but also stabilising African urban population and developing a sense of attachment of the land. At present the priorities of urban planning in Zambia are as follows : (a) housing, (b) preparation of development plans, and (c) integration of different parts of towns and cities.

After independence, the government took positive steps for planning of towns and urban areas. First in this series was the *Copperbelt Development Plan* which was produced in 1965. Later studies were by planning bodies on the various aspects of urban problems. Subsequently, development plans were also prepared for urban centres, such as Lusaka, Kitwe, Ndola, Chipata, Mongu, and the like. However, some of these plans are still awaiting implementation. At least two plans have been prepared for Mongu.[38]

Distribution of Urban Centres

Zambia is a country having a unique organisation of space through urban centres. The size and function arranged over space have a tilt towards the capital city, Lusaka. The old line-of-rail is the main focus with 16 big urban centres containing about 92 per cent of the urban population of Zambia, or 28 per cent of the total population of this country in 1969 (Fig. 6.3). Almost all the non-African population is distributed along this line. The small towns are dispersed reflecting an unsystematic hierarchy and metropolitan colonial pattern of organisation. In 1980 census, 33 new towns were added, out of which 13 are in Southern Province.[39] These new towns are small and contribute to only 4.57 per cent of the total urban population. The population of these towns is less than that of Luanshya in Copperbelt Province. These towns have developed either around railway siding, or near mine, harbour, big settlement, administrative posts or missions. With the addition of these towns, the tendency of clustering of urban centres has become more pronounced. Kansanshi, Kalengwa and Nampundwe are the new mining towns. Katima Mulilo, Mulobezi, Nakonde and Sinazongwe, are transport points. Batoka, Chisekesi, Chisamba, Kaleya, Magoye, Mbabala, Nega–Nega, Zimba and Kapiri Mposhi are on the old line-of-rail. In addition, new towns like Kafue George, Chirundu, Maamba, Chongwe, Chibombo, Masaiti and Rufunsa are not very far away from this rail line. For the first time clustering of towns around the provincial headquarters towns has taken place. Around Mongu, Limilunga and Mamushakende have been declared as towns. Mungwi is not very far from Kasama (Fig. 6.4).

The addition of 33 towns has not changed the Zambian urban scene even marginally. According to the population, Zambian urban centres can be grouped into seven classes (Table 6.1). Out of total of 85 urban centres, 27 are in the group of 2–5,000, followed by 19 in 5–10,000

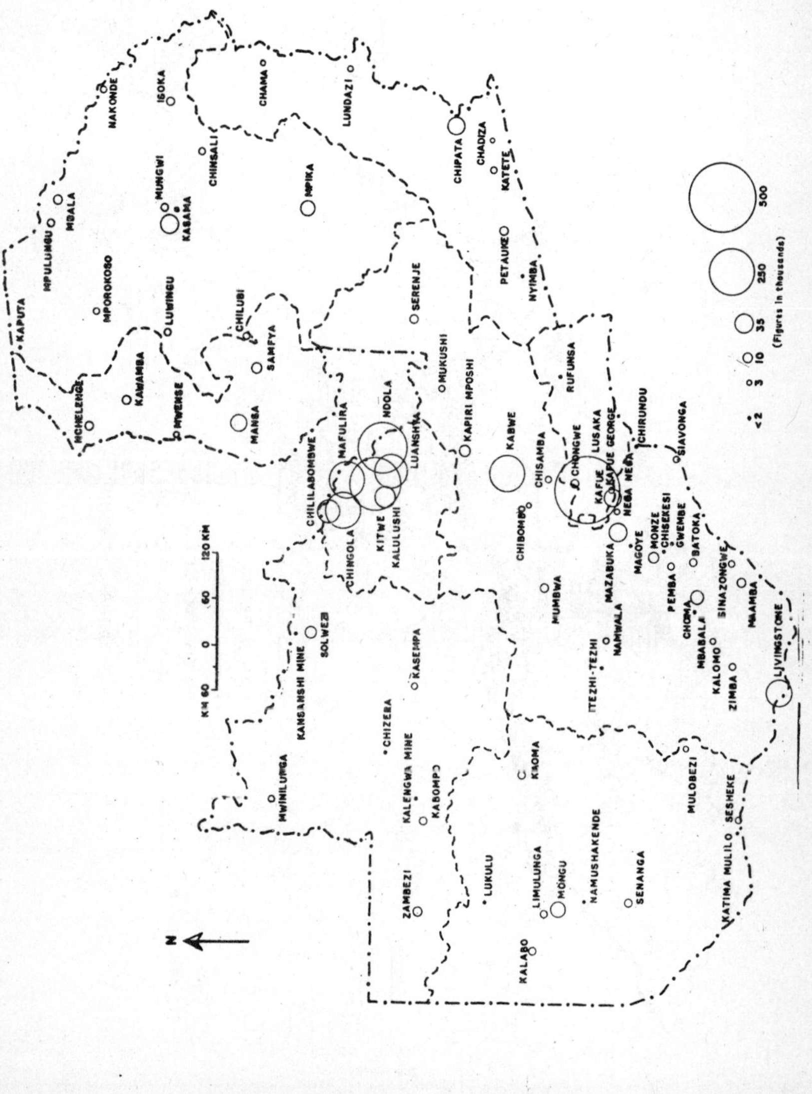

Fig. 6.3: Distribution of Urban Centres, 1980

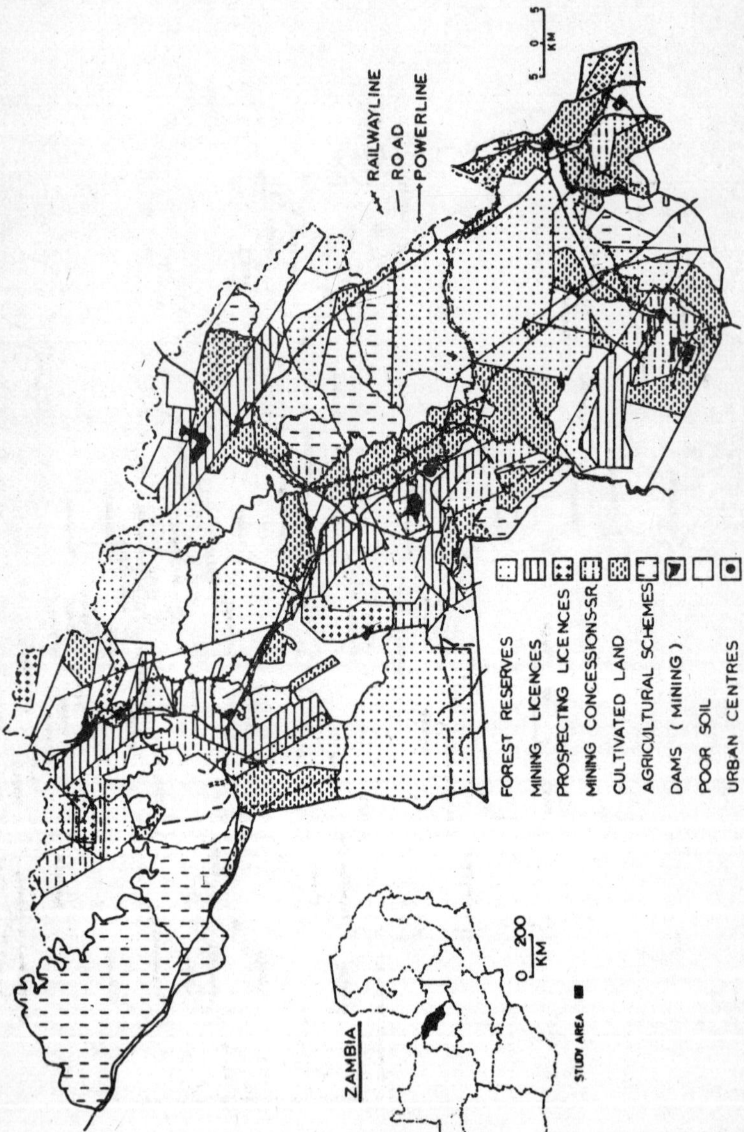

Fig. 6.4: Urban and Mining Complex of Copperbelt

persons. In the cities over 100,000 population, 5 out of 7 are in Copperbelt Province. They contribute to about 70 per cent of Zambia's urban population. In total, the largest number of urban centres are from Southern Province and most of these centres are along the line-of-rail.

Table 6.1 : Distribution of Urban Centres, 1980

Province	*Below 2,000*	*2,000–5,000*	*5,000–10,000*	*10,000–20,000*	*20,000–50,000*	*50,000–100,000*	*Above 100,000*	*Total*
Central	—	4	2	1	—	—	1	8
Copperbelt	—	1	—	—	—	2	5	8
Eastern	1	4	2	—	1	—	—	8
Luapula	—	1	2	1	1	—	—	5
Lusaka	2	—	1	—	1	—	1	5
Northern	1	4	4	1	2	—	—	12
North-Western	3	2	2	1	—	—	—	8
Southern	6	9	2	2	1	1	—	21
Western	3	2	4	—	1	—	—	10
Total	16	27	19	6	7	3	7	85

Source : 1980 Census of Population and Housing, Preliminary Report.

The 1980 census data related to the economic activity of the urban population is not yet available. Based on 1969 data, the economic activity can be identified as (a) professionals, (b) technical, (c) administrative, (d) clerical, (e) sales, (f) service, (g) agriculture, (h) production, (i) semi-skilled labour and (j) labourers (Fig. 6.2). In this year, substantial urban population was engaged as labourers, professionals and in services. Since, the growth of urban population has still been considered high during 1969-80 period, there is a possibility of heavy rural-urban migration contributing large increase in the number of labourers, semi-skilled and the like. However, in 1969, administrative, semi-skilled and production sectors more-so-ever have similar percentage of persons engaged in 17 urban centres.

Copperbelt Urban Region

The Copperbelt urban region provides an unparalleled example of urban agglomeration in Africa. This area of 7,667 km² (extending 160 km in length and 50 km in width) contains 7 urban districts and 7 large urban centres of Zambia. It also includes number of comparatively small centres, which are comparable with the sizable settlements in rural districts. This extraordinary development of Little England[40] in African soil has no well formed functional hierarchy in space and towns having even large population and functions failed to increase their influence to a desirable extent (Fig. 6.4).

This region of Zambia is well planned and has most complicated land holding rights. Forest reserves and agricultural scheme also cover a large portion in this urban region.[41] For scholars, planners and tourists, Copperbelt has a special interest. It has been successful in controlling social, economic and functional aspects throughout Zambia, though Lusaka is its real rival. Kay remarks that in the Copperbelt and the railway line zone 'the resources and facilities are under-used and continue to attract development'.[42]

The Copperbelt is the most urbanised area of Zambia. The urban centres, except Ndola, are located on ore-extracting sites. Ndola which started with the slave trade, developed as a Gateway to Copperbelt. The commercial, distributive and administrative functions are concentrated here. Kitwe, with more than 314 thousand population, at present, is Ndola's biggest competitor, and is the second largest town of Zambia.[43] It is only 56 km from Ndola and occupies a central position in the Copperbelt.

The Copperbelt towns usually have twin townships one for the mine and the other of the administration. Both the towns have different management boards, land rights, buildings, and planning bodies but make a single settlement complex or a political city (Table 6.2). The city centre at the border of both the townships serves the total settlement. Kitwe, Luanshya, Mufulira, Chingola and Chililabombwe have twin townships. Kalulushi and Chambeshi are purely mining settlements. The hanging and crippling waste material dumps, which were once at the border of the urban settlements, have posed problems for urban planning.

Gardiner[44] has rightly observed that the Zambian towns were built by and primarily designed for an expatriate ruling minority. The Copperbelt towns provided ample facilities for Europeans who were having one of the most affluent society in the world having two to three cars per household. Townscape was characterised by European recreational interests with golf course, clubs, boat clubs, etc. All the towns had airfields. The city centres have a proto-type character with similar banks, departmental stores, Indian shops and buildings.

Table 6.2 : Population in Cities Having Mining Activities, 1980

City	*Population in Mine Township (%)*	*Population in Municipal Council (%)*	*Total Population*
Chilalabombe	33,834 (54.63)	28,094 (45.37)	61,928
Chingola	82,681 (56.68)	63,188 (43.32)	1,45,869
Kalulshi	41,807 (70.60)	17,406 (29.40)	59,213
Kitwe	85,868 (27.28)	2,28,926 (72.72)	3,14,794
Luanshya	61,513 (46.54)	70,651 (53.46)	1,32,164
Ndola	3,096 (1.10)	2,79,343 (98.90)	2,82,439
Kabwe	10,049 (7.00)	1,33,587 (93.00)	1,43,636
Total	3,18,848 (27.97)	8,21,195 (72.03)	1,140,043

Source : 1980 Census.

Apart from the towns, this belt contains farms, agricultural plots, agricultural small holdings and African townships. Except the latter all are underused. The agricultural holdings on relatively poor soil of the Copperbelt[45] are used for raising perishable products like milk and butter, piggeries, orchards and vegetables. Chambeshi, Garneton, Kalulushi, Chibuluma, Fisenge, Kansuswa, Kasompo and Twapia were once having separate management boards.[46] All these settlements are served by the six towns.

The population in this urban region is continuously increasing since the mining activities started in this area, however, growth rate has declined recently. Migration from rural areas to these centres has been a matter of much interest to the scholars.[47] In 1963 its population was about 487 thousand which increased to 1,146 thousand in 1980. The ratio of this population to that of the whole of Zambia is steadily increasing indicating comparatively higher concentration of population which it continues to attract. On the other hand, the percentage of this population to the urban population of the country has gone down from 71 per cent in 1963 to 47 per cent in 1980. This is due to the recession on the price and demand for copper and comparative increase in urban population elsewhere in the country, the largest one is in Lusaka followed by towns in the south of this capital city lying along the old line-of-rail.

Morphology of Zambian Towns

It may not be very difficult in evolving a model of Zambian towns. with a few exceptions, there are sufficient reasons to suggest similarities in the process of shaping the urban morphology. These processes have been influenced by colonial legacies, pressing housing problems, and after independence by the policies of the present government based on humanism. Since almost all the towns originated during the early colonial period, the impression of the colonial policies are still prominent on the townscape. Owing to these legacies, it would be difficult to reshape the Zambian towns altogether in order to adjust with the policies of the present government which no longer approves the segregation of areas within towns according to cost, density or race. However, some towns have originated after independence, and they clearly reflect the approach of the present government.

Town/City Centre

As mentioned earlier, the old plans of towns have been on grid pattern. Along the old line-of-rail, railway sidings, which later assumed the status of railway station, have been associated with such plan. This combination has been common in all the towns along the old line-of-rail including Livingstone, Lusaka, Ndola and Kabwe. With time, the towns expanded in all directions and this grid layout became the nucleus or city centre. All the commercial, administrative and transportational establishments are located here. In a town like Mwinilunga, it contains a few shops, administrative offices and petrol pump.[48] In a provincial headquarters town of Kasama, bank, departmental stores, wholesale shops, and the like can be noticed. However, in the capital city of Lusaka, the city centre contains regional and national headquarters of banks, commercial houses and parastatal bodies. Government offices, mission of other countries, book shops etc. are located here. Ndola has been the commercial and distribution centre of Zambia. Its city centre also serves parts of Katanga in Zaire.[49] The landuse map shows the activities of this place (Fig. 6.5). Still there are gaps in the city centre which are not built up. This leaves scope for further development in accordance with the changing priorities. However, if one visits these places, he would be impressed by the planned layout. The shops mostly contain consumer goods having marginal relevance with the development of vast rural area of the country.

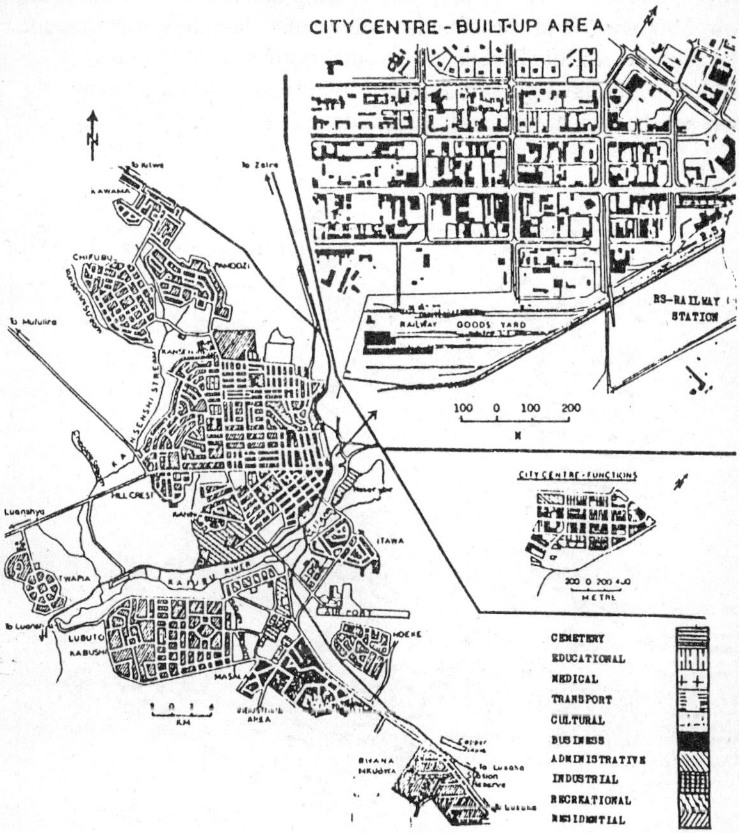

Fig. 6.5: Ndola

Low Density Residential Areas

Residential areas for Europeans have always been selected with reference to the city centre. In most cases such low density areas have been close to the city and are well connected. However, there were private residential areas for Europeans outside the council boundaries. With the growth of towns, such areas created problems for urban planning. Manner's private (European) township created problems for the planning of Ndola at its initial stage.[50] Olyampia Park (now

Chikonkoto) within, and Roma and Kabulonga outside the Lusaka council boundary were European housing areas. Handsworth Park (now Shikoswe) and the Chama valley small holdings were pseudo rural complexes of Europeans in the northeast of Lusaka. Their planned layout having a very low density of bungalows with swimming pools are the typical feature of these elite pockets (Fig. 6.6)

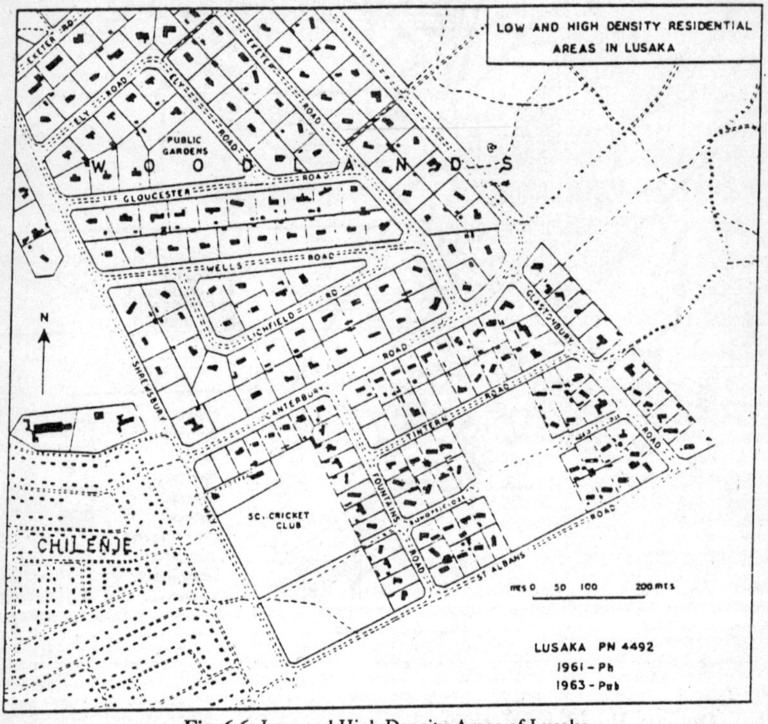

Fig. 6.6: Low and High Density Areas of Lusaka

High Density Residential Areas

The Zambian towns were initially planned for European population. Later it was realised that African population cannot be possibly excluded from towns. They were required as skilled and un-skilled workers and as house boys. The original plans were modified in order to include African quarters which were known as location, or high density area or Messenger's Compound etc. African residential areas were separated from the city centre or European areas by a distinct physical and cultural features. The messengers' compound in Mwinilunga is separated by Solwezi-Kalene Hill Mission Road (Fig. 6.7). In Kasama, the European residential areas was located on a high ridge in a grid patterns, where the African location was squeezed in between the ridge and the Muliansolo stream. In the location, the houses are sub-standard and arranged in a combination of triangular and grid-pattern. Broken and vacant houses are also noticeable here with a minimum of social public amenities. In Mansa, the north-south road separates the African quarters from other areas. Masala in Ndola is located in the south of the Kafbu stream. Later other African townships, such as Luboto and Kabushi, developed adjoining to it. Chifubu on the other side of Kansenshi stream is another high density area which developed north of the European quarters. Pamodzi and Kawama developed close to it. Twapia, an octagonal shaped African high density residential area was included in this town after independence. In Chipata, Lunkwakwa stream separates African quarters from other areas. In Chapter VII, the development of African housing areas in Lusaka and Ndola have been discussed in details

Every location is served by a small complex having a school, community centre, some bars and shops for basic needs. But, during the colonial days, African needs were met by the so-called second class trading areas. The shops in these trading areas were of Indians, and were not elegant in appearance. The location of these trading areas were not very far from the European or first class trading areas. In Lusaka, it is in the southeast of the city centre. In Ndola, both the trading areas appear to be in continuation. In smaller towns, such distinction is not always possible. However in Chipata, the second class trading area is more dominating. Indians were invited by the British South African Company (BSAC) to settle in this town for trading, and as mentioned earlier, a separate area was allotted to them in its original plan (Figs. 6.1 & Fig. 6.8). However, Indians continue to stay behind or above their shops. In Ndola, Lusaka and Chipata, Indians have a separate housing area meant for them. They have their temples, Hindu Halls, Mosques and Gurdwara (Sikh temple).

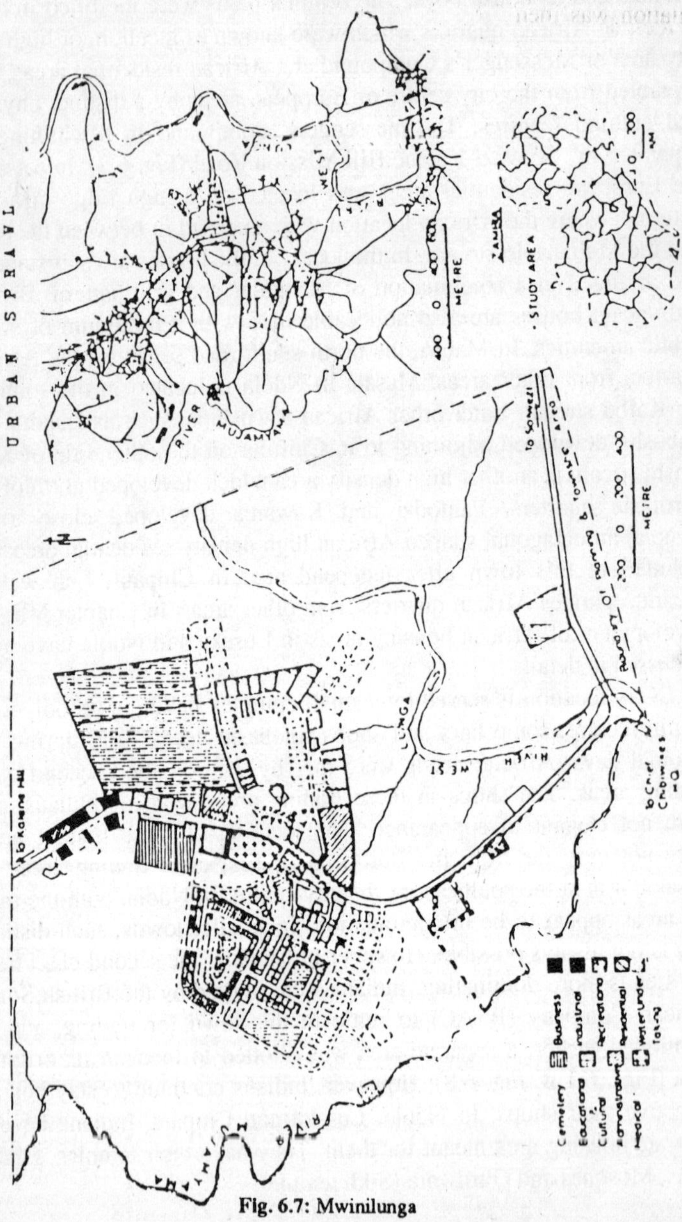

Fig. 6.7: Mwinilunga

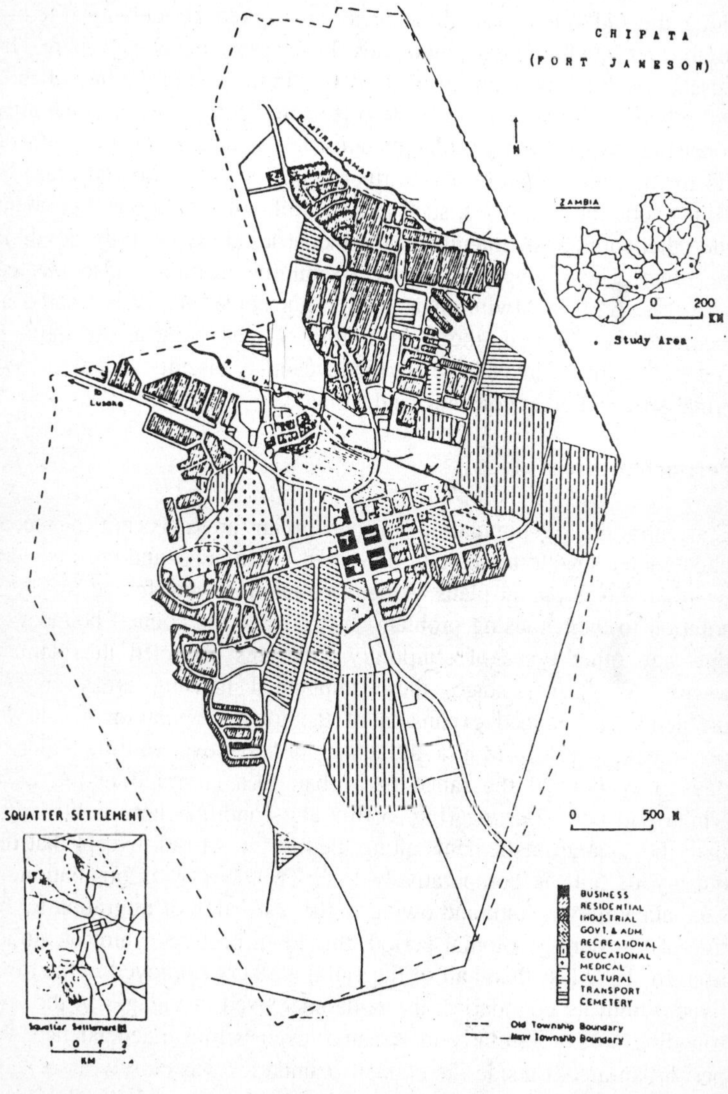

Fig. 6.8: Chipata

ındustrial Area

Every sizable Zambian town has an industrial area. In the provinces along the old line-or-rail these areas are served by railway. Mostly small and medium size industries have been developed here. In Lusaka, there are two industrial areas, one in the east of the line-of-rail, and other in the south of the Matero Housing area. In Ndola, such area consisting copper and petroleum industries, is located in the south of the town, Bwana Mkubwa is further south of this industrial area. In Livingstone the industries, such as saw mill, cold storage and garment and other small-scale manufacturing industries are lying in the south of the town. The Livingstone motor assembling factory is also located here (Fig. 6.9). In Mwinilunga town, a pineapple factory is located in the north. In Mongu, the light industrial area is near the market. Generally, these areas have garment, candle, biscuit, suitcase, food processing and other consumer industries.

Peri-urban Areas

Concentration of population in peri-urban areas is not a recent phenomena. Owing to scarcity houses in urban areas and enforcement of urban development plans, African population were forced to find a solution to their housing problem. Just outside the council boundaries huts and other types of temporary structures encircled the planned towns. At a later stage, these unplanned housing areas created problems for planned expansion of the town. Population growth in peri-urban areas of Mansa attracted attention even during colonial days. Kay noticed the range peri-urban area surrounding the town which had poor housing (Fig. 6.10). The condition here is no better than the squatter settlements along the old line-of-rail, except that the density of huts is comparatively low. The density of population in Luapula Valley is high and owing to the restriction of migration to the line-of-rail during colonial period, this town became centre of attraction. In 1959 less than half of the 1,400 workers employed in the town lived within its boundaries; the remainder lived in villages in the surrounding area.[51] Similarly in Kasama, even before independence, the peri-urban area, outside the council boundaries was closely associated with the town. Both have developed nearly along the Mpika Road and aggregated at the other side of the forest boundary. In order to provide social amenities to the peri-urban areas, the idea is to relocate population into a planned layout (Fig. 6.11).[52] In the case of Mongu, the

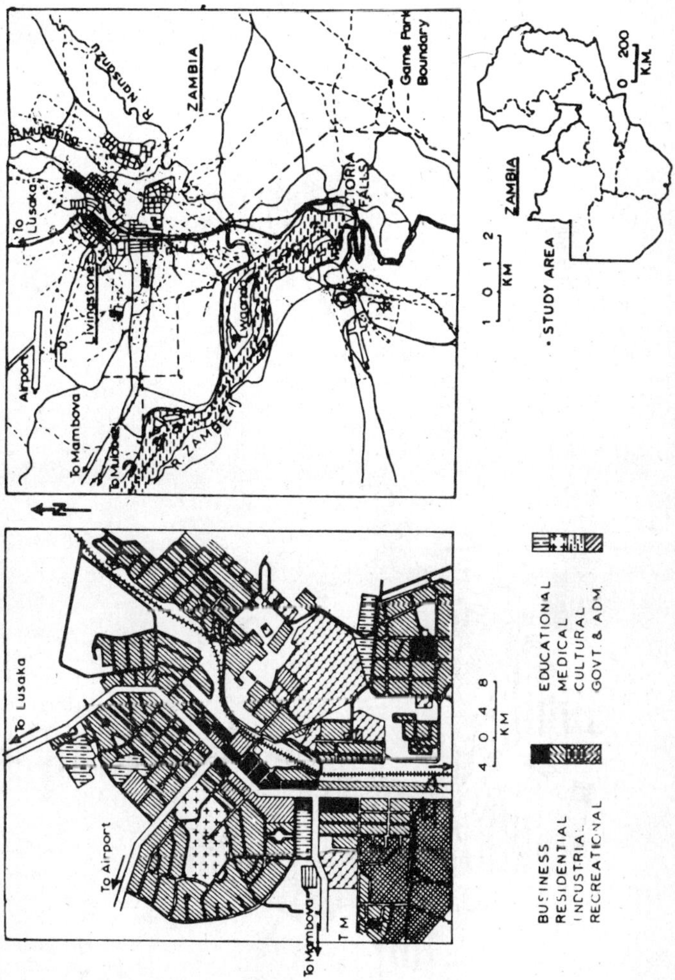

Fig. 6.9: Livingstone

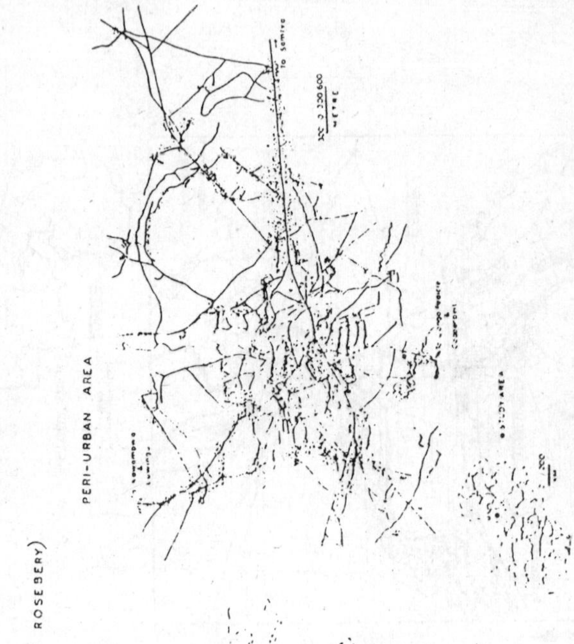

Fig. 6.10: Mansa

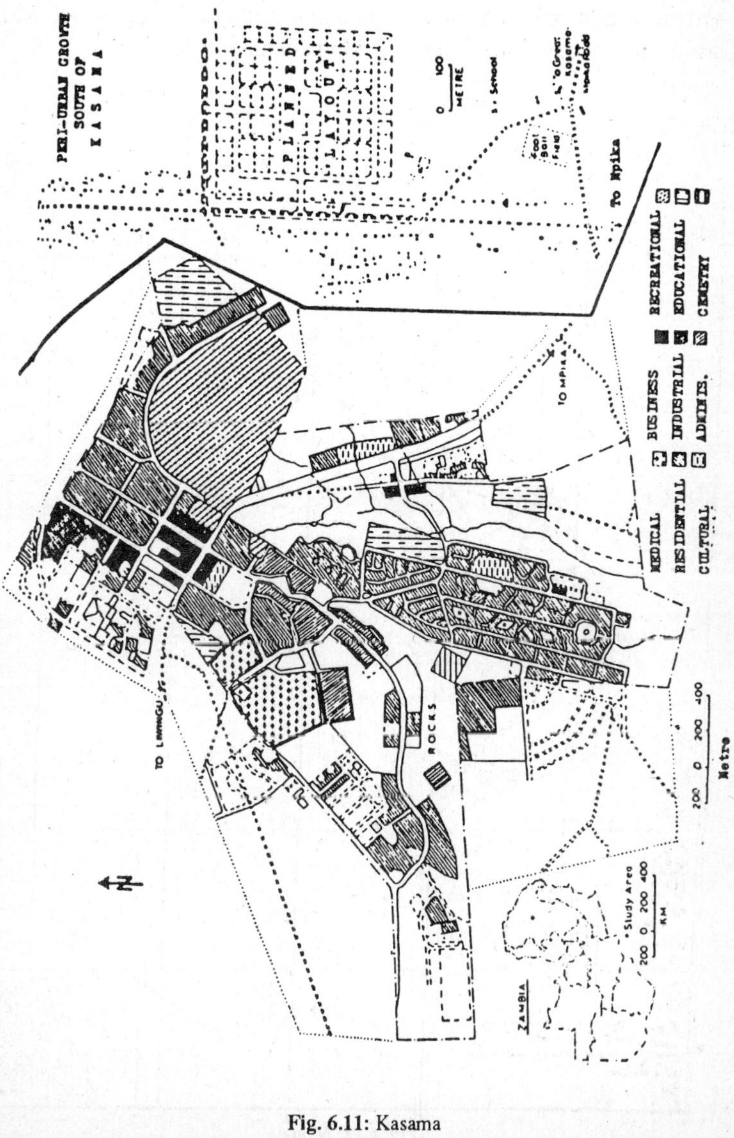

Fig. 6.11: Kasama

nearby Zambezi flood plain is thickly populated. This zone is not wholly included within the new council boundaries (Fig. 6.12). In other cities along the old line-of-rail and Chipata, squatter settlements have grown within and outside the planning authority boundaries, which would be discussed in details in the next chapter.[53]

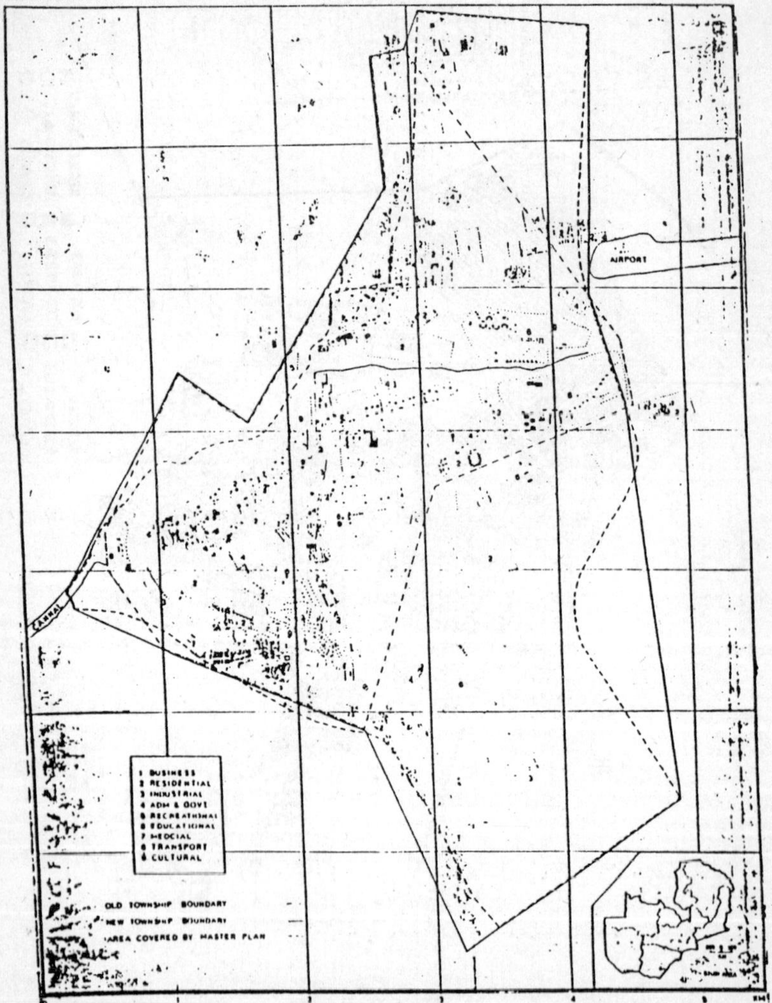

Fig. 6.12: Mongu

The most important aspect of the morphology has been the close functional relationship between the town/city centre with the low density areas which were for European during colonial days. Along the line-of-rail this area is served by a railway station. The bus stand is also not very far from this place. The so-called second class trading area is not very far from the city centre as well. Previously Indians were living around this trading area. Now they have a separate residential area which do not exactly fall on the general density pattern of residential area (Fig. 6.13). The high density residential areas were away from the city centre and are poorly connected. In city like Lusaka, they surround the city centre and low density areas. High density areas are now

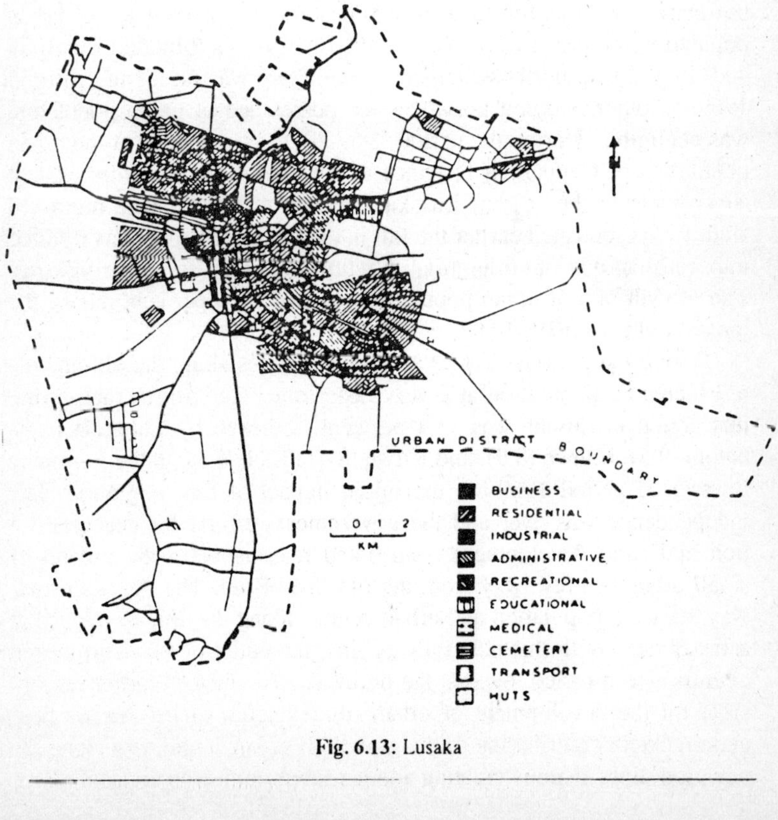

Fig. 6.13: Lusaka

served by a small shopping complex. Industrial area is a distinct zone, mostly planned and served by a railway line. There are also complexes of institutions for specific purposes, such as university, airport etc. In between these complexes are the squatter settlements. They have grown since the colonial period owing to the acute housing problem which exist in Zambian towns.

Recent Urbanisation

The history of urbanisation in Zambia is not very old. In chapter 3 the pattern of rural-urban migration indicates the rate of urbanisation in this African country. However, within a very short time Zambia has become one of the most urbanised state among the developing countries. As explained earlier, the urban centres are not of indigenous origin. These centres were established for serving colonial interests, but became centres for African urbanisation. The percentage of urban population increased from 20.5 in 1963 to 29.4 in 1969 and finally to 43.0 in 1980. In north-western province, there was no urban centre in 1969. In other outlying provinces the percentage of urban population was negligible. During the period 1969-80, the percentage of the urban population of Copperbelt Province to the total decreased from 62.4 to 47.1; while in the case of Lusaka Province this percentage improved slightly. As indicated earlier the fall in the prices of copper has resulted into considerable out-migration or return-migration to native villages. The growth rate of urban population reduced by 6 per cent during the intercensal period 1969-80.

During the period 1963-69, the urban centres along the old line-of-rail increased population at a very faster rate. The growth rate during this period in Lusaka was 13.4 per cent, followed by Chingola (9.6), Ndola (9.5), Kabwe (8.9), and Kitwe (8.4) (Table 6.3). In the following intercensal period 1969-80, the initial impact of free migration after independence was over and the governments efforts for decentralisation and rural development contributed reasonably to the growth of small urban centres away from the old line-of-rail. The Tan-Zam railway attracted population and urban centres along this line developed at a faster rate. With this new railway line, the outlet of this land-locked country was directed towards the northeast. The factors earlier responsible for the development of urban centres south of Lusaka are upto certain extent contributing to the growth of urban centre now along the new rail line, thereby creating another urban-industrial corridor along

Table 6.3: Population of Large Urban Areas, 1963, 1969 and 1980

Large urban areas	*1980 Census*	*Av. annual Growth Rate (%) 1969-80*	*1969 Census*	*Av. Annual Growth Rate (%) 1963-69*	*1963 Census*
Chililambombwe	61,928	3.0	44,862	4.6	34,165
Chingola	145,869	3.2	103,292	9.6	59,517
Kabwe	143,635	7.3	65,974	8.9	39,522
Kalulshi	59,213	5.7	32,232	7.2	21,303
Kitwe	314,794	4.2	199,798	8.4	132,027
Livingstone	71,987	4.3	45,243	5.4	33,026
Luanshya	132,164	2.9	96,282	4.2	75,332
Lusaka	538,469	6.8	262,425	13.4	123,146
Mufulira	149,778	3.0	107,802	5.0	80,609
Ndola	282,439	5.3	159,786	9.5	92,691
Total Urban (Including small towns)	2,440,419	6.7	1,192,116	8.9	715,020

Source : 1980 Census.

Table 6.4 : Urban Areas and Growth of Population, 1963 - 80

Urban Areas	*Population ('000)*			*Contribution to total Population Growth (%)*	
	1963	*1969*	*1980*	*1963-69*	*1969-80*
Large Urban Areas (LUA)	682.0 (95.4)	1,117.8 (93.8)	1,760,677 (75.3)	91.3	78.0
Other Urban Areas	33.0 (4.6)	74.3 (6.2)	4,97,892 (24.7)	8.7	22.0
Total Urban	715.5	1,192.1	2,258,569	100.00	100.00

Note: Figures in parentheses denote percentage
Source: Central Statistical Office, Lusaka.

the Muchinga escarpments.[53] From Table 6.4, it is apparent that the ratio of population in Large Urban Area (LUA) to the total urban population is continuously reducing from 95.4 per cent in 1963 to 75.3 per cent in 1980. Their contribution to the total population growth has also been reduced. At the same time, other urban centres have made a significant contribution towards much desired pattern Zambian urbanisation. The most significant contribution is due to the growth of provincial headquarters towns. During the intercensal period of 1969-80, Kasama in Northern Province experienced over 300 per cent change, followed by Mansa (283%), Mongu (199%), Chipata (150%). Several new towns were recognised which are small and widely distributed all over the country. Hopefully, these urban centres will become focus for urbanisation in Zambia in near future.

REFERENCES

1. Brelsford, W.V. Abandoned Bomas : a consolidated list, *Zambia (Northern Rhodesia) Journal*, Vol. VI, 1965, pp. 293-308.
2. Chienji (8° 39′ S, 29° 10′ E) established around 1890 later reopened twice in 1890 and 1929, and finally closed in 1933.
3. Koka (9° 3′ S, 30° 46′ E) was a temporary settlement in Chief Chibes Kunda's area in Chinsali district.
4. Katumbi (10° 48′ S, 33° 33′ E) had administrative functions from 1906 to 1909 near the present Malawi Zambia border.
5. Brelsford, *op. cit.*.
6. It became an administrative centre as early as 1902. The town attained the status of Village Management Board in 1920; Town Management Board in 1930; Municipal Council in 1932; and City Council after independence. The council boundary has now been increased from 68 km^2 to 1,091 km^2, i.e. to the extent of Ndola Urban District vide Brelsford, W.V., Abandoned Bomas : a consolidated list, op.cit. (See Old Ndola). Also see Gardiner, John, *Some Aspects of the Establishment of Towns in Zambia During the Nineteen Twenties and Thirties*, Davies, D.H. (Ed.), Zambia Urban Studies, No. 3, Institute of African Research, University of Zambia, 1970, pp. 4-8. Further see *Copperbelt Development Plan* (1965), Copperbelt Planning Authority, Ministry of Lands and Natural Resources, Government Printers, Lusaka, 1965.
7. Kalungwishi (9° 30′ S, 29° 21′ E) was deserted due to sleeping sickness in 1908 in Luapula Valley. The classic example is the 7 sites of forts : (a) Chinunda, March 1896, (b) Fort Zameson, or Fort Patridge, renamed Fort Jameson, 5 December 1895, (c) Present Fort Jameson, October 1898, (d) Fort Patrick, April 1898, (e) Fort Young, 5 July 1896, (f) Fort Young, 27 June 1894, and (g) Fort Horgenes. Chaplin, J.H., A note on the forts of the Eastern Province. *The Northern Rhodesia Journal*, Vol. IV, 1961, pp. 462-8.
8. Stephenson, J.E., Chirupula memories of abandoned bomas No. 16. Mwomboshi, *Zambia - Northern Rhodesia Journal*, Vol. VI, 1965, p. 72 (also see p. 114).
9. Thomson, Mr. Justice J.B., Memories of abandoned bomas; Cheingi. *The Northern Rhodesia Journal*, Vol. 11, 1965, pp. 67-77.
10. There was a demand in 1898 to open Boma at Mongu, i.e. after agreement of Lewanika and Coryndon. Welliams quotes B.S.A.C. Report of 1889, which

states that Lealui was opened in October, 1897. Mongu locally means Pumpkin. See Williams, G.D.B., Some early mail runner service, *The Northern Rhodesia Journal,* Vol. IV, 1961, p. 603. Also, Jordon, E. Knowles, Mongu in 1908. *The Northern Rhodesia Journal*, Vol.I I, 1959, pp. 60-72.

11. This name was after Lord Rosebery, who was an imperialist and friend of Cicel Rhodes and Dr. Jameson. He was Prime Minister of the Liberal Party at the time of the establishment of the settlement by H.T. Barrington. See Brelsford, W.V., A further note on European place names, *Northern Rhodesia Journal*, No. VI, December 1952, p. 42. Meri Meri Sohontwi and Johnson Falls Sites were attempted for building this administrative post. See Calendars of the *District Notebooks* (Luapula Province): 1798-1965, V-1, National Archives of Zambia, Lusaka, p. 33; also see Brelsford, W.V., Abandoned bomas : A consolidated list, *op. cit.* Makintosh, C.W., some pioneer missions of Northern Rhodesia and Nyasaland, in *The Occasional Papers of the Rhodes Livingstone Museum No.1-16*, Manchester University Press for the Institute for African Studies, Lusaka, 1974, pp. 249-96. Gouldsbury, Cullen and Hubert Scheane, *The Great Plateau of Northern Rhodesia—Being some impression of the Tanganyika Plateau*, Edward Arnold, London, 1911 (for missionary activities see pp. 230-50).

12. Fox, H. Wilson, The development of Rhodesia from a geographical standpoint, *The Geographical Journal*, Oct., 1916, pp. 289-310.

13. The first site is claimed to be Old Drift, settled in 1968 which was ultimately abandoned owing to unhealthy conditions. The Old Drift also claimed to be known as Clarke Drift, after F.J. Clarke, who opened a store and a bar at this point. Old Drift is located at the narrowest point on the River Zambezi, between Victoria Falls and the Zambezi Rapids. Further, whether the Anderson Drift or Sikuti's Drift is different from the Old Drift is still uncertain. The Livingstone Development Plan, prepared by A.S.C.O. (in page 20), describes the first settlement at Anderson's Drift. For Old Drift see The Memoirs of Henry Rengeley, *Zambia-Northern Rhodesia Journal*, V.VI, 1965, p. 174. See also Gordon, D. and Brelsford, W.V., European place names of major geographical features, *Northern Rhodesia Journal*, No. II, 1950, pp. 64-700 (especially see p. 68). And also see Gelefand, Michael, *Northern Rhodesia in the Days of Charter*, Basil Blackwell, Oxford, 1961, pp. 221-2.

The chronology of Livingstone can be arranged as follows: 1905-establishment; 1907—Capital of Northern Western Rhodesia; 1911—Capital of Northern Rhodesia; 1913—Formation of the Village Management Board, later called Town Management Board; 1928—gained the status of Municipality, first in Northern Rhodesia; and—1935-capital was removed to Lusaka. Since then the town lost its importance in following manner: (a) during the time of Federation, when the development was concentrated in Southern Rhodesia (1953-63); (b) after independence, since then the border to south is often closed; (c) completion of tar road from Lusaka to Mongu; and (d) the completion of Tan-Zam Railway line. See Rodway, C.G. Reedon, Livingstone in early days, *Supplement to Rhodesian Recorder*, December, 1958, p. 22. Also Kay, G., *A Social Geography of Zambia*, University of London Press Ltd., 1967, p. 33.

14. The term appears to be adopted from Gulf Countries. It is a misnomer of 'Banla', meaning trader.

15. Named after British South African Company's President Dr. Leander S. Jameson. It was also headquarters for B.S.A.C. and Northern Charterland Exploration Company.
There exist other forts in the surrounding of fort Jameson, *viz.* Fort Patric, Fort Young and Fort Hargreaues. See Chaplin, J.H., A note on the forts of the Eastern Province, *Norther Rhodesia Journal*, V. IV, 1961, pp. 462-8. See also the map on page 463. Also "The Prison provided the 'Fort' to Fort Jameson, having been designed as a stronghold in case of trouble", see Page, Thomas, "Early days in Fort Jameson", *Northern Rhodesia Journal*, V. III, 1956, p. 4.
In the year 1902, on 9th July this settlement was declared a 'Township', thereafter water and sanitation facilities were provided, See Gelefard, Michael, *Northern Rhodesia in the Days of Charter*, Basil Blackwell, Oxford, 1961, p. 214.
16. Lusaka gained the status of Village Management Board in 1913, Municipal Board in 1953 and City in 1960. Along with Lusaka Broken Hill (Kabwe), Luanshya, Mufulira and Kitwe gained municipal status in 1953, and in the following year, Chingola was also raised to this level.
17. Collins, J., *Lusaka : The Myth of the Garden City*, Zambia, 1969, p. 4; *Lusaka—The New Capital of Northern Rhodesia*, produced for private circulation by Jonathan Cape, London, 1935.
18. Collins, *idem.*
19. Davies, D.H., *Lusaka, Zambia : Some Town Planning Problems in an African Capital City at Independence*, Zambia Urban Studies, University of Zambia, 1973, pp. 7.
20. Gelefard, Michael, *op. cit.*, 1961, p. 212.
21. Greenwood, Alan and John Howell, Urban local authorities, in Tordoff, William (ed), *Administration in Zambia*, Manchester University Press, and University of Wisconsin Press 1880, p. 163.
22. Berg, E.F., The development of a labour force in sub-Saharan Africa, *Economic Development and Cultural Change*, 1965, Vol. 13, pp. 395-412.
23. Davidson, J.W., *Northern Rhodesian Legislative Council*, Faber & Faber Ltd., London, 1947, p. 31.
24. Department of Town & Country Planning, *Low Cost Residential Development in Lusaka*, Research Unit, Lusaka, 1972, p. 3. See also Simmance, Alan, J.F., *Urbanization in Zambia*, International Urbanization Survey, The Ford Foundation, 1973.
25. Wood, Anthony St. John, *Northern Rhodesia : The Human Background*, Pall Mall Press, London & Dunmow, 1961, p. 37.
26. The native tax in Northern Rhodesia is a poll tax imposed by the Native Tax Ordinance of 1930 on male natives over the apparent age of 18 years. Lockhart, C.R., F. Sandford and S. Gore-Browne, *Report on Native Taxation Committee*, Government Printers, Lusaka, 1937, pp. 2-3. For policies during early colonial rule, vide Datha, K., *The Policy of Indirect Rule in Northern Rhodesia : 1924-1953*, Ph.D. thesis, University of London, 1956.
27. Mitchel, J. Clyde, *African Urbanisation in Ndola and Luanshya*, Rhodes-Livingstone Communication No. 6, Lusaka, 1954 (3rd. in 1966), p. 18.
28. Logan, W.N., Native administration in Northern Rhodesia, *Race Relations*, Vo' VI, No. 2, 1939, pp. 50-9.

29. Wilson, Godfrey, *An Essay on the Economics of Detribalisation in Northern Rhodesia*, The Rhodes-Livingstone paper No. 6, Manchester University Press, 1968 (first published in 1942), 2 Vols.
30. Kapferer, Bruce, *The Population of a Zambian Municipal Township*, Institute for Social Research, Communication No. 1, Lusaka, 1966, pp. 8-9.
31. Mitchell, J. Clyde and A.L. Epstein, Occupational prestige and social status among urban Africans in Northern Rhodesia, Pierre L.Van den Berghe (ed), *Africa — Social Problems of Change and Conflict*, Chandler Publishing Co., California, 1965, pp. 198-220 for urbanization in Copperbelt vide Berger, Elena A., *Labour, Race and Colonial Rule : The Copperbelt from 1924 to Independence*, Clarendon Press Oxford, 1974.
32. Local authority means council authority.
33. *Second National Development Plan*, Ministry of Development Planning and National Guidance, Lusaka, 1971, p. 48.
34. Davis, D.H. (ed), *Zambia in Maps*, University of London Press, 1971, p. 89.
35. Doxiadis Associates, *Kafue Master Plan*, Final Report, DOX - ZAM -A9 Sep. 1967.
36. S.N.D.P., *op. cit*., p. 27.
37. Collins, John, Recent trends in urban housing policy in Zambia, unpublished paper, Lusaka, Aug., 1973, p. 7.
38. *Copperbelt Development Plan*, Government Printers, Lusaka, 1965. *Kabwe Quinquennial Review of Development Plan*, Municipality of Kabwe Planning Authority, 1967. Doxiadis Associates, *Kafue Master Plan and Communities Layout*, Final Report, Dox - 2 AM - 49, 1967. Doxiadis Associates, *Urban Centres : Selection of Sites and Programmes*, Dox-ZAM - AS2, 1969. A.S.C.O., *Mansa Development Plan - Preliminary Report*, Lusaka 1969, A.S.C.O., *Ndola Development Plan*, phase I, Vol. I, A.S.C.O., *Development Trends for the Ndola and Luanshya Regions*, - A.S.C.O. *Site Selection of 4,000 plots of the City Council of Ndola*, Ministry of Local Government and Housing, Lusaka, 1972. Doxiadis Associates, *Lusaka : Existing Conditions*, Dox-ZAM - A38, Lusaka. Doxiadis Associates, *Monga Development Plan*, Dox-ZAM - A26 Lusaka, Development of Town and Country Planning, *Monga Development Plan : 1973 - 2000*. Research Unit, Lusaka, 1973.
39. The 33 new towns have been calculated by comparing the list of 1980 census towns with that of the initial/provisional list of 1969 census towns. Some of the towns identified in the latter census initially were no longer considered as towns. As a result in North-Western Province urban population in 1969 has been shown nil in the Preliminary Report of 1980 Census of Population and Housing.
40. Kay, G., *A Social Geography of Zambia*, London, 1967, p. 29.
41. Dawtrey, Brain, Copperbelt Province farming settlement schemes, in Eligie, Ian D.(ed.), *Kitwe and its Hinterland*, Zambia Geographical Association, Handbook series No. 3, Lusaka, 1975, pp. 133-48.
42. Kay. G., *ibid*, p. 87.
43. Berg, L.M. Vanden, Kitwe : The growth of mining town, in Elgie (ed), *op. cit* pp. 99-112.
44. Gardiner, John, *Some Aspects of the Establishment of Towns in Zambia During the Nineteen Twenties and Thirties*, Zambia Urban Studies, Lusaka, 1970, p. 28.

45. *Report of a Soil and Landuse Survey of the Copperbelt*, Deptt. of Agriculture, 1956, and Clothier, J.R., *A Report on the Agricultural Possibilities in Selected Areas on the Copperbelt*, 1936.
46. Copperbelt Development Plan 1965, op. cit. pp. 1-52.
47. Berger, Elena, A, *Labour Race, and Colonial Rule : The Copperbelt from 1924 to Independence*, Clarendon Press, Oxford, 1974 (Ch.II : The mine labour force, pp. 12-18). Short, Robin, *African Sunset*, Johnson, London, 1973, (Ch. 6 : *Copperbelt - The Melting Pot*, pp. 108-26). Powdermaker, Francis L., *The Northern Rhodesia Copperbelt, 1899-1962, Technological Development upto the End of the Central African Federation.* Manchester University Press, 1971. Blake, W.T., *Central African Survey : Facts and Figures of Rhodesia and Nyasaland*, Alvin Redman, London, 1961 (for towns see pp. 98-110).
48. Mwinilunga means overlord of Lunga. Kalene Hill Mission in the north developed earlier to the Mwinilunga *boma* and competes with it in attracting functions, establishments and development. Mwinilunga along with Kasama and Mansa came under planning authority in 16 November, 1962 by Cap. 475 - Old cap. 123. For general description of 1950-65, see Short, Robert, *African Sunset*, Johnson, London, 1973. (Chapter 8 : Mwinilunga - The unwearied sun, pp. 129-50).
49. Its city centre is not only of regional, provincial, or national importance but also of international significance. Lubumbashi (Zaire) has to depend on this town for its primary needs, such as sugar, salt, candle and garment. The Indian shops in this city centre, dealing with the wholesale of such items have gained reputation even in Zaire (formerly Congo). The city centre consists of real estate, financing, accounting, insurance establishments; hotels, banks, garages, cinema halls, post office, departmental stores; and number of especialised shops of medicines, jewellery, motor and stationery.
50. Gardiner mentions that the 'uncoordinated development in Ndola was checked by the decision, taken in 1929, to include the developed part of Manner's township standing adjacent to the public township (Ndola proper) within the area administrated by the Management Board'. Gardiner, *op.cit.*, p. 8.
51. Kay, George, *op. cit.*, 1967, p. 61.
52. "In some other localities such as the Kasama and Fort Rosebery peri-urban areas, the improvement of water supplies by the application and advanced technology has led to increase local concentration of population". Kay, *op. cit.*, 1967, p. 51.
53. In Ndola the population in the urban area increased during 1963-69 to 92.06 per cent while in the peri-urban area it was 205.71 per cent. The total increase was 109.07 per cent. A.S.C.O., *Ndola Development Plan, Phase I*, Vol. I, p. 50. In 1980 site and service/shanty towns have 57 and the peri-urban areas have 4.8 per cent Lusaka's population. (Vide Table).
54. Jauhari, A. and P. Nag, Rural development in an underpopulated developing country of Africa : Zambia, in Singh, R.L. *et al.* (eds), *Geographic Dimensions of Rural Settlements*, National Geographical Society of India publication Varanasi, 1976, pp. 248-61.

7

SQUATTER POPULATION AND HOUSING PROBLEM

IT is deplorable feature in the third world countries to add the worst type of shelters to the urban settlements. These habitations are either deep rooted in the political structure of the country, or exist due to migration policies, or due to racial and economic segregation of the population. After independence, owing to free movement and better chances of economic progress, the weaker section of the population was forced to find out an alternative to the increasing housing problem in the towns. In Zambia, this problem became acute by the non-availability of private or government owned houses. Squatter settlements became the consequence of prevailing situation in the Zambian towns. These settlements as urban shelters are known in different parts of the world as squatters, shanty towns, discriminated settlement (Buraku), bindovilles, bario, barriada, favela, hoover-villes, brong-brong, kampong, laperla and el faguito. Such settlements within planning authority boundaries in Africa and Latin America are different from the slums of European, American or Indian cities in respect to growth of population, location, rent and control of land, but have similar social and economic characteristics. Population residing within council boundaries in densely mushroomed hutments which are below the minimum recognized standards and without legal rights is known as squatter population in Zambia. (Fig. 7.1)[1]

Housing Situation

The crowding in houses has been felt particularly in urban centres even before independence. The colonial government imposed certain restrictions to check migration to urban areas. After 1964 the independent government changed the colonial policies which led to crowding in urban houses. Later, this government took a series of steps in solving

Fig. 7.1: Nguluwe/Chaisa Squatter Settlement

urban housing problems. As a result the towns and cities which were practically having no privately owned houses, now have a good number of individually owned dwelling units.

The census data of 1963, 1969 and 1980 are not always comparable. However, some estimation can be made regarding the housing conditions. In 1963 Census of Africans, about 40 per cent of the occupied rooms in rural areas were brick built, compared to 96 per cent in the urban areas. There are certain variations from this average if the provinces are considered separately. In the present day Western Province (then Barotse-land), only 5 per cent rooms were of bricks, while in Copperbelt Province (earlier known as Western Province) had 91.4 per cent of this building material. Rest of the rooms were made of 'pole and dagga'. Out of a total of 1,474,586 rooms, 53.4 per cent were brick built. Average number of persons per room was 2.3 only. In rural areas single room dwellings were more, while in urban areas the maximum number of dwellings (32.7%) were having 3 rooms.

In 1969 out of 879,134 dwelling units (not rooms), 45.73 per cent were constructed with pole and dagga walls, 25.92 per cent by burnt bricks or concrete blocks and 21 per cent by kimberly bricks. These percentages vary considerably for different provinces. In Copperbelt and Luapula provinces, the percentage of dwellings with pole and dagga walls was below 20 per cent. Excepting Copperbelt and Southern provinces, large number of dwellings were having grass roofs (Table 7.1). About three-fourth of the dwellings with asbestos roofs were located in urban areas. The situation in 1980 changed substantially. The number of dwellings constructed by pole and dagga reduced to 27.5 per cent. On the other hand, there were more houses of burnt bricks (40%). The urban dwellings were having either burnt brick or kimberly brick walls, and corrugated iron sheets or asbestos roofs. The rural dwellings continued to have grass roofs.

There has been substantial change in the ownership pattern of the dwelling units which reflects the governments policy towards housing. The dwellings owned either by the government, local authority, companies or by private landlords have increased their number as well as share to total houses. On the other hand, though the number of dwellings owned by the occupants increased by 34 thousand, their percentage decreased from 79.65 in 1969 to 65.25 in 1980. During the same period number of persons per dwelling increased from 4.62 to 5.05 (Table 7.2). The number of dwellings increased by only 28 per cent while population added 40 per cent in 1969-80 period.

Table 7.1: Dwellings Classified by Material of Construction of Roofs and Walls

(in percentage)

Provinces	*Material of construction of walls*			*Material of construction of roofs*					
	Total	*Pole & Dagga*	*Burnt Bricks Concrete Blocks*	*Kimberly Bricks*	*Grass*	*Asbestos*	*Corrugated*	*Thatch*	*Grass*
Copperbelt	150,678	15.18	61.47	20.23	0.70	42.13	29.28	7.47	14.09
Northern	121,994	47.37	13.13	33.56	0.74	1.33	3.73	6.03	80.12
Luapula	870,72	19.88	15.30	48.95	9.90	0.74	2.43	7.09	81.81
North-Western	59,006	58.32	8.58	23.79	4.15	1.00	3.64	10.89	73.61
Eastern	120,326	81.16	9.09	3.72	0.27	1.12	4.44	5.26	68.58
Central & Lusaka	146,875	33.57	38.82	23.53	0.82	19.92	24.04	11.09	41.46
Southern	98,585	44.92	31.05	16.03	1.36	22.78	9.43	8.14	5.40
Western	94,600	82.88	4.56	1.78	8.76	0.91	3.63	15.81	70.10
Zambia	879,134	45.73	25.92	21.00	2.75	13.68	12.09	8.62	56.49

Source : Census of Population Housing 1969, First Report, C.S.O., Lusaka.

Though there has been a housing crises, each household occupied one dwelling unit. About one-fourth of the dwellings were having one room, while the percentage of houses with 2 rooms were 30.81, and with 3 rooms were 23, i.e. the maximum number of dwelling units were having 3 rooms or less in 1980. In rural areas, about 17 per cent and in urban areas about 25 per cent houses were having more than 3 rooms. About one-third of the dwelling units were occupied by household of size varying from four to six persons. The household size of 7 persons or more was found in about 30 per cent of the dwellings. In urban areas the largest number of dwellings were occupied by household of this size. The crowding in dwellings can be estimated from Table 7.3. Mostly the larger size of households (7+) occupy dwellings having three rooms.

Table 7.2 : Ownership Patterns of Dwellings, 1969, 1980

(In Percentage)

Ownership	*1969*	*1980*
Government	4.22	8.55
Local Authorities	6.08	8.60
Companies	7.31	11.26
Private Land Lords	2.74	6.35
Owned by Occupants	79.65	65.25
Total dwellings	879,134	1,125,627
Total Population	4,056,995	5,679,808
Average number of persons/ dwellings	4.62	5.05

Source : 1969 & 1980 Census.

Table 7.3 : Dwelling units by Number of Rooms and Occupants, 1980

Number of Occupants	*Total Housing Units*	*Number of Rooms*					
		Total	*1*	*2*	*3*	*4*	*5+*
1	10.71	100	51.85	28.13	11.96	5.04	3.02
2 - 3	25.25	100	36.64	34.83	17.15	7.02	4.36
4 - 6	34.41	100	23.14	34.36	24.68	11.07	6.75
7+	29.63	100	10.24	24.19	30.02	20.03	15.51
Total	100.00	100	25.80	30.81	23.00	12.05	8.34

Source : C.S.O., Lusaka.

Distribution of Squatter Settlements, Population and Dwellings

From the earlier description, it is evident that the squatter population is associated with the urban centres. Squatter settlements with their population and dwellings are only within the planning authority boundaries. The large urban centres have more potential for employment and attraction of population but have comparatively lesser proportion of amenities and facilities. The larger the size of urban centres, the greater is the number of squatter settlement with sizable population and dwellings. The pressure of population per squatter dwellings is also high in the larger urban centres.

Table 7.4 : Squatter Settlement, Population and Dwellings in Zambian Towns.

Town/Urban Centre	*Total Urban Population*	*Squatter Dwellings*	*Squatter Population*	*% of Squatter to total population*
Kitwe	1,70,404	2,224	10,008	5.8
Ndola	1,28,579	6,326	28,467	22.2
Mufulira	95,767	346	1,557	1.6
Luanshya	88,776	293	1,318	1.5
Chingola	78,326	1,248	5,616	7.2
Kabwe	50,326	6,666	30,000	59.3
Livingstone	45,585	1,110	50,000	11.0
Chililabombwe	35,404	903	4,063	11.5
Chipata	13,500	1,150	5,175	38.4
Kafue	12,500	2,010	9,045	72.2
Mongu	11,000	1,380	6,210	56.4
Choma	8,964	500	2,250	25.1
Kasama	8,824	—	—	—
Mazabuka	6,931	819	3,685	53.1
Mbala	4,821	800	3,600	74.6
Chameshi	2,370	183	823	34.8
Lusaka (Estimated)	2,38,100	17,316	95,240	40.0

Source : Doxiadis Associates, 'Urban Centres' : Selection of Sites and Programme, DOX–ZAM–A62, July 1969, p. 10.

In 1974, the three large urban centres of Zambia, i.e. Lusaka (39), Kitwe (35) and Ndola (21) have the maximum number of squatter settlements.[2] The percentage of squatter population was less in Kitwe, however in Ndola it was considerably high, while in Lusaka it was then about 42 per cent.[3] The squatter dwellings have similar trend as well

(Table 7.4). Earlier in 1969, among the towns along the old line-of-rail, Kabwe has 59 per cent and Livingstone has 11 per cent of its population residing in squatter settlements. The newly planned town of Kafue had 72 per cent of its population lodging in eleven squatter settlements consisting of about 2,010 squatter dwellings. The provincial headquarters towns are slowly adding squatter population to their urban complex. Chipata town is the Eastern Province has four settlements with 5,190 population and 1,150 dwellings, while Mongu in the Western Province has 5,055 and 1,380 respectively. The *boma* towns do not have significant size of squatter population. The concentration of such population is along the old line-of-rail and in the provincial towns with the exception of Mbala town.

Squatter Population Before Independence

The squatter population in Zambia have their roots in the colonial period. Their distribution pattern is similar to those of Tripoli (Libya) or Latin American countries, where the squatter settlements have surrounded the towns. The rapid urbanisation, introduction of money economy and inadequacy of houses provided by the council authorities are some of the factors which encouraged the growth of squatter population in Zambian towns at early stage. The private holdings were then uncommon in urban Zambia. The houses are either of the councils (city, municipal, township or rural), or of the government, or owned by parastatal bodies. Owing to this reason, the housing facilities are restricted within the urban area boundaries.

The different land holding systems and building designs is strange to the uprooted rural population in the towns. However, financial problems is the most important aspect for selection of such shelter of temporary nature. The high cost–low density housing areas are privately owned by Europeans or Indians, or belong to the government. The low cost housing capacity of an urban centre and job opportunities determine the index of growth of squatter population.

During the colonial days, the African residential areas were known as 'high density areas' or 'low cost housing areas' or 'location' or 'municipal location'. The civic authorities were responsible for providing accommodation to the African urban population. In 1951, it was felt that more than twice over the allocated amount is required for local authority for African housing. From this amount, a large sum was for African civil servant housing schemes in the years 1952-56. A standard two roomed house was then costing £200. It was expected that local authorities will increasingly facilitate Africans who have the cash and competence to build their own houses in urban layouts by the scale of plots at nominal figures and the provision of service conditions. The squatter settlements were illegal compounds of unplanned dwellings of various building materials and became an alternative solution to the housing problems in towns.[4] These settlements, not looking strange to rural population, had a degree of convenience over the location houses, though they lacked in amenities, such as water, removal of garbage and the like. In order to reside in these settlements marriage certificate was not required. No administration as that of location was imposed on them and there was no restriction on the number of persons staying in such dwellings. The residents would not lose their houses if they lost their jobs. These settlements were free from police interference and selling of local beer. The small fields around them made an additional advantage for a squatter household. The private landlords made a business by collecting about £1 per month for each hut during the colonial days.[5] The Europeans and Indian employers, who could not manage accommodation in municipal location, could easily get a hut in these squatter settlements for their employees. Further, the employers found it cheaper to employ men from such settlements. Hence, the high rent in location with strict administration was not preferred to such settlements. Garneton, near Kitwe is an example of squatter settlement which was started by the African workers employed in the nearby farms during colonial period. Here neither the government nor the European farmers took interest in the development of this settlement. On the other hand, Malota, the oldest African housing area in Zambia located in Livingstone town in the south received much attention from the colonial government. But, with the passage of time the ownership right over the holding became more complicated. Both, the examples of colonial urban Zambia not only provide an insight in to the then urban situation, but also, indicate how these settlements have changed in form and function after independence.

Garneton : A Squatter Settlement in Copperbelt

This settlement is also known as North of Garneton, which is 10 km northwest of Kitwe City and the adjoining Garneton small holdings. It lies in the Kitwe urban district.[6] Migrants to this settlement left their rural areas upto the year 1957. Since then the flow of the uprooted rural migrants was slow upto the independence. This again increased in 1964 but later the flow of migrants became feeble. Most of the household heads except the recent migrants were employed. The migrants were at first employed in Itimpi Small-holdings, when this settlement was used as a place residence of the labourers (Fig. 7.2). As noted in respect of other squatter settlements there is a higher percentage of migrants who have spent less time along the old line-of-rail, indicating thereby the direct migration to this area. About 34 per cent of the households have previous residence in authorised housing areas while 51 per cent lived in other squatter settlements, indicating a large volume of internal circulation among squatter population. Further, 9 per cent households had residence in other towns along the old line-of-rail, while only 6 per cent have migrated from the rest of Zambia. The maximum migration from the rural area was experienced during the period 1960-69 when 46 household heads (34%) migrated to this settlement. The migration occurred mainly for two reasons : (a) need for own accommodation; and (b) jobs without the provision of accommodation. The other reasons were unemployment or seeking employment or desire to live close to the friends or relatives.

The settlements consists of 131 dwellings. Only 8 (6%) of the total households shared four dwellings. The ratio of dwellings to households is 10.0 : 10.6. The average number of persons per household is 4.43, having 2.07 adults on an average. The children below 7 years is only 0.75 per household. Maximum number of households (81%) have below 6 persons. The adult sex ratio is 10.7 males for 10.0 females. Highest number of dwellings (38%) are two roomed while only 18 per cent of the dwellings have a single room. The average number of persons per dwelling and per room is 4.7 and 1.8 respectively.

Of the 127 (98%) dwellings occupied by the owners, 107 are built by the household heads; only 8 or 6 per cent have received them as a gift. The cost of building of popular type of houses had been between K 50-100. From 7 or 5 per cent households pay rents while 3 or 2 per cent are lodging free.

The largest income group concerning 70 per cent of the households earns between K.20 and 60 in 1972. Only 4.76 per cent males were unemployed against 3.59 per cent of the females. While males have a negligible number not looking for work, this figure as usual rises to 89.92 per cent for females. Nearly 5.44 per cent males and 2.87 per cent of females work as salesman and saleswomen respectively. Males are mainly employed in services (24.48%), such as watchman.

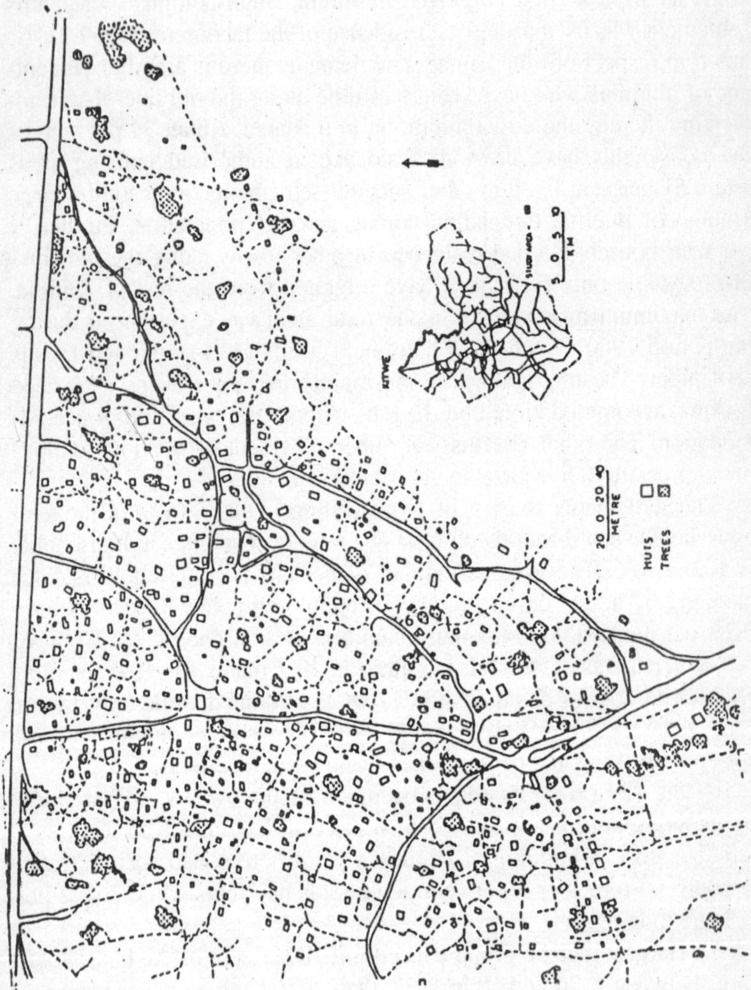

Fig. 7.2: Garneton

servants, or cooks; and as production workers (48.9%). The original profession of agriculture and forestry have been reduced to 12.92 per cent. The percentage of students is negligible.

The place of work for 33 per cent of the people is Garneton. Mwambeshi area and Industria in Kitwe city are other popular places of work. As usual, the largest number go to work on foot and 36 per cent on bicycles. Since there is a school in the nearby Garneton small holdings, about 79 per cent of the children attend this school. Only 19 per cent of children have never received any formal education. The household heads, apart from 34 per cent who have no formal education, about 41 per cent are educated upto more than Grade-5.[7]

The squatter settlement consist mostly of rectangular huts of pole and dagga, with thatched roof, though linearly arranged along a footpath of 10-12 feet wide. A glance at the map clearly shows that the vegetation, house and open space relationship (Fig. 7.2). While touring over the area it can be noticed that the vegetal cover is gradually diminishing due to increase in number of houses and kitchen gardens. The low vegetal cover causes high temperatures and dry dusty atmosphere. It has four shops and the goods are supplied either by vans or the shopkeeper buy them from the so-called "second class trading area". The materials of houses and open use of land make things worst. Kitchen gardens and poultry are popular. Water is a problem and the life is monotonous here.

Malota: The Oldest African Residential Area

Malota is the oldest among Zambian squatter settlements. Livingstone town (1905) was planned on grid pattern needed residential areas for African employees. The government then allotted plots of 50 x 50 feet. Nearly 512 plots were demarcated and the Africans were allowed to put up their houses. No title or lease was issued against such occupied plots. This resulted squatter settlements on this framework. Malota settlement, apart from the general squatter characteristics, is more complicated owing to its long history and changing land possession.

In July 1972, there were 128 absentee landlords in Malota[8] out of which 38 surveys of absentee landlords reveal some interesting cases of complicated land possession. Most of these landlords have shifted to authorised housing as Dambwa or Libuyu in Livingstone town. Only 5 have moved out of this town. The present tenants have in no case stayed more than 4 years on such plots. Mostly the present residents pay rents varying from K.4 to K.8. The rent is collected by some representatives of the absentee landlords who may not even stay in the settlement. Apart from these tenants, a few relatives of absentee landlords reside here without contributing any rent. In some cases ownership is transferred to the caretakers. Further, five cases were recorded of landlords having more than one plot. The extreme case is of a landlord having 3 plots with 37 tenants. The picture becomes more complex when these plots are sold to other persons who neither have a title or lease. The official records do not indicate the wife's name and whether they are actually present there or not. This is due to the fear that the land may not be transferred to wives' name. These plots have proved to be assets, as they are popular housing areas close to the place of work (Fig. 7.3).

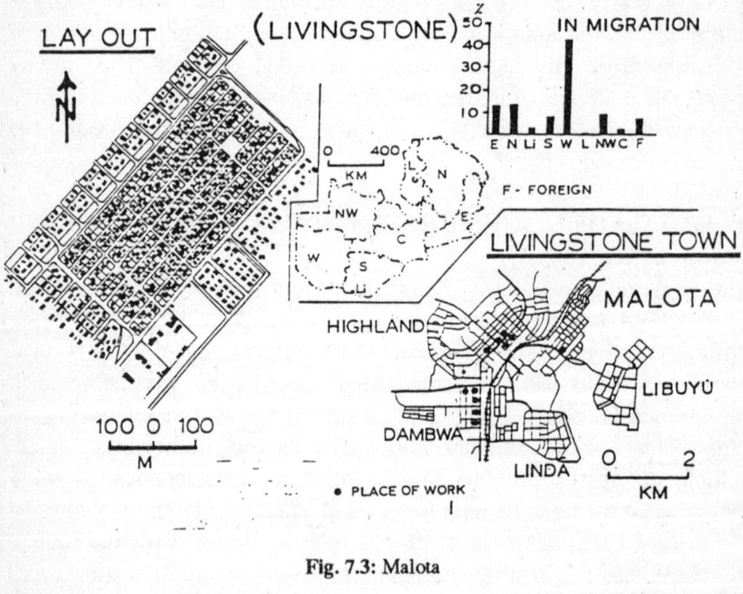

Fig. 7.3: Malota

The present landlords in whose name the lands are allotted are mostly outside of Livingstone, including 7 per cent foreigners, mostly from Malawi. Out of 100 samples (20% of the total of 512), only eight were from Livingstone; four belonged to the Southern Provinces; thirty nine were from Western Province, primarily from Sesheke, Mongu and Kaoma districts; eight from Zambezi district of North-Western Province; twelve from Eastern Province; fourteen from Northern Province and the rest came from Luapula, Copperbelt and Central province which constitute negligible percentage.

Of the above samples, fourty-three self-employed, including three in curio and five in charcoal makings. Only eleven were in government service, while seventeen were in the private concerns and five were engaged in Municipal Corporation of Livingstone. The places of work are located in business centres and industrial areas while the location markets have largely attracted the self-employed persons. Most of the plots have two houses. It is served by three nearby primary schools. The business area and Libuyu Market are approximately equidistant. The general character of the settlement is not much different from other squatter settlements located in the different parts of the country. The houses are rectangular and large with dirty drained footpaths. The open drainage and foul smell deteriorate the general health of the people of Malota.

The Council has been up-grading the settlement and a loan of K.185 was sanctioned for up-grading the plot on monthly deduction basis at the rate of K.3.35. From 1972, total facilities for up-grading the settlement have been provided by the Council. The reselling deals which vary from K.50 to K.200 per plot have now to be brought to the notice of the "Malota Up-Grading Office".

Squatter Population after Independence

After independence the migration was decontrolled. Africanization of jobs and earlier attraction for cash wages and European goods brought heavy influx to urban areas. It was a problem for the present democratic government to check migration in early years of its regime. The squatter population grew at a very fast rate. Their settlements became an organic part of an urban system of Zambia. In the First National Development Plan, a small number of high standard of housing was discouraged and the policy was to permit greater number of small and less expensive units. The government was to spend £4.20 million each year on the low cost housing.[9] The Commissioner of Lands was made responsible for these settlements. The stress was laid on site-and-service scheme which fitted with poor income groups.[10] Before the beginning of the Second National Development Plan, 17,298 site and service plots were approved under self-help housing programme which was launched in 1965. In addition, ten self-help townships had been developed before independence.[11] In the Second National Development Plan these settlements were recognised as assets both in social and financial terms. During this plan period (1972-76), the urban growth rate was expected to be 6.84 per cent annually, the proportion of Zambians living in urban areas was expected to rise from 30.2 to 36.5 per cent and an additional 85 thousand urban households were expected to be formed.[12] The emphasis was to upgrade these settlements by providing social and communal services. Government institutions, consultants, and the like organised their departments and obtained voluntary services from foreign countries and international organisations to upgrade such blighted settlements. Social Action in Lusaka (SAIL) and parallel to it in Kitwe (SAIK) have objective to develop and help such upgrading process, and the World Bank also expressed its willingness to provide financial assistance.[13] However, self help low cost and high density housing scheme started much earlier before independence. As mentioned earlier, Malota was the first example in this regard. Chibuluma, (1,062 houses) in Kitwe, Fisenge (220) in Luanshya, Kansuswa (403) in Mufulira, Kasompe (447), Maploto (24), Chibolya (337), New Kanyama (720) in Lusaka, Mukobeko (250) in Kabwe and Twapia (2214) in Ndola were other self help schemes constructed before 1964.[14]

The official self help scheme now known as site and service programme was initiated in 1965. Under this programme, 30 per cent of the six thousand housing plots were to be provided per year for the next 5 years, i.e. a total of nine thousand plots. These plots were subsidized by the government, loan at lower interest rates were provided and ablution units were constructed.

The governments efforts under this scheme were no match with rate of increase of squatters in the urban centres. Doxiadis associates were asked to prepare a crash programme for the settlement of squatter population which was later known as the Special Programme of Action for settlement of squatters. Kaunda Square (I) in Lusaka was developed under this action programme after 1969. Between 1969-1972, there was no change in the policy, however the designs were altered. In the Second National Development Plan the policy basically remained the same, in addition, the individuals were allowed maximum freedom. In 1972, an agreement was made between the Ministry of

Local Government and Housing and the African States Consulting Organisation Zambia Ltd. to carry out consultancy services in respect of the design layout of housing programmes in Ndola, Luanshya and Livingstone as provided for in the SNDP. The housing units were to be provided for the following Council areas (Table 7.5).

Table 7.5 : SNDP Housing Units in Ndola, Luanshya and Livingstone

Councils	*Self-help*	*Low-cost*	*Medium cost*	*Total*
Ndola City Council	2,100	1,500	400	4,000
Luanshya and Livingstone Municipal Councils	1,100	500	400	2,000

Source: ASCO Development Trends for the Ndola, and Luanshya Regions, Ministry of Local Government and Housing, Nov., 1972 1&2.

Low Cost Housing and Growth of Squatter Population

The growth of squatter population must be seen in relation to the availability of dwelling units in the low cost housing areas of the towns. The high and medium cost housing areas have lesser number of dwelling units and are mostly under the control of the councils or owned by private or parastatal bodies. The influx of population is ineffective in the high and medium cost housing areas. It has been noticed that the fewer dwelling units in municipal location have given rise to unofficial (squatter) housing areas. Copperbelt and the towns along the old line-of-rail have always been the centres of attraction for rural population and the better employment opportunities have accelerated such migration process. The growth of dwelling units did not keep in pace with the growing population which resulted in the formation of squatter settlements.

In December 1958, it was recorded that 28.7 per cent of all African employees lived in municipal locations, while 57.8 per cent in private premises and 13.5 per cent in squatter settlements (Table 7.6). In the mining towns, 20.6 per cent resided in municipal location, 71.7 per cent in mines or in employer's compounds whereas only 7.7 per cent in squatter settlements. The percentages in non-mining urban areas of Ndola, Livingstone and Lusaka was 44.3, 31.3 and 24.4 respectively. Mines provided houses for almost all of their employees, while the railways provided for 81 per cent, and in other industries it varied from

Table 7.6 : Housing of Urban African Workers Employed in Towns, 1958

Town	*Total Workers*	*Percentage of Workers residing in*		
		Municipal Houses	*Employers Compounds*	*Unauthorised Compounds*
Kitwe	13,604	18.6	73.8	7.6
Luanshya	14,803	24.0	73.7	2.3
Mufulira	18,311	13.3	68.7	18.0
Chingola	11,270	31.0	68.8	0.2
Kabwe	4,091	18.5	78.6	2.9
Total				
Mining Town	62,079	20.6	71.7	7.7
Ndola	16,818	44.8	27.0	28.2
Lusaka	8,700	45.5	27.9	26.6
Livingstone	6,970	41.4	46.4	12.6
Total				
Other towns along line-of-rail	32,488	44.3	31.3	24.4

Source : Department of Labour, Lusaka, Government of Northern Rhodesia, Lusaka, December 1958.

Note : Excluding employees of the government, municipalities, domestic servants, self employed and unemployed.

30 to 70 per cent (Table 7.7). Obviously, the remaining employees had to seek shelter within their social circles or in squatter settlement. Further, non-industrial employees, such as domestic servants, who were not provided with accommodation, added to these settlements. Ndola and Lusaka had the highest number of employees living in squatter settlements though they also had the highest number of employees residing in municipal houses. In the following paragraphs, an attempt has been made to highlight the growth of low cost housing and squatter population in respect of Ndola city. Such case study envisages the facts prior to independence and after.

Ndola - A Case Study (1954-73)

Ndola has experienced a rapid growth and development during the colonial period and was unable to meet the housing demand of the African urban population. As early as 1954, about 4 thousand dwelling

Table 7.7 : Housing of Urban African Workers in Different Industries 1958

Industry etc.	*Total Workers*	*Percentage of workers residing in*		
		Municipal Houses	*Employer's Compounds*	*Unauthorised Compounds*
Mines	33,090	—	100.0	—
Railways	3,188	15.2	81.0	3.8
Quarries, lime workers, small mines etc.	3,408	9.2	72.3	18.5
Butcheries, Mills Butchers	3,355	73.2	9.5	17.3
Small-scale industries	3,592	19.9	66.2	13.9
Printing, saw mills Bricks, Metals, and Machineries	7,820	48.9	36.8	14.3
Garages	2,399	74.6	2.0	23.4
Construction	21,159	30.0	37.2	32.8
Wholesale and retail	9,387	79.2	7.0	13.8
Transport Office	4,663	47.1	40.5	12.4
Hotels, Cafes	2,053	61.0	23.6	15.4
Sundry Services	953	74.6	4.0	21.4
Total	94,567	28.7	57.8	13.5

Source : Department of Labour, Government of Northern Rhodesia, Lusaka, December 1958.

Note : Excluding workers employed by the government municipalities, domestic servants, self-employed and unemployed.

units were planned with ablutions for each block of units. It was estimated that 5 thousand employees were not properly housed, and a programme was finalised to build some 2 thousand dwelling units each year since 1956. The total dwelling units in July 1956 was 7,394 only while 3,567 persons were on the waiting list. However, by January 1957 the number of dwelling units increased to 7,794 only, on the other hand, the waiting list rose to 5,809 persons indicating a large rise in the demand for housing (Table 7.8). In 1958, it was estimated that about 3 thousand employees were living as lodgers or sub-tenants, out of which 6 thousand were living in Masala Main Location. By then African women were getting employed in the city and there was a demand for a hostel for employed and unemployed African women.

During this period hundreds of employed Africans were living illegally in other housing areas, and in each case the employers were notified. However, a few employers complied with the provision of the law (Employment of Native Ordinance). It was estimated that number of employed Africans not properly housed in Ndola was 2,750 out of which one thousand in Main area, 750 in Chifubu, 500 in Kabushi and 500 in other areas of the city.

Table 7.8 : Housing Units and Waiting List in Ndola, 1957

Housing Units	*July*	*January*	*Difference*
Rentable Units of Housing	6,418	6,690	272
NRG Units of Housing	839	839	—
Contractors Housing Units	137	265	128
Total Housing Units	7,394	7,794	400
Waiting List for Housing	3,567	5,809	2,242
Total	10,961	13,603	2,642

Source : Ndola City Council
Note : NRG-Northern Rhodesia Government

By 1962, the council made provision of about 332 houses by initiating two infilling schemes in Masala and Kabushi. This was in addition to one thousand houses for the employees of Rhodesian Railways. There was also demand for better houses. On the other hand, lowest income group people were unwilling to move to the council houses. As a result in June 1962, about one thousand houses were lying vacant in the three main council housing areas (Table 7.9).

Table 7.9 : Council Houses in Ndola, 1962

Council Housing Areas	*Houses*		*Single Room Quarters*	
	Occupied	*Vacant*	*Occupied*	*Vacant*
Chifubu	4,250	75	222	3
Kabushi	2,396	50	236	834
Main	4,416	—	144	—
Total	11,062	125	662	862

Source : Ndola City Council.

Owing to the unpopularity of single room quarter in Kabushi, they were converted to three roomed houses. By June 1964, there were 552 mud hut occupants in Ndola. Council decided to house 225 families in the commuted housing units in this area, and to demolish the mud huts as soon as possible. By then sufficient number of serviced plots were available in Masala for approximately 115 better standard houses. Tenants having small houses applied for such transfer. Council earmarked the resultant smaller houses for the mud dwellers or squatter population, whenever they are vacated. For remaining 100 mud dwelling families, the Town Engineer proposed double-storied and terraced flats as a possible solution to be made in an area adjacent to Masala. These were attempts to bring the problem of squatter population under control and there was a scope to do so. However, there was a continuous demand of houses from the new and old establishments. It was estimated that approximately 500 additional dwelling units per year would be required for next few years.

On the contrary, over 300 dwelling units were lying vacant in 1959 probably owing to high rent, though the council was building then at the rate of 100 dwelling units per year.[15] During the same time, about one thousand employees were living in illegal housing areas which were mostly named after their employers. It was felt that the council was unable to look after the housing needs for all the employees and so the council made a representation to the Commissioner for Local Government to force the employers to arrange houses for their employees. The bewildering position of housing is also evident from the position of 1968, In July, about 9,953 persons were on the waiting list, but this figure rose to 10,152 by August and 10,182 by September, while only 42 persons were allotted houses in the previous and 81 in the latter months. In January 1970, about 13,348 persons were on the waiting list.[16]

With the government initiative for larger private ownership of houses of dwelling units by providing facilities to site-and-service schemes, eight per cent of houses in different locations in Ndola were privately owned, out of which Lubutu alone had 1,366. However, the council owned houses accounted for 88 per cent in October 1973.

An attempt has also been made to study ten low cost housing areas and twenty-one squatter settlements in Ndola city on the basis of the data available since March 1964 (Table 7.10). The population increased by 140 per cent during the period 1964-73, while the dwelling units during the same period increased to 64 per cent only. The population in all the squatter settlements of Ndola city was estimated at 5.34 per cent in 1958 which increased to 12.5 per cent in 1973, indicating the increasing housing problem.

The growth of population in the low cost housing areas was less than the unofficial and even high cost housing areas of Ndola. The high cost residential areas, *viz*. North Rise, Ndola Central, Itawa or Kesenji experienced a growth of 214 per cent between 1963 and 1971 while low cost housing areas had only 172 per cent increase. In comparison to official housing areas registering 92 per cent of growth, the unofficial housing areas experienced 206 per cent rise. The overall growth of population of the city was only 109 per cent during this period.[17]

Table 7.10: Dwelling Units in the Townships of Ndola City

Township	1964 Mar.	1965 Jan.	1966 Nov.	1967 Nov.	1968 Nov.	1969 Nov.	1970 Nov.	1971 Nov.	1972 Nov.	1973 Nov.
Masala N	614	1877	2024	2011	1953	1908	1895	1643	1643	1643
Masala S	2417	2210	2217	2217	2217	2226	2226	2226	2235	2235
Chifubu E	4398	2167	2165	2286	2314	2314	2314	2314	2314	2414
Chifubu N.		2365	2365	2437	2437	2437	2437	2437	2437	2417
Kabushi N.	2991	2928	4291	4665	1987	1987	1987	1987	1987	1987
Kabushi S.					2678	2678	2678	2678	2678	2678
Luboto					763	1138	1138	1952	1998	2035
Ndeke								707	921	921
Pamodzi									562	800
Twapia										31
Total	10428	12545	13062	13616	14349	14688	15028	15944	16775	17082
Growth (%)	--	20.30	4.12	4.24	5.38	2.31	2.31	6.10	3.21	1.83

Note : Total growth from 1964 to 1973 is 39.17 per cent.
Source : Ndola city council.

Composition of Squatter Households

Composition of the squatter households is closely linked with the availability of jobs and the age of the settlement. The settlements of recent origin have a larger number of males among the adult population, and the number of children is negligible. Such trend is found in Kankoma (Kitwe), Magazine (Kitwe) and Federnici (Ndola) squatter settlements. The older settlements, which in many cases have a larger number of females, attain the average sex ratio of the district. Out of twenty-four squatter settlements in Greater Kitwe, eight have numerical dominancy of females among the adult population. All these settlements are old and senile. However, the norm is of male dominancy. In settlements, such as Kalingalinga, Chibolya, Old Kanyama and George Compound in Lusaka, the overall sex-ratio was recorded as 103, 103, 104 and 108 males per 100 females, respectively (1969 census).

The longevity of a settlement could also be understood from increasing number of children in the settlement as well as in individual household. Chipulukusu (Ndola), which was settled in 1943, has 23 per cent males, 22 per cent females and 55 per cent children. Similarly, in the older squatter settlements of Greater Kitwe, such as Mulenga (62%), Kapili (58%) and Chisokone (57%), the percentage of children is higher; while in the new settlements, such as, Kandabwe, Mindola Dam and Kankoma, it is negligible. Malota (Livingstone) has 58 per cent of its population as children. Fifty-three per cent of Ndola's squatter population consist of children.

The household size is smaller in the newly settled compounds. A household head who migrated first looking for a job, adds his wife (wives) and children with the passage of time. Other members of the extended family also join in the future.[18] Visitors are unavoidable part of the squatter households. In the old settlements, such as Miseshi, and Kalumfwa, about six persons per household was recorded. During the studies of squatter settlements of Lusaka, 5.04 persons per household in George Compound and 4.6 in Kalingalinga were registered.[19]

Migration

As already mentioned, heavy migration to urban areas has resulted in the formation of such unauthorised settlements. With the exception of Malota settlement (Livingstone), these settlements are not more than one generation old. The population is generally new and has migrated from distant places. The place-names of the settlements or a part of it have a bearing on the place of origin of migrants, such as Chipata or Zambezi.

In the first instance, the migrants are economically low inproductivity. The migrants in these settlements generally belong to the same district which is away from the old line-of-rail. The squatter population in Livingstone is from its natural hinterland, i.e. the districts of Western Province and Zambezi district of North-Western Province. The natural flow of population from relatively densely settled areas of Eastern Province is towards Lusaka. Similarly, the squatter settlements of Copperbelt attract a large number of migrants from Bhapula, Northern and North-Western provinces.

It is interesting to note that during the peak year of migration, i.e. 1964 (the year of independence) and 1970, the percentage of unemployed and illiterate migrants was also maximum. According to the Kitwe City Council (KCC), the educational standard of the literates is between Grade-3 and Grade-7 (60%), while there is negligible population with Form-2 level of education.

In 1972, it was recorded that the maximum number of the heads of the households lived only upto four years in the towns along the old line-of-rail before moving to the squatter settlements of Kitwe. According to K.C.C., the previous residences of 37 per cent of the squatter population were in the authorised areas while 42 per cent lived in different areas within Greater Kitwe. Only 13 per cent were from other areas along the old line-of-rail. Similarly, in Mwaziona (George) in Lusaka, 40 per cent of the household heads have lived previously in Lusaka, in almost equal numbers in unauthorised areas and low cost housing areas. Among the residents of this squatter settlement, 30 per cent were resident in Lusaka before independence, but only 13 per cent were resident of the same settlement. During the period 1969-73, 48 per cent of the sample household heads moved into this settlement. Of these 322 persons 189 were newcomers to Lusaka and remainder came from elsewhere in the city.[20] In the first instance it indicates that a considerable number of persons who are urbanised and lived in authorised areas do not like to return after the expiry of their jobs. Large number of squatter population show high inter-squatter settlement movement. This is mainly due to the tendency among the people either to come nearer to a town in order to be benefited from the urban facilities, or to stay closer to their place of work. The settlements nearer to the city/town centre are popular for labour circulations. Owing to such circulations, a considerable number of new arrivals are found in these settlements. Many persons could no longer stay with relatives, while some would like to have a separate accommodation. Those who had expensive or small house would move for a preferable change. A few movements were also due to demolition activities by authorities, such as, settlement control offices. Some persons have migrated in order to establish business in squatter settlements.

The regional towns, away from the old line-of-rail, have squatter settlements with highly detached huts belonging to local population. The internal and inter-settlement circulation is negligible as the number of squatter settlement are few and the household economy is also dependent on agricultural produces. Hence, the land under the possession of the squatter household becomes an important factor for movement of squatter population.

Employment Structure

Squatter settlements are linked with the multifarious job opportunities provided by urban centres. Since employment is the determining factor, most of the settlement are functionally related to the place of work, while on the other hand, the source of water supply ultimately determines the actual site. In most of the cases the settlements are closer to the place of work and are connected with a small foot-path. The settlements, such as, Zamtan, Sawyers, Mindola Dam, Chambeshi Siding and Robert's Compound in Kitwe would clearly predict their employment structure. However, these settlements are likely to be deserted with the completion of the project (Fig. 7.4). In Lusaka, the work place of a large number of household heads of George complex in 1973 was in nearby Industrial Area and City Centre.[21] In another study of the same complex reveals that 81 per cent of the household heads were wage-employed mostly falling in the occupational status of 'Production and related Workers'.[22]

The desertion of a settlement is not a rule but it is an exception. A settlement, which may have grown with a specific source of employment, multiplies its employment structure with the passage of time. New arrival to towns make it a base for hunting job. It is difficult to find a settlement having no unemployed youth. In Miseshi and Kamfisa II in Kitwe, 22 per cent of the adult males are unemployed. Among the other sex, the majority of them do not look for jobs and usually engaged in the household chores. However, the popular source of their employment is as saleswomen, though, it has never exceeded more than 12 per cent of the adult females. The popular source of male employment is in production and transport industry, for example in Kalumbwa (Kitwe), all the adult males were employed in this sector. The settlements based only on the primary economy, such as, agriculture and forestry including charcoal making, are distant from the place of secondary and tertiary centres of activities, i.e. from city/town centres. Sawyer's and Robert's-Ndeke compounds (Kitwe) have upto

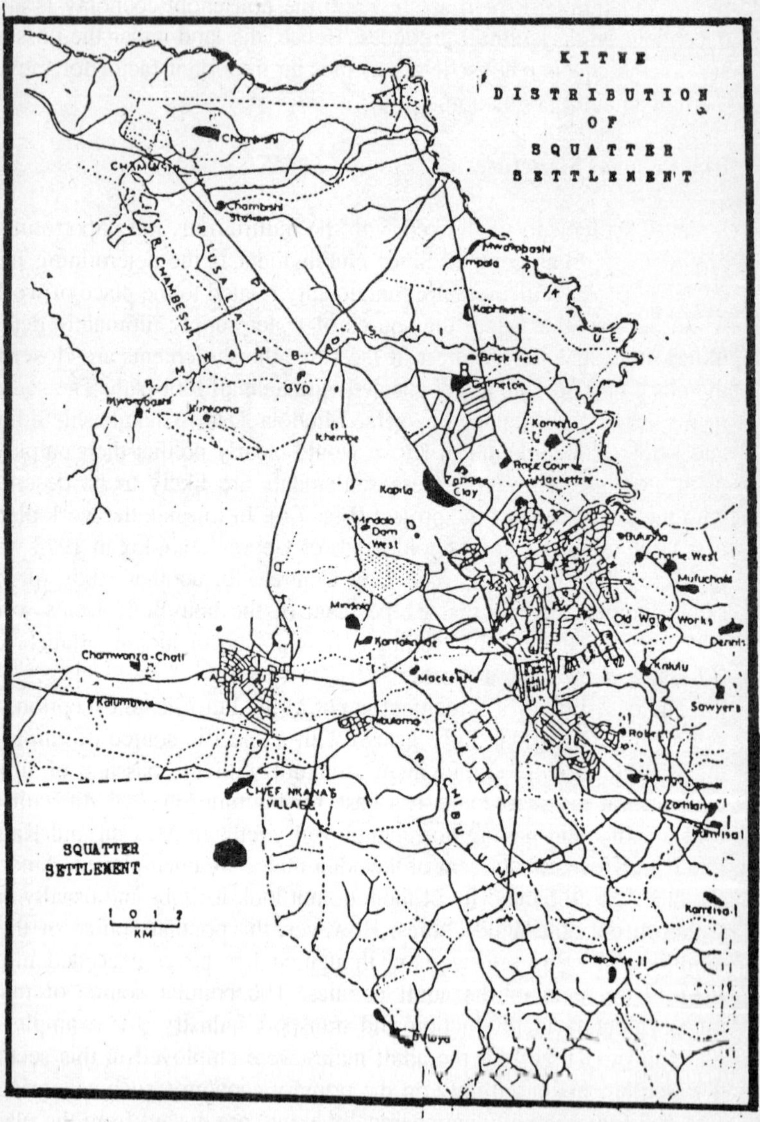

Fig. 7.4: Distribution of Squatter Settlements in Kitwe

75 and 79 per cent of the adult males engaged in this sector. Services is the third popular sector on employment. The unproductive group consists of students which have never increased to more than 10 per cent. In Kitwe, a few settlements have preponderance of female students over males. This indicates the growing interest of the females in education, on the other hand, the males are more willing to secure jobs. The employment in professional, technical, clerical or administrative activities is unpopular among both the sexes.

The squatter settlements primarily provide cheap accommodation for the blue collar labour force. Figure 7.4 shows the distribution of such settlements in Kitwe city. The pattern indicates that generally persons employed in some place in the town, live in the nearby settlement. With the increase in the size of settlements, the place of work decentralises. In the case of Mindola Dam settlement in the western part of Kitwe city, the place of work of 87 per cent workers is in Nkana West/Rokana. For this city, the popular places of work are City Centre, Industrial and Nkana West/Rokana. The daily journey to these places is made either on foot, or bicycles or by bus. However, in these seventeen settlements a reasonable number of persons are self-employed, within or around their respective settlements.

A sizable settlement which has accumulated population with time, requires services and related establishments, according to the local standards. This leads to self-employed persons and establishments, such as, shops or beer halls and units for cycle repairing or brick-laying. It was found in Ndola City that the ratio of self-employed persons to the total is about 1:4. It is likely that the area of operation of a self employed persons may also include areas outside the squatter settlement in which they are residing. Though, a large number of such persons are in secondary and tertiary sectors, their number in primary sector in some of the settlements is substantial. In a recent study of Chaisa, Chawama, Chipata Garden and George squatter settlements in Lusaka, a similar trend was found. In these settlements, about 75 per cent are employed in formal sectors, while rest are self employed.[23]

Informal Activities in Squatter Settlements

In several studies squatter settlements have been mentioned as informal housing areas. After favourable changes in laws, the legal status of such settlements have improved. Government or the concerned council is providing some assistance under upgrading programmes. However, there are a lot of activities within or around these settlements which are not directly or indirectly related to government, or council sponsored programmes or supported by the organised sector. Recently, the contribution of the informal sector has been considered to be valuable in the development of the economy. Several studies have been made in this regard, particularly in the squatter settlements of Lusaka.[24] Persons engaged in this activity are mostly self employed and looking for better employment opportunities elsewhere.

These settlements of exclusively cheap residential character have establishments to satisfy their needs which are similar to those of big villages. The shops in a squatter settlement have a bush character, i.e. a single shop satisfies all the primary needs of the entire settlement. The number of establishments does not always depend on the population base. The squatter shop, commonly known as grocery shop, deals with bread, coco-cola, medicines, maize flour and the like, over and above those articles sold in a village shop. These settlements do not have government institutions (an exception is Chipuluku, Ndola, has a clinic and primary school), but 'UNIP'offices are located there which generally look after the administration.

The local needs create demands for the establishments as groceries, small markets, butcheries, beer halls, bars and bottle stores. The last three are harmful as they sell alcoholic drinks which exploit the local population. The markets within the settlements are maintained by the council. The council also provides educational and health services. In Kalingalinga (Lusaka), there is one primary school and a clinic. In Mwaziona and its surroundings,[25] UNIP runs two primary schools, one of which was built on self help basis. The community centre is a focal point for social activities in the squatter settlements, similar to the location. It is a place for having school, clinic, women's club, meetings and literacy classes.

The population or households per establishment varies considerably in these settlements. Due to temporary nature, a shop or a bar often closes down. Three markets in Mwaziona settlements and its surrounds serve 41,358 persons. Each market serve on an average nearly 14,000 persons only. Ngulwe with 8,497 persons has a small market. Chawama and Nyerere with 19,780 have a single large market. All these are in Lusaka.

In Ndola, only Chipulukusu (9,639)[26] and Sinia (2,433) have markets while other squatter populations do their marketing nearly with a maximum distance of 9 kms. Similarly, the population base, to support a bar, shop or butchery varies considerably. According to a survey of the Department of Town and Country Planning a shop needs 144 households in case of Kalingalinga, 88 in Old-Kanyama and 50 in Buleni, all in Lusaka. Anglew squatter settlement (Ndola) with 1,458 people, has two groceries only. Chipulukusu in north of Ndola has 30 groceries, 1 butchery, 4 bar halls and 3 bars, while Kntolomba having one-third population of the former, has 5 groceries, 3 butcheries, 1 beer hall and 2 bottle stores. It would be misleading to suggest any definite population base for such establishments as it varies with the taste of the residents and the distance from shopping areas which differ from town to town.

The settlement away from city centres do not attain maturity and hence lack in functional organisation and establishments. In these settlements, the gardens make physical separation among the households – a diffused pattern of settlement having relatively vague boundaries. In comparison to Lusaka, the functional organizations is weak in Ndola as well as in Kitwe while it is weaker in squatter settlements of other towns such as Chipata or Mongu. These settlements provide patterns of possible co-existence of different peoples of Zambia with feasible environmental and socio-economic adjustments.

Planned and Unplanned Housing Areas in Lusaka

The complications in planning the capital city has discussed in the earlier chapters. The statutory and unstatutory development exist side by side which has shaped the present morphology of this city. Owing to this reason, it has been an interesting case for the study of squatter population and settlement. For no other urban centre in Zambia, this aspect has been studied in so details. Several useful contributions have been made so far in understanding the genesis of the problem. Some studies have been on the squatter problem in the city as a whole, while other studies are on the housing conditions, or the site and service scheme or the growth of individual settlements which are sizable. But, a survey of existing literature on this issue will reveal that a geographical explanation to the whole problem of squatter development is still lacking.

The acute housing problem in the then Northern Rhodesian towns was more prominent in Lusaka. The limited housing facilities forced African population to find an alternative to the unfavourable policies in colonial urban development plans. Kamwala and Chibolya which were included in the Bowling Plan of 1933, did not prove to be sufficient to accommodate Lusaka's African population. Kabwata developed before 1945 and Chinika in 1947. After 1948 Urban Housing Ordinance, it became for the first time necessary to make provision for housing for every African employed within council boundary. This ordinance forced to develop additional African quarters in Lusaka. In July 1957, there was a backlog of 8 thousand houses which was expected to increase to over 11 thousand in 1962 unless new houses were built. African Affairs Committee set out a programme for the provisions of permanent housing and service schemes in order to clear the backlog.[27] As a result, New Chilengi (1960), Chibolya (1951) and Matero (1952) developed as African housing areas. It was agreed in 1957 that Chibolya African Township be retained as a permanent African Housing area. No more houses were to be permitted there and after 2 years the position was to be reviewed with an aim to making a definite time limit to the existence of this African township. The slopes in the absence of rock outcrops and better drained soils of the Ridgeway area, made suitable for septic tank method of sewage disposal. The African quarters have followed the ridge and the sewage line.[28] The other African housing areas also developed along the same sewage line here after the enforcement of statutory plans. These high density areas are New Kamwala (1962), Libala I and II (before 1962) and Libala III and IV and Chilange South, stage I and II (1965).

It was felt that the high density areas for Africans were not sufficient for the growing population of Lusaka. Squatter settlements developed surrounding the town. Kalingalinga, quarries, Marrapodi, Kanyama and George are the squatter settlements from the colonial days. They account for about ten per cent of the Lusaka's population 1963.[29] However, there were large number of villages around Lusaka having similar characteristics. Around 1966 the then existing squatter settlements expanded in all directions, while new settlements sprang up in the intervening vacant space. In 1968, there were 12,107 names on the waiting list for all types of houses in a total of nine estates. During the period June 1965 to December 1967, a total of 2,312 houses were either allocated or reallocated. Our of which only 275 (12.9%) were given to persons removed by demolition schemes, and 991 (22%) to persons who were self-employed or employed in commerce and industry. It was estimated in 1968 that over 1,300 new housing units will have to be constructed.[30]

The physical structure of squatter settlements from air photos appears to be mushroomed, thatched tin roofed huts. The air photographs used in the study of Mwaziona or George squatter settlements reveal that it grew from a few large farm houses and small villages. During the period 1960-62, there was hardly any change. This was the period when there was no out-migration. In 1962-65, i.e. the period around independence when restriction on migration was relaxed, the infilling process was more significant then out-migration. Moreover, in a photograph of 1968, the expansion of settlement could be observed.[31] In another study of the same settlement, the expansion of the George from 1960-77 in 7 phases was mapped. The composite map indicates the recent trend of growth towards the north, while the vacant spaces inside the settlements, still exist. Its population has increased from 570 in 1958 to 56 thousand in 1976.[32] However, the 1980 census reports that the population of the settlement (including Mwaziona, Kizito and Soweto) was only 46,655 (24,913 males and 21,472 females).[33]

In the study on urban development of colonial Lusaka, Rothman has identified 5 periods of study from 1905-64. Each of Lusaka's five historical periods presented novel situations which required varying degress of adaptations on the part of African community. This study traces how the ruling communities enforced new legislations, ordinances and sanctions in order to mett the changing urban situation for the African population.[34]

The SNDPs policy of squatter upgrading made a provision of K 26.5 million to Lusaka Housing Project in 1974. This was financed by the Zambian Government, the World Bank and UNICEF. Legal Provision for upgrading was made under the Housing (Statutory and Improvement Areas) Act of 1974. The features of this projects were upgrading of Chawama, George, Chaisa, Chipata and Garden squatter settlements involving servicing of about 17 thousand dwellings; preparation of 7.6 thousand overspill plots for resettlement of people removed from the original squatter areas for development; and site and service scheme provision for 3.2 thousand plots in normal schemes and 1.2 thousand plots in basic schemes. The whole idea was to improve the housing standard in Lusaka.[35] However, 42 per cent of Lusaka's population was still living in squatter settlement areas. The contribution of such informal housing to the total capacity of urban housing in Lusaka is one of the outstanding examples of self-reliance during the first 10 years of independence.[36] Several studies have been made on the role of informal sector in urban areas. How a system has developed without the support of the government? How the Zambian humanistic society having its roots in rural areas, has modified with time and space?

Other studies have also been made between 1974-80 regarding various aspects of squatter settlements, self-help schemes, upgrading of squatters and low cost housing areas. These studies were made by Lusaka Housing Project Unit Evaluation Team (LHPET), Lusaka City Council Housing Project Unit (LCCHPU), National Housing Authority. Institute for African Studies (Urban Community Reports), some of these reports are published while most of them are mimiographed volumes. These studies deal wit a variety of subjects which were more significant during this period for Lusaka's development. Laws were then implemented which provided legal acceptability to the upgrading of squatter settlements. On the other hand, in order to control the growth of squatters, no person was allowed to occupy or continue to occupy vacant land and the local authorities were asked not to allow unauthorised buildings in their respective jurisdiction.[37]

During this period (1974-80) several squatter settlements in Lusaka were partly or wholly upgraded either by site and service scheme or by self-development. The 1980 census records four types housing areas. In the category of "Site and Service/Shanty Townships", there are 26 areas which constitute about 37 per cent of Lusaka's population (Table 7.11). If we consider the sex ratio in these townships, it appears that female in-migration has been directed to such inexpensive housing areas of Lusaka. Here the population density has been high and the process of normalisation the sex ratio has been relatively more effective. The households are becoming more complete.[38]

Table 7.11 : Lusaka — Males, Females and Sex-Ratio According to Types of Housing Areas, 1980

Housing area	*Male*	*Female*	*Total*	*M/1000F*
1. Site & Services/ Shanty Room	156,997 (56.85)	149,658 (57.16)	306,655 (57.00)	1,049
2. Peri-urban Areas	13,731 (4.97)	12,091 (4.62)	25,822 (4.80)	1,136
3. Low/Medium-Cost Housing Areas	60,241 (21.81)	58,546 (22.36)	118,787 (22.08)	1,029
4. High Cost Housing Area	45,207 (16.37)	41,535 (15.86)	86,742 (16.12)	1,088
Total Lusaka	276,176 (100,00)	261,830 (100,00)	538,006 (100,00)	1,055

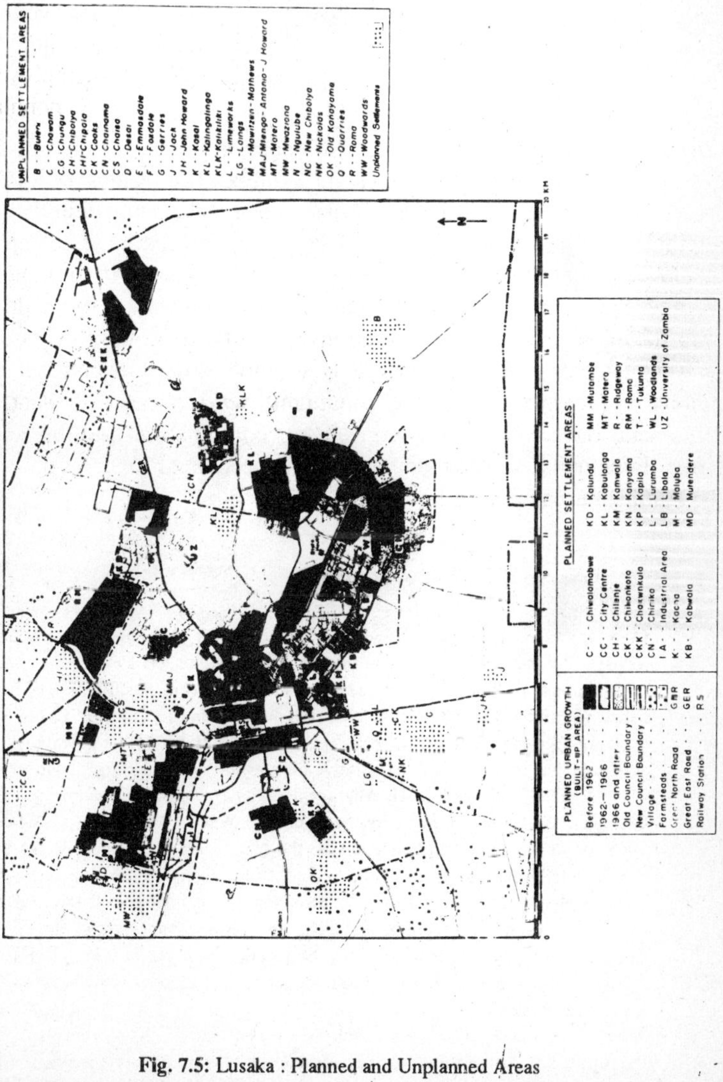

Fig. 7.5: Lusaka : Planned and Unplanned Areas

Conclusion

In the present study, the squatter population has been considered as a part of the urban population. Within the Zambian towns, their district is linked with the place of work. However, the working population in the older settlements have to go to several places for their earnings. Since, construction of houses is not in pace with the growth of population, these settlements become receiving areas for the standing unemployed labour force in the towns. The family composition of squatter population indicates the sex-ratio in favour of males, nevertheless, there is an overall preponderance of females in Zambia. The names of these settlements or a part of it have a bearing on the place or origin of the migrants or place of work. The phases of migration can be linked with the development or economic policies of the government. In the course of time, the squatter settlements add sufficient population to create a base for maintaining social institutions like schools or health centres, or establishments like grocery shop or bottle store. Government of Zambia is providing social and community services because squatter settlements have been recognised as assets both in social and financial terms. Eventually, squatter population has become an integral part of the Zambian urban population.

REFERENCES

1. Eyre, L. Alan, The shanty towns of Montego Bay, Jamaica, *Geographical Review*, Vol. 62, 1972, p. 394. In this article the author has claimed that 'only one geographer, Lucien Parisse, has made shanty towns as specific field of published research'. Vide Parisse, Lucian, Les Favclas dan la Ville : le Casde Rio de Janiro, *Rivista Geografica*, Vol. 70, 1969, pp. 109-30. Also see Howton, F. Williams, Cities, slums and accultrative process in the developing Countries, in Meadov, Paul and Ephrain H. Mizravchi (eds.) *Urbanism, Urbanization and Change : Comparative Perspectives*, Addision-Wesley Publishing Company, 1969, p. 433. Yuzo, Uchida, Report on the experience of Japanese slums improvements, Paper presented in the Second World Congress on Human Settlements, Calcutta, December 1984. See also Nag, P., squatter population in Zambian towns, in the Proceedings of the pre-conference Symposium of the I.G.U. Commission on population Geography, Sao Paulo, 1982, pp. 113-26 (mimio).
2. Figures within the parenthesis indicate the number of squatter settlements in the associated urban centres.
3. *Seminar on Planned Urban Growth in Lusaka*, 19 and 20 November 1974, Department of Extra Mural Studies, Institute for African Studies, Lusaka.
4. *Second Review of the Ten-Year Development Plan of Northern Rhodesia*,

Government Printers, Lusaka, 1951, p. 20.

5. John, Anthony St., *Northern Rhodesia - The Human Background*, Pall Mall Press, London and Dunmow, 1961, p. 91.

6. "The site was originally known as Itempi and was divided into agricultural holdings for retired mine-workers. This scheme failed to attract sufficient support, so ten-acre plots were offered to general public.....As Kitwe expanded, the demand for peri-urban residences increased and plots were sub-divided, most are now three, four or five acres only". Vide, Kay, G., *A Social Geography of Zambia*, University of London Press, 1967, p. 93.

7. Kitwe City Council, Kitwe.

8. Monthly report ending July 1972 of Municipal Council of Livingstone. Information was also collected from Livingstone Municipal Council, and Malota Up-grading Office.

9. *First National Development Plan*, Ministry of National Development and Planning, Government Printers, Lusaka, 1966, p. 47.

10. The up-grading in Kitwe has developed beautiful houses through site-and-service schemes. The city councils provide loan in the form of housing materials and assistance. Kaunda in Lusaka is an example of such development.

11. National Housing Authority, *Self Help in Action : A Study of Site and Service Schemes in Zambia*, Research Study No. 2, Lusaka, June 1975, p. 2.

12. National Housing Authority, *Op. cit.*

13. "Do our squatters Need World Bank Aid?", *Daily Mail*, February 7, 1974.

14. National Housing Authority, *Op. cit.*, p. 4.

15. "New Houses Stand Empty while Africans live in Broken-down Houses", *Ndola News*, December 16, 1958. For Lusaka see Council sets 11,000 Houses Target for Africans, *Northern News*, July 31, 1957.

16. Information provided by the Director of Housing, Ndola City Council.

17. For comparison see *Low Cost Residential Development in Lusaka*, Department of Town and Country Planning, Research Unit, Lusaka, 1972.

18. *Lodgers and Houses in New Kanyama : A Survey*, Department of Community Development, Research Unit, 1966.

19. Lundgreen, Thomas, Schlyter, Am and Schlyter, Thomas, *Kapwepwe Compound : A Study of an Unauthorised Settlement*, University of Lund, Department of Architecture II B, Sweden, 1969. Schlyter, Ann, Thomas Schlyter, *George — The development of a Squatter Settlement in Lusaka, Zambia*, Swedish Council for Building Research, Stockholm, 1980. Also see Witola, Zeilter, *A Socio-Economic Survey of Kalingalinga*, Department of Community Development, Lusaka, p. 7.

20. Department of Town and Country Planning, *Mwaziona : A Study of an Unofficial Housing Area*, Development, Planning and Research Unit, Lusaka, 1973, pp. 43-50.

21. Department of Town and Country Planning, *Mwaziona: A Study of an Unofficial Housing Area*, Development and Research Unit, Lusaka, July 1973, Figure 12, pp. 51-63.

22. Schlyter, Ann, Upgrading George revisited in Ratodi, Carole and Ann Schlytor, *Upgrading in Lusaka : Participation and Physical Changes*. The National Swedish Institute for Building Research, Gavle, 1981, p. 27.

23. Todd, Dave and Chistopher Shaw, *Education, Employment and the Important*

Sector in Zambia, Urban Community Research Unit Report No. 2, Institute for African Studies, Lusaka, u.d., pp. 21-30.

24. Todd, Dave and Chistopher Shaw, *Education, Employment and the Informal Sector in Zambia*, Urban Community Research Unit, Institute for African Studies, University of Zambia, Lusaka, Report No. 2, u.d. (for employment in squatters in Lusaka, see pp. 21-30); Todd, Dave, Alfred Mulenga and Chris Muplmila, *Marketers and Urban Growth* (A study of five Lusaka Markets) , Urban Community Report No. 1, 1978 (?); Todd, Dave, *Small Scale Manufacturing in Lusaka: A Comparison of Markets and Small-scale Industry Sites*, Urban Community Report No. 2, September 1980 (mimio).
25. Mwaziona and its surroundings include Desai, Freedom, New Chibolya and Paradise Compounds.
26. Figures in parenthesis indicate total population of each settlement.
27. Council sets 11,000 – Homes Target for Africans, Northern News, 31st July, 1957.
28. Department of Town and Country Planning, *Low Cost Residential Development in Lusaka*, Research Unit, Lusaka, 1972, p. 10.
29. Kay, G., *A Social Geography of Zambia*, University of London Press, 1967, p. 127.
30. *Report of the Commission of Inquiry into the Affairs of Lusaka City Council*, Government Printers, Lusaka, November 1968, pp. 11-12.
31. Department of Town and Country Planning, *Mwaziana : A Study of an Unofficial Housing Area*, Research Unit, Lusaka, 1973.
32. Schlyter, Ann, Upgrading George Revisited, in Carole, Rakodi and Ann Schlyter, *Upgrading in Lusaka : Participation and Physical Changes*, The National Swedish Institute for Building Research, Gavle, 1981, pp. 21 & 22.
33. *1980 Census of Population and Housing*, Preliminary Report, Central Statistical Office, Lusaka, 1981.
34. Rothman, N., *African Urban Development in the Colonial Period : A Study of Lusaka, 1905-1964*, Ph.D. Thesis (History) , Northwestern University, Illinois, 1972, (Microfilm : Ann Arbor, Michigen). Periods of study : 1905-27, 1927-39, 1939-46, 1946-53 and 1953-64.
35. Todd, Dave, *Small-Scale Manufacturing in Lusaka: A Comparison of Markets and Small-Scale Industry Sites*, Urban Community Reports No. 2, Institute for African Studies, Lusaka, September, 1980 (mimio) , pp. 13-5.
36. Seminar on Planned Urban Growth in Lusaka, *Department of Extra - Mural Studies, Institute for African Studies, Lusaka, 19 & 20th November, 1974 (B 3 : Housing, Site and Service in Lusaka). See also* Pasteur, D., Financial Resources for Urban Services and Development in Lusaka : A Case Study and an Exercise, *Development Administration Group, Institute of Local Government Studies, University of Birmingham*, 1978.
37. L.H.P.T., Lusaka Reports : *Study of Plot Use in Site and Service Scheme and a Squatter Area in Lusaka*, Working paper, 2, 1976; George 1976, *Initial Results of the First Primary Sample Survey*, W.P. 4, 1977; *George Overspill Consolidation: Preliminary Results*, W.P. 12, 1977; Mulenga, Alfred D., *A descriptive Analogy of the Physical Process*, W.P. 24, 1978; Mulenga, Alfred, D.; *Mutual Help Block Making Garden Overspill*, W.P. 23, 1978; Rakodi, Carole, *The Affordability of the Options Offered by the Lusaka Squatter Upgrading and*

Site and Service Project, W.P. 15, 1977; Rakodi, Carole and Catherine Mwanamambwa, *Community Development and Change : The Community Development Process in Chawama and George,* Lusaka, W.P. 10; Singini, R. E., George 1978. *Primary Surveys I and II - Comparisons,* W.P. 21, 1978. Todd, David, *Cost of Housing,* 1979; Banda, M.C., *Observations of a Pilot Mutual Help Scheme in Nyerere* (Chawama Complex), W.P. 3, 1977, Banda, M.C., *Observation of a Mutual Help Scheme in Desai (George Complex),* W.P. 13, 1978; Banda, M.C., *The House Construction II,* First Draft, W.P. 31, 1979; Banda, M.C., *Community Participation in the Upgrading Process (First Draft),* W.P. 36, n.d.; Mulenga, A.D., *The Chaisa/Garden Community Development Process,* Lusaka, W.P. 17, 1978; Rakodi, C., *Research Design,* W.P. 1, 1976; Rakodi, C., *Lusaka Housing Project Unit : The Collections Systems, First Report,* W.P. 18, 1978; Banda, M.C., *People Buying Plots and Houses in Chawana Overspill and Chawama Existing. The Newcomers,* W.P. 29, 1979. Lusaka City Council Housing Project Unit (LCCHPU) Reports, Lusaka : *The Facts,* u.d., *George Complex Operation Review (Phase I),* u.d. National Housing Authority, Lusaka : *Aided Self-Help Housing. House Types with Built - in Ablution Block,* 1972; *Request to the International Bank for Reconstruction and Development for a loan to Finance a Service Plot and Squatter Upgrading Programme,* 1973.

38. Nag, P., The role of women in internal migration in Zambia, *Population Geography,* Vol. 5 (1& 2) , 1983, pp. 60-9.

8

DEVELOPMENT OF POPULATION SETTLEMENTS

ZAMBIA is a large land-locked nation state now under a highly centralised administration of One Party Participatory democracy. This country came under the European colonisation comparatively at a later stage and hence the process of so called modernisation under the connotation of imperial powers was experienced late in this part of Central Africa. As mentioned earlier, the colonial development was obviously based on exploitable resources. The developmental infrastructure has been dominated by physical and environmental conditions, and the overall economic activities in space were organised on this framework. The two decade year old republic government has reorganised the country into a single administrative system. The modern transportation system of roads and railways developed a par excellence position. The old line-of-rail still continues to attract development. Copperbelt has attained a special position in the organisation of settlements and population. It has been able to draw socio-economic contours over the territory. In addition to environmental and functional barriers, the large game parks have added to settlement gaps at the regional level while forest resources and mining rights have resulted in such gaps at the local level. The problems of Zambia have been enormous, but not beyond control. There is a lot of scope for development in every sector. Judicious management of resources and redistribution of population can solve some of the most pressing problems of the country. Excessive concentration of population in favoured places and continuation of this trend has to be checked. This has to be done by (a) development of rural areas and settlements, (b) development of resources, and (c) diversification of the economy. Government Republic of Zambia is fully aware of these problems, and taken certain measures for the development of population and settlements.

National Development Plans

The policies in the national development plans regarding population and settlement are implicit and explicit. The explicit policies regarding rural and urban development have been mentioned in the earlier chapters. However, the implicit policy measures, such as rural development for checking migration to urban areas, have been less effective owing to several socio-economic reasons. On the other hand, the explicit measures, such as development of towns and cities by self-help schemes have made these places more attractive. As result, migration of population continues to urban centres along the old line-of-rail.

The first attempt for planned development of the country was made by preparing the Ten-Year Plan of 1947-56. The broad objectives of the original plan for Northern Rhodesia which was reviewed in 1948 remained the same. The immediate objectives were more food, more dwellings and better roads (FDR).[1] Obviously, these measures were with colonial interest. A large sum was kept aside for European agriculture, marketing and the development of the secondary industry. To a great extent the objective for higher food production was met soon. On one hand there were attempts to depend on increased mechanisation in order to meet the shortage of the African Labour force, while on the other hand the government was trying to revolutionise African agriculture. One of the measure was to identify improved farmers and peasant farmers (Chapter 5).[2] But, this scheme was more effective in Mazabuka, a district along the old line-of-rail. However, by 1950 the results of these measures were promising. In the same plan, a reasonable sum was allotted for African housing in urban areas. This explicit measure encouraged African population in having their own houses resulting into permanent nature of settlement away from their tribal areas. The 1961-65 Plan included a rural and economic development plan, but it was basically for European population. Majority of African population was not involved in development process. Rural areas away from the old line-of-rail remained unaffected. The requirements of the African population took second place even in such enormously important fields as health and education.[3] Till then, there was no priority for the development of the majority population and their settlements.

Immediately after independence, a new plan was prepared with a basic aim of developing certain essential services, such as defence, internal security, transport and communication, and most important aims were education and agriculture. This was the *Transitional Development Plan* which was later taken over by the *First National Development Plan 1966-1970*. The basic aim of this plan was to develop human resources. One of the objective was to increase employment by at least 100,000 jobs, including jobs in rural areas. This objective was also with an aim to increase incomes of the rural population 'who at present are only supporting their own families and not contributing in any other way to the nations wealth. These people will then be able to buy the goods that the new industries will be making in towns'. The another more explicit objective was to provide more and better houses as an essential part of a better standard of living, and to raise the general level of social welfare. The additional objective was to develop infrastructure, such as transport and communication. All these policies, implicit or explicit, encouraged migration of the population to the urban centres. Raise in the level of education and training increased the number of persons suitable for administrative and technical jobs. Such enterprising population crowded the urban areas leaving behind the rural areas underdeveloped.[4] This plan was however, based on revenue returned from the sale of copper which was considered to have a stable price in the international market.[5] The plan covering four and half years period (July 1966-December 1970) brought about substantial achievements in economic and social development. Moreover, the such achievements as well as failures provided basis for the fomulation of strategies for the next plan which started in January 1972. The year 1971 was designated as a year of consolidation of the gains already achieved by the country.[6]

The Second National Development Plan for the period from January 1972-December 1976, emphasize on rural development even more than the earlier plan. Increase in agricultural production and efficiency was considered to be the essential for increasing employment opportunities in rural areas. However, regarding rural small scale industries, it was then considered that "the emphasis on rural development and generation of rural employment depends on the implicit linking of increases in production and efficiency with the use of modern agricultural techniques which do not displace labour but which absorb labour".[7] Regarding housing, high priority was given for the construction of low-cost housing units, community development by involving people in their own development and self-help schemes, in coordination with other government agencies was considered essential for improving the level of living of the general population in rural and urban areas. The degree to which a country's housing needs are met was thought to be important measure of social, political and economic progress. Overcrowding was seriously felt in urban areas only. This situation was expected to be worsen with continuing migration from rural areas and pattern of demographic growth in urban areas . In order to meet the required housing needs in urban areas the ideas of "home ownership" and "serviced plots" were initiated by the government, which as we have noticed in chapter 7 have worked out with considerable success. However, such initiative for solving urban housing problem made urban centres more attractive which in turn encourage rural-urban migration.

After a lapse of almost three years, the Third National Development Plan (TNDP) of K. 3,354 million was launched in October 1979. The objectives of the plan were not altogether different from the earlier plans. As expected, more emphasis was given for the development of rural sphere. The main objectives were as follows:

(i) The adoption of a more labour-intensive technology to generate the fuller employment;
(ii) To give the highest priority to rural development, emphasizing the expansion of the production based on agriculture, the promotion of village and small scale industries, and the creation of infrastructural and extension facilities to benefit subsistence process and small-scale farmers;
(iii) To promote industrial production based on local raw materials;
(iv) To reduce the disparities in levels of income between rural and urban sectors;
(v) To expand education and training facilities both in quality and quantity; and
(vi) Obtaining, with reasonable price stability, target growth of 6 per cent per annum in real G.D.P.[8]

Development Framework

The Second National Development Plan was aware of the problems of Zambia and the planning framework of the First National Development Plan. The areas away from the old line-of-rail, mentioned earlier as 'rural areas', were given priority in terms of strategy, objectives and allocation of funds. The aim was to fill the gap between the disparate rural and urban areas. In S.N.D.P., the planning machinery was tuned up for a continuous planning process. At National level, Development Planning Division (DPD) or Central Planning Office was the basic agency to draft, review and implement the plan. The D.P.D. also co-ordinates the ministries, its programmes and 'ensures inter-sectoral and inter-regional coherence of all sectoral plans' of different ministries. In addition to above it also assists parastatal bodies to function in coherence with the aims and objectives of the S.N.D.P. The parastatal bodies are directly attached to planning units of ministries which are responsible for sectoral planning in consultation with D.P.D.

The D.P.D.also have Area Development Units *viz.* Regional Planning Units (RPU); and Provincial Planning Units (PPU). The R.P.Us are given 'all the necessary assistance to province in the formulation of plans and policies concerning regional and urban development aimed at achieving better balanced inter-regional development in the country'. While 'the development of inadequately staffed P.P.Us is a task which cannot be accomplished in a short period of time'. However, 'close and continuous co-operation between the D.P.D., the P.P.U.s and the Department of Town and Country Planning (DT&CP) is indispensable for making possible integrated regional planning'. The D.T.&C.P. is made responsible to prepare Development Plans, in advance, for all the potential settlements and this department has been entrusted with the planning and development of either the existing planned urban settlements or new settlements. The existing unplanned rural settlements were left to provincial, district and ward development committees for achieving the national goals. Extensive publicity was made to organise the country in this new system. The fieldwork experience indicates that this task cannot be accomplished during the second plan period. A mature settlement system, of the proposed nature, will drift more towards economic organisation of space and will be oriented towards the economically potential or functionally responsible settlements, i.e. as expected, towards the ward centres, instead of social or cultural centres as chief's headquarters.

Three ministries mentioned earlier, were directly held responsible for settlements in Zambia. The Ministry of Rural Development has four divisions directly dealing with not only the development of unplanned rural settlements but even cultivating planned rural settlements. These divisions are Land Use Services, Project Division, Department of Co-operatives and Tobacco Board of Zambia. The other divisions do indirectly affect the unplanned rural settlements such as Veterinary and Tsetse Control Services. On the urban scene, Ministry of Land and Natural Resources is involved in purchasing farms etc. for unplanned urban settlements or squatter settlements and Ministry of Local Government and Housing is responsible for the development of low cost housing, for providing loans to site and service scheme, and for the development of planned urban settlements.

The remaining ministries are more responsible for national, regional and provincial programmes, such as construction of roads or electrification. These programmes affect the development of rural and urban settlements. Such ministries and their agencies have more co-ordinated activities in urban areas, while in rural areas intensive co-ordination is experimented through the I.D.Z. programmes, and S.N.D.P. had high hopes on it.

Issues in Development

Functions and services especially in rural areas, away from the old line-of-rail, are loosely organised with large functional gaps, vacuum of settlements over large areas, and limited population base which resulted into a weak foundation for development in the country. Hierarchy of functions and services based on such loosely organised space comes in the way of development. Unbalanced sex ratio, heavy migration of a particular age group to urban areas, rural-urban dichotomy with virtually no common economic dominator pose problems in the development process. Such factors have retarded the development of the country into one functional system. In order to develop the country with a new perspective, following aspects have to be taken into account:

- (a) Linking local economy with the national economy;
- (b) Connecting settlements to national transportation and communication system;
- (c) Breaking isolation of settlement pockets;
- (d) Identification of secondary and tertiary establishments based on local resources;
- (e) Formation of settlement hierarchy from the grass-roots;
- (f) Discouraging rural-urban migration;
- (g) Weakening of the monopoly of Copperbelt, Lusaka and old line-of-rail;
- (h) Development of potential centres away from the main transport line, including the old line-of-rail;
- (i) Discouraging squatter settlements.

There are several interrelated issues, such as schooling in rural areas, rural development, environmental management, housing, changing rural and urban social system, industrialisation and the like. These aspects can be discussed along with the above mentioned issues responsible for the development of population and settlement in Zambai. The legacies of the colonial policies have been so apparent in Zambia that a determined effort can only transform the whole situation in the desired direction. The changes in meeting this challenge will make the process of development more perplexing in the years to come.

Development through Growth Poles

A central place may be defined as a place whose prime function is the provision of a wide range of goods and services to a dispersed settlements around it.[9] Considerable theoretical studies and the application of the central place theory have come forward in different cultural areas of the world. Christaller[10], Losch[11], Berry[12] and others have contributed to the understanding of such focal nature of services and functions in the form of settlements arranged in an hierarchical order. There are various aspects of the central place study, which may not however, be possible to examine here in detail. These aspects are : (a) threshold values, (b) hierarchical arrangement of functions and services, (c) nesting of complementary regions, (d) marketing, administrative and transport principles, (e) space and size relationship of settlements, (f) principle of least effort, and (g) Loschian Landscape - city rich and city poor.

A service centre as an agglomeration of services and function has a zone of dominance intensity around it.[13] In recent years the central place region or complementary region is thought to be more nodal, complete, real and natural than other regions and hence is used as a catchword in planning. Zambian settlements are influenced by the role of money-economy and transportation. In settlement planning, central place based development becomes utmost necessary. However, modifications have been suggested.

Studies of Central Place Development

Studies have been made by different authors and organisations to understand the central place system and its role in the development of

Zambia. Kay[14], Siddle[15], Van Den Berg[16], Doxiadis Associates[17], German Consultants[18], Jauhari and Nag[19], Department of Town and Country Planning[20] and Kaunda[21] have contributed in this field. Berg's study was primarily a review of the work done previously. He critically examined the proposal and plans suggested by Doxiadis Associates and German Consultants. His constructive criticism will be helpful to academicians and planners. Zambian Government engaged Doxiadis Associates to make plans of 16 rural townships throughout the Country[22], but such proto-type, expensive town-plans are 'to remain on the shelves for many years to come'.[23] Nitambu[24], Mwinilunga district, which is off the main transport lines, and surrounded by functional barriers hardly indicates good reasons for its location. Siddle drawn 56 km (35 miles) circles around each scheme of rural development and identifies the areas which are not served. President Kaunda prefers Primary Service Centre with 10,000 population having economic, social and community services. Since Primary Service Centre cannot be expected to meet the requirements of rural development programmes so he proposed *bomas* or sub-*bomas* as secondary services centres. D.T.& C.P., in Central Province, has recognised the existing hierarchy of centres in four grades.[25]

Survey of Existing Conditions

It would not be out of place to mention the use of provinces as units for further study. A province makes a more comprehensive unit, where the degree of similarity is high, especially in central place studies where each province has an average of about 9 towns, the lower administrative unit, *viz.*, the district does not necessarily become viable. Prior to 1980 census, some of the districts do not even had a single town. However, Ndola Rural District of Copperbelt Province or Gwembe of Southern Province are not similar to the provincial character and are exceptions.

For the purpose of the present study the list of towns is based on 1980 Census. The service centres, (which are not necessarily towns) are semi-deterministically chosen. About 500 centres were identified throughout the country. Further, scanning was done keeping in view the central functions available there. A regular transport link was thought to be of utmost importance. Further, missions, post office, U.B.Z., Secondary school, tourist centre or hospital were considered as useful establishments in rural areas. The settlements having atleast two such establishments were considered as service centre.[26] The nature of a neighbourhood has been discussed in detail in Chapter 4. The number was estimated with the help of different data, records and maps and finally confirmed by a 100 samples of areal photographs. The data on rural markets was based on Godel's work.[27] Such markets are either associated with service centres or neighbourhood centres. Nearly 150 out of the 1,093 markets (i.e.14%) are year-round which only indicates the unstable condition of rural central places. Again a lesser number of rural markets then the service centres shows a weak organisation of the rural economy (Table 8.1).

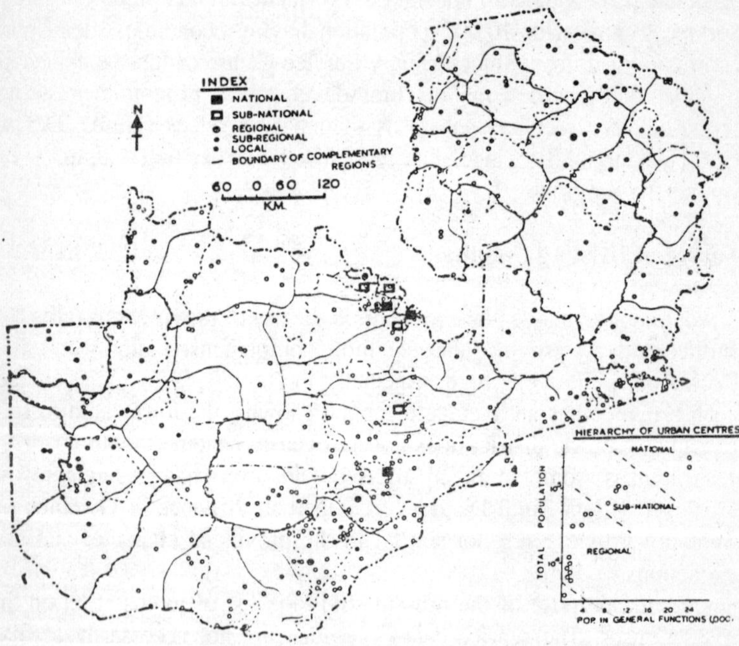

Fig. 8.1: Distribution of Central Places

In order to find out a hierarchy of towns of higher order service centres, a semi-deterministic approach was adopted. The 1969 Census provides only the data of economic activities of 17 towns, which include all the city, municipal and township councils (Fig. 6.3). A hierarchy was made on a graph (Fig. 8.1) by Plotting total population and population engaged in central functions. Replacing the later by the number of establishments, a similar pattern is noticed. Three national level centre, *viz.*, Lusaka, Kitwe and Ndola (all city Councils); four sub-national *viz.*, Chingola, Luanshya, Mufulira and Kabwe (all municipal councils); nine regional centres were identified as sub-regional centre (Table 8.1).

Table 8.1 : Number of Urban and Service Centres and their Spacing (in km.).

Province	*Villages*	*Neighbourhood centres estimated*	*Rural markets*	*Service centres*	*Towns*	*District*
1. Central Lusaka	4,617 (5.4)	460 (17.0)	103 (36.0)	44 (55.0)	11 (109.9)	8
2. Copperbelt	1,863 (4.2)	100 (15.5)	17 (34.8)	20 (40.3)	8 (64.1)	8
3. Eastern	5,563 (3.8)	900 (9.4)	283 (16.8)	40 (44.9)	8 (99.3)	6
4. Luapula	2,599 (4.7)	520 (10.6)	98 (24.3)	19 (55.4)	5 (107.5)	5
5. Northern	4,150 (6.3)	1,000 (13.0)	219 (27.8)	37 (66.7)	12 (118.6)	9
6. North-Western	4,820 (5.5)	440 (18.1)	92 (39.5)	35 (63.9)	8 (134.0)	6
7. Southern	2,947 (5.7)	460 (14.5)	226 (20.8)	58 (41.3)	21 (68.1)	9
8. Western	5,913 (5.0)	700 (14.4)	55 (51.2)	38 (61.9)	10 (120.2)	6
Total	32,472 (5.1)	4,980 (13.2)	1,093 (28.1)	293 (54.5)	85 (100.4)	57

National level centres have large population engaged in central functions but their relative importance in terms of area served is less. The sub-national centres all mining towns along the old line-of-rail, have character similar to the former. The establishments pertaining to the central functions are concentrated in such centres. The complementary regions of regional centres are also in extra district areas (Fig. 8.1). Provincial headquarters and the remaining old line-of-rail towns are in this group, with large population engaged in central functions and large areas to serve. The remaining sub-regional centres are small in size and distributed all over the country. The complimentary region approximately covers a district, but the potentialities to serve are less. The local centres are 293 and serve large pockets. They have moresoever evolved on traditional set-up Zambia's future development hinges on such centres. The neighbourhood centres could not be mapped. In these settlements, rural health centre or/and the primary schools are often found alongwith one or two general stores. The population size of such centres are about 200 persons.

Table 8.2 : Distribution and Spacing of Service Centres

In Kilometres)

	Total	*Provinces along the old line-of-rail*	*Provinces off the line-of-rail*
National			
No. of Centres	3	3	—
Hypothetical spacing (km)	515.4	276.3	
Actual spacing (km)	—	195.0	
R_x Value	—	0.70	
Sub-National			
No. of Centres	4	4	—
H.S. (km)	350.7	195.2	
A.S. (km.)	—	81	
R_x-Value	—	0.41	
Regional			
No. of Centres	9	5	4
H.S. (km)	231.7	147.9	386.8
A.S. (km)	—	95.0	365.0
R_x-Value	—	0.64	0.94
Sub-Regional			
No. of Centres	36	10	26
H.S. (km)	128.7	109.1	141.4
A.S. (km)	—	96.0	135.0
R_x-Value	—	0.88	0.96
Local			
No. of Centres	293	123	170
H.S. (km)	50.2	42.7	54.6
A.S. (km)	—	25.5	30.0
R_x-Value	—	0.53	0.55
Neighbourhood			
No. of Centres	4980	1020	3960
11.7	14.9	12.0	

To throw light on the distributional arrangement of Service Centres, R_X values (Chapter 4) were calculated in (a) the old line-of-rail provinces and (b) the rest of the country. The most uniform pattern of distribution is of sub-regional centres. The local centres are randomly distributed. The sub-national centres show a tendency to cluster along the old line-of-rail. There is a high regularity of regional centres away from the old line-of-rail. Though R_X value for the three national centres is 0.70. Ndola and Kitwe are only 59 km apart, while they are 320 and 356 km from Lusaka respectively (Table 8.2).

Proposed Process of Transformation

For a sound developmental methodology, it is imperative to consider integrated growth of rural-urban areas, hierarchy of settlements, linkage pattern of transport and communication, integration of social and economic services, appropriate technology, organisation of space, and the like. The above postulates can, however, be viewed within Growth Pole Concept.[28] The unsystematic fashion of the transformation of rural habitat through urban centres, causing more problems than remedies, can be reorganised if the transformatory forces are appropriately integrated with the balanced settlement system. The agents of transformation in rural areas, as mentioned earlier, could be associated with the growth pole hierarchy. Moreover, a critique on growth pole approach in relation to the concerned issues will not be possible here. A few modifications may be mentioned in the following analyses. The organisation of space also takes into account of social institutions or the transformation is thought to be operative in socio-economic space. Further, these forces are supposed to be lucid in habitational areas only. The habitational areas include the settlements, fields, industries, mines, roads and the like.

In Zambia, the rural-urban continuance stretches from an isolated village in tribal space to highly urbanised districts. The growth pole model is elaborated here in order to integrate the country into one functional system. The model mentioned below is meant to transform the tribal space to economic space as well as to enhance the rural habitat from below subsistence economy to industrial economy (Fig. 8.2). Five stages have been traced for such transformation:

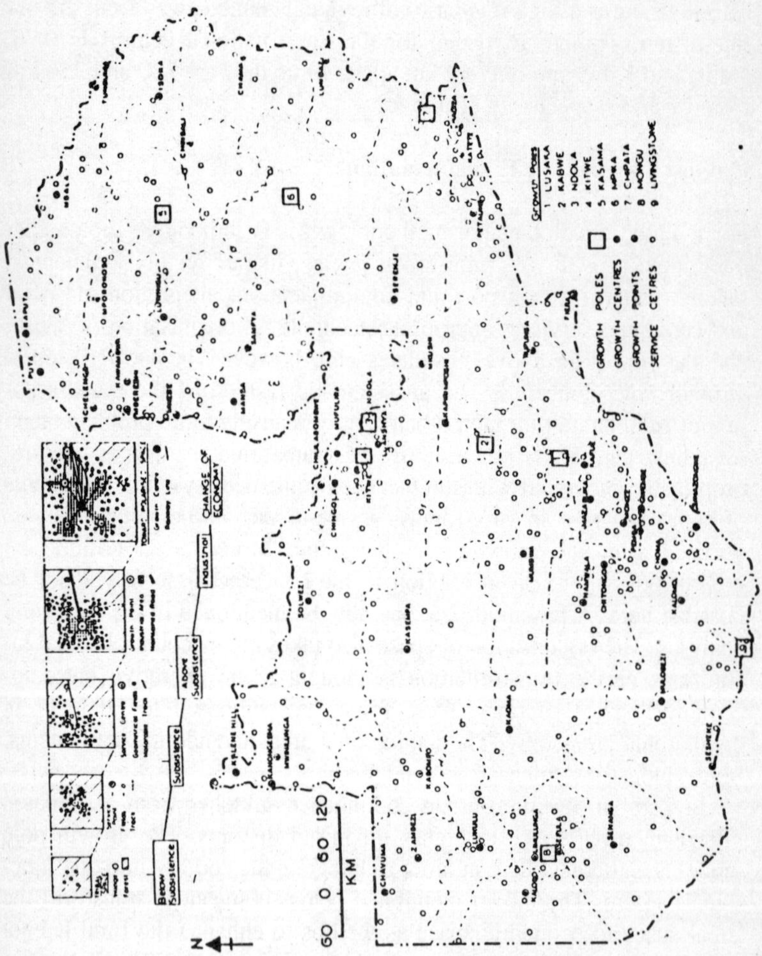

Fig. 8.2: Planning through growth poles

Stage 1: Tribal space ; economy below subsistence level; hunting, fishing etc.; isolated settlement sites; fields not permanent; practice of Chitimene system (shifting cultivation); formation of Basic village.

Stage 2: Economy approaching towards subsistence; monocrop; development of tracks or foot-paths; location of a few social institutions; permanent habitational sites but temporary fields; formation of service point.

Stage 3: Subsistence economy; multi-crops; introduction of secondary functions and related institutions; rough motorable tracks; additional social institutions; permanent fields with geometrical shape; development of rural-urban links; and formation of Service Centres.

Stage 4: Economy above subsistence level better transportational links with maintained roads; introduction of tertiary functions; industries and higher order establishments; radial spread of transport arteries; substantial labour force; and formation of Growth Points.

Stage 5: Towards the formation of polarized space; concentration of tertiary and industrial establishments, and commercial, banking and financial institutions; domination of economic rather than social functions; rail and air links; formation of Growth Centres or Growth Poles.

Nature of Centres

It is however, necessary to discuss what should be the nature of centres or growth foci and how they are partially or wholly helpful in the transformation of rural habitat in the framework of the model, discussed earlier. Fig. 8.2 shows the distribution of poles over Zambian territory. The national centres and sub-national centres are recognised as growth poles. The nine regional centres have the characteristics of growth centres, and they are able to serve extra-district areas. The nature of 35 sub-regional centres is similar to the concept of growth point, and serve an area approximately equal to a district. The service centres are dotted all over the country to serve pockets of settlements around them. For the order of neighbourhood centres, a term service point has been coined here. They are likely to serve 5-10 villages. Including a few growth points, the service centres and service points are rural in nature (Table 8.3). In the perview of Zambian habitat transformation a five ordered growth foci are discussed in addition to a basic village. For the purpose of rational transformation it is necessary to discuss the nature of centres which are to function as indispensable part of a greater system.

Basic Village

The basic village or the lowest order of administrative-cum-occupance unit must have substantial rural economy, primarily based on agriculture and household industries. Some kind of secondary functions may be attached to it. Following minimum amenities should be provided: (a) drinking water, (b) a shop for daily necessities, and (c) link with service point. Sandaliya (Mansa) and Pemba (Chipata) villages, mentioned earlier, fulfil these requirements.

Service Point

A service point located at the centre of neighbourhood should be well connected with the surrounding rural habitat; and by a motorable track to a service centre. Weekly market, agriculture camp, rural health centre, co-operative centres and bus service may be provided to such points. They are to service about 750 persons, covering an area of 140 km^2. Kasama (Kasama) and Nakonga (Mongu) villages need upgrading in order to become a service point.

Table 8.3 : Nature of Centres

Order of Centres	*No. of Centres*	*Av. Pop: of Centre*	*Pop. Served (1969)*	*Area Served km^2*	*Equivalent Growth Pole legend*
National	3	200,000	1,352,298	247,967	Growth Poles
Sub-National	4	90,000	579,556	106,261	Growth Poles
Regional	9	10,000	253,566	46,494	Growth Centres
Sub-regional	36	3,500	78,017	14,306	Growth Points
Local	293	600	11,759	2,156	Service Centres
Neighbourhood	4980	200	762	140	Service Points

Service Centres

Service centres are the most significant order of settlements for the socio-economic transformation of rural habitat of Zambia. Most of them are already connected by bus service and provided with hospital, post office, co-operative centre and the like. It is to serve about 12,000 population in 2,000 km² area. It should be connected to growth point with maintained road. Substantial secondary and tertiary functions are required for this order of growth foci. Chiwala (Ndola) and Mungwi (Kasama) are the examples of service centres.

Growth Point

Growth Points of sub-regional order are generally urban centres. They are well established and connected with maintained roads. In the present set-up the diffusion of innovations quickly reach upto these points. They need banks, petrol pump, big departmental stores, hospital (specialised in gynaecology), small industrial set-up based on local resources, garage, large co-operative and a permanent grain market etc. They are to serve about 7,000 persons and 12,000 km² area. These foci should be well connected with growth centres or growth poles. Few of the towns are matured growth points; however, others need some of the functions; mentioned above.

Growth Centre

The fifth level in the hierarchy of growth foci is limited in number, nevertheless, of national significance. A growth centre should contain large departmental stores; large industrial estate, commercial activities; banks, financial, calculating and auditing firms; higher order of educational, technical and vocational institutions and large hospital with specialised facilities. These centres on an average should serve about 250,000 persons and 45,000 km² area. Air service, railways and inter-regional roads should be attached with these centres. Growth centres are meant to create growth impulses in the areas associated with them. Livingstone, Kasama, and Kabwe towns have most of these significant functions. Chipata or Mongu need a few more functions to become a growth centre.

Growth Poles

These growth foci of national importance should be well interlinked with other growth poles and growth centres. There should be concentration of commercial, banking, industrial, financial and manufacturing activities; and able to control the social, economic and political functions over the territory. The highest order of educational and medical institutions are to be located at these poles. Lusaka, Ndola and Kitwe cities do have such characteristics, however, unable to represent precisely the whole of the country owing to the colonial heritage. These poles must reveal the national character.

The role of the poles of various orders vary only in the size and scale of operations and are complementary to each other. They are rural as well as urban centres. The functions and institutions arranged in this hierarchy are in the context (a) preventing the population flow to the urban centres and creating squatter settlements; (b) providing sufficient job opportunities in rural areas; (c) stabilising rural population; (d) developing local resources; and (e) horizontal and vertical integration of functions for balanced settlements system. In brief, the growth pole approach provides a strategy for the integration of different level of transformatory forces through rural and urban centres. Moreover, the system of transformation is in coherence with the developmental methodologies of the Second National Development Plan.[29] A service centre is associated with a ward; a growth point with district; and a growth centre or growth pole with a province. However, as the neighbourhood is not an administrative or habitat unit, its service point cannot be integrated with S.N.D.P. framework. In near future such points will be most important tool for propagating growth impulses in rural areas and must be included in the transformation process.

The above reorientation of rural and urban centres not only provide expeditious apparatus for the transformation but also indicate the relevant modifications at every order of centres. Zambia awaits for transformation towards more promising, attractive and propitious rural habitat: an aim repeatedly propounded in the successive national development plans. The urban structure along the old line-of-rail is to be challenged by more commendable rural habitat. It is nevertheless, felt that there is a herculean task in front of the national planners to mould different socio-economic and political institutions for transformation in a rational direction. However, stipulation is necessary at every step while the goal hinges on how rational, effective and timely efforts are made for the transformation of the Zambian settlements.[30]

Railway Line Model

The existing pattern of the railway line has successfully developed an economic belt along it. Keeping in view of such developments, railway lines are proposed throughout the country, according to priority on the basis of population and settlement growth (Fig. 8.3). Such model will integrate the higher orders of poles and hence, almost all the settlements in the Zambian territory.

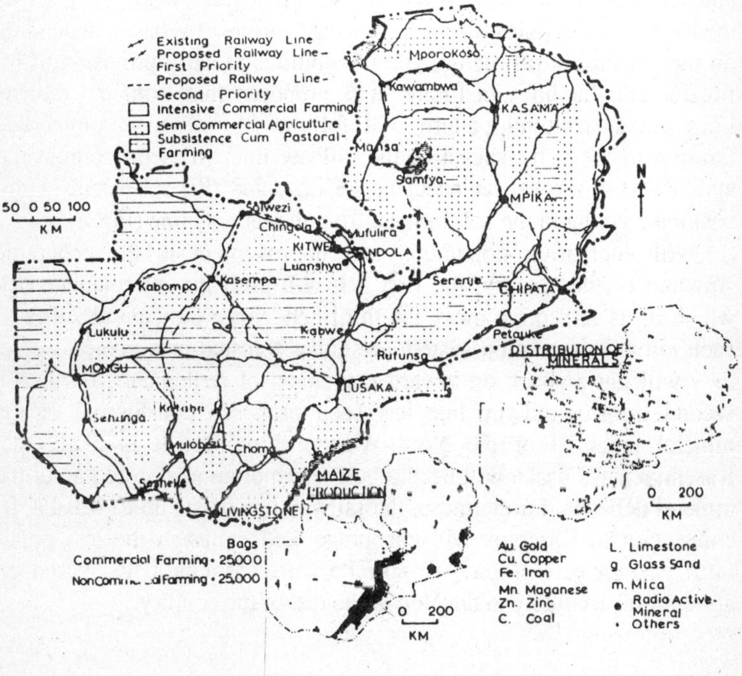

Fig. 8.3: Proposed Railway lines

In order to successfully organize this country, development process should include (a) National level, (b) regional level, and (c) local level policy programmes. First priority to be given to areas:

(i) Near the existing order of poles;
(ii) Good soil, water and suitable climate;
(iii) Near the existing transport lines;

(iv) Near the existing markets; and
(v) Having already developed infrastructure in nearby areas.

Equal emphasis has, however, been given to the remote and less populous areas which have to progress in the national interest; and for their development, a railway circulation system has been proposed. This railway net, however takes into following consideration: (a) existing population nodes and belts; (b) continuity of transport facilities, and (c) national interest. Within these broad framework, new settlements or growth poles are to be selected on priority basis, depending on the existing infrastructure and possibilities of early provision of infrastructural facilities in future. It is proposed that from the railway lines the agricultural pattern will follow: (i) intensive commercial farming in the belt, nearest to the railway line; (ii) semi-commercial agriculture in the belt adjacent to the first; and (iii) subsistence-cum-pastoral farming in the belt farthest from the railway line (Fig. 8.3).

With increasing population and improvement in the economic structure of the country, the first belt will push the intermediate belt which in its turn drive away the third belt. Since the central zones of each railway circulation system are either forested or a game reserve, they will put a check on inward movement of settlements. Further, a second priority railway line has been proposed considering of the mineral potential of the North-Western Province. It is likely that Kasempa and Lusaka will need a bulk transportation system due to the mineral deposits. Furthermore, the railway line exists up to Kataba, its connection to Kasempa will encourage settlements in the less populated eastern part of the Western Province. Similar belts, based on agricultural are likely to develop in the rest of the country.

REFERENCES

1. *Second (1951) Review of the Ten-Year Development Plan of Northern Rhodesia*, Government Printers, Lusaka, 1951. Further, this plan was revised several times during the ten-year period, by a new plan for 1957-63, and grew into the Development Plan for 1961-65.
2. *Zambia's Plan at Work 1966-1970*, The Office of National Development and Planning, Lusaka, n.d., p. 4.
3. *Zambian Plan at Work 1966-70, Op. cit.*, p. 4.
4. *First National Development Plan 1966-1970*, Office of National Development and Planning, Lusaka, July 1966, p. 5.
5. Davis, D.H., Regional inequalities and the First National Development Plan,

1966-70, in Davies, D.H. (ed.) *Zambia in Maps*, University of Lonaon Press Ltd., 1971, pp. 116-19. Six representative indicators were selected for mapping each of the then eight provinces. These indication were (a) urbanization, (b) manufacturing, (c) banking services, (d) personal levy payments, (e) secondary schooling, and (f) hospital beds. The author concludes that 'the spatial pattern on the map is not immediately apparent, these being no clear-cut dominance of either line of rail or outlying regions' (p. 118).

6. *Second National Development Plan, January 1972-December 1976* (SNDP), Ministry of Development Planning and National Guidance, Lusaka, December 1971, pp. I & VII.
7. Ziche, J.B., Beharrel and T.T. Hartman, Relative importance of labour input in agricultural development : The Zambian Case, *Journal of Rural Development*, 1974, pp. 111-41. Also, S.N.D.P., *Op. cit*, p. 53.
8. William, Geoffrey J., Zambia - Physical and Social Geography, in *Africa : South of Sahara 1982-83*, Europa Publication Ltd., 12th ed., pp. 1179-93.
9. Nag, P., Zambia : A Geographical Analysis of Settlement Planing, Ph.D. Dissertation, Banaras Hindu University, Varanasi, 1976.
10. Christraller, W., *Central Places in Southern Germany*, Translated by Bakin, C.W., Prentice-Hall, Englewood, Chiffs, 1966.
11. Losch, A., *The Economics of Location*, Yale University Press, New Haven, 1954.
12. Berry, B.J.L. and Garrison, W.L., Functional basis of central places hierarchy, *Economic Geography*, Vol-34, 1958, pp. 145-54, and Berry, B.J.L. and W.L.Garrison, recent development of central place theory, Paper and proceedings, *Regional Science Association*, Vol. 4, 1958, pp. 107-20.
13. Singh, O.P., Central place regions for planning in Uttar Pradesh, *National Geographical Journal of India*, Vol. XXI, 1975, p. 98.
14. Kay, G., *Social Aspects of Village Regrouping in Zambia*, Institute of Social Research, University of Zambia, Lusaka, 1967.
15. Siddle, D.J., Rural Development in Zambia: A Spatial Analysis, *Journal of Modern African Studies*, Vol. 8, 1970, pp. 271-84.
16. Van Den Berg, L.M., *Central Place Theory*, Occasional Studies No.5, Zambia Geographical Association, Lusaka, 1972.
17. Doxiadis Associates, *Zambia : Organisation of the Countryside*, DOX ZAM-A48, 1969, also *Rural Townships in Zambia*, General Report, DOX-ZAM-A12, 1967.
18. Gesellschaft fur regional stukturent wicklung, E.V., *Southern Province : Prospects of Regional Development*, Born, 1971.
19. Jauhari, A.S. and Nag, P., Rural development in an under populated developing country of Africa : Zambia in Singh, R.L., *et al.* (eds.), *Geographic Dimensions of Rural Settlements*, National Geographical Society of India, Varanasi, 1976.
20. Department of Town and Country Planning is working out for Central Places in Central Province, Zambia, D.T.&C.P., Research Unit, Dec., 1971.
21. Kaunda, K., *Zambia's Guide Lines for Next Decade*, Zambia Information Service, Lusaka, 1968.
22. Doxiadis Associates, *Op. cit.*, 1967.
23. Van Den Berg, *Op. cit.*, p. 15.
24. Doxiadis Associates, *Ntambu Development Plan*, DOX-ZAM-A33, Dec., 1968.

25. Department of Town and Country Planning, *op. cit*. The grading of centres are based on a point system based on Table 25 of the report.
26. Other establishments can be added in this list. They are: (a) Rural Health Centre, (b) Primary School; (c) Agricultural Camp; (d) Postal Agency; (e) NAMBoard Centre; (f) market; (g) flying doctors; (h) Chief's Headquarters; (i) Local Court; (j) Police Station; (k) Transport route or, (l) Commercial Centre.
27. Godel, Feo L., *An Analysis of Zambian Agricultural Camps*, July 15, 1972, Ministry of Rural Development, Lusaka, p. 16, (Unpublished).
28. Harmansen, T., *Growth Poles and Growth Centres in National and Regional Development : A Synthetical Approach: A Survey of Concepts, their Origin, Development and Application*, Part I, UNRISED, Geneva. Also idem *Spatial Organisation and Economic Development : The Scope and Task of Spatial Planning*, Mysore, 1971; Kukulinski, A.R. (ed.), *Growth Poles and Growth Centres* , UNRISED, 1972; Misra, R.P., *Growth Poles and Growth Centres in India*, Mysore, 1971; Nicholas, vide, Growth poles: An evaluation of their propulsive effects, *Environment and Planning*, Vol. I, 1969, pp. 198-208; Van Den Berg, L.M., Central Place Theory, *Op. cit.;* and Doxiadis Associates, *Urban Centres : Selection of Site and Programmes*, DOX-ZAM-A52, July 1969.
29. *Second National Development Plan*, Ministry of Planning and National Guidance, Government Republic of Zambia, Government Printers, Lusaka, 1971.
30. Nag, P., Role of rural and urban centres in the transformation of rural habitat of Zambia, in Singh, R.L. *et al.* (eds.), *Rural Habitat Transformation in World Frontiers*, National Geographical Society of India Publication, Varanasi, 1980, pp. 424-34.

9

RETROSPECT AND PROSPECT

ZAMBIA has a set of problems and prospects which are to certain extent exceptional. This country is gifted with a very low population density but with high literacy rate, rich minerals and reasonable forest wealth. On the other hand, this country is land-locked and economy is based on transportation of heavy minerals, the cost of which depends on trends in the world market. The distribution of population is lop-sided. Copper and its byproduct cobalt are the main source for export earnings. To a lesser extent, zinc, lead and coal are produced. Tourism is an additional source of foreign exchange earnings. With all sincere efforts of the government, it has not been possible to diversify the economy away from dependence on copper. As a result, with a fall in earnings from copper, there has been an economic crisis. The gaps between rural and urban incomes has increased. Average household income in urban areas is now four times that in rural areas.[1] The richest 2 per cent of the entire national household income is the same amount as the poorest 50 per cent.[2] The concentration of population along the old line-of-rail has increased. In the successive national development plans attempts have been made for rural development in order to check these problems. Some of the efforts have shown positive results. Literacy and percentage of population attending schools have increased. The roof and building materials have changed. Squatter settlements have been brought under site and service schemes. A method has to be worked out in order to solve Zambia's problems with whatever resources available. Certainly population and settlements can play a vital role in the development and planning processes. Land is probably the most important resource of the country. A mechanism for the economic development through population and settlements has to be integrated with the national development plans. This process of economic development should be complementary with the development of population and settlements. Zambia is not dissimilar than other developing countries. Uncertainty due to international influences beyond their control, compulsions within the country and commitment for a humanistic society have to be taken into consideration in evolving the mechanism for change, transformation and development.

The line-of-rail with Copperbelt makes a unique feature of corridor development as north-south axis in the middle of the country. The present administration of 'One Party Participatory Democracy' has 9 provinces. 57 districts, 273 chiefs' territories and 32,472 villages. About one-fourth of the land is under permanent settlement while over 40 per cent comes under the control of planning and extension services. Large areas are covered by water bodies, game parks and forest reserves while lowlying areas are infested by tsetse flies which discourage human population. Further, the distribution of population is also effected by the different tribal and colonial settling processes, which have played an important role in the past.

Historical Aspects of Development

The peopling and settling processes in this part of Africa is the outcome of the tribal and colonial organisations during the different historical phases. The colonization processes can be traced in five phases which have fabricated the present settlement pattern. There are certain evidences which indicate the nature of settlements before A.D. 1500. Second phase (A.D. 1500-1850) is dominated by the migration from the north (Zaire). During the third phase (1850-1890) external threats by the Portuguese, Swahilis and slave-traders affected the Zambian settlements. In the fourth phase (A.D. 1890-1964), the colonial settlement pattern emerged on the tribal space. The Europeans divided this territory into three types of lands, *viz.* (a) Native Reserves; (b) Native Trust land, and (c) Crown Land. These three types of land evolved different patterns of settlements which were divorced from each other. However, at a later stage, the tribal and colonial settlement organisations have some degree of synthesis, through missions, administrative headquarters and transport points.[3]

In order to evaluate the role of the Indians, their settlement process has been studied in the light of the overall settlement process in the concerned area. There are evidences indicating the presence of Indians during the pre-colonial period. It was probably such evidences as the architecture of the ruins, names of territories, the presence and domination of the caste system instead of tribes and similar links, which raise possibilities of links of the areas lying on both sides of the River Zambezi with India.[4] However, the presence of Indian population during the colonial period is owing to the historical accident of a common colonial era. The intercontinental Crown administration sought solutions for interrelated problems involving the land and peoples of Asia and Africa. In the case of relatively populous Asia, it was their people who were made to migrate and settle on lands in different parts of the colonial world, including Africa, particularly in Zambia. The role of Indians has changed after independence, when there was an acute shortage of trained personnel for overall social and economic development of the country.[5]

Population Trends

The population of Zambia is likely to increase from 5.7 million in 1980 to 11.8 million by the turn of the century (Table 9.1). More than one million population has increased from the time last census has taken

Table 9.1: Population Projection, 1980-2000 (Medium Variant)

Age group	*Population in Thousand*				
	1980	*1985*	*1990*	*1995*	*2000*
0-4	1,126.0	1,331.8	1,634.0	1,992.1	2,404.9
5-9	917.1	1,057.8	1,263.5	1,563.9	1,921.9
10-14	753.0	894.6	1,035.5	1,240.9	1,540.5
15-19	597.6	738.7	879.5	1,020.2	1,225.1
20-24	476.0	583.4	722.8	862.7	1,003.0
25-29	382.5	462.5	568.5	706.3	845.3
30-34	306.0	370.5	449.5	554.3	890.7
35-39	249.4	295.3	358.9	436.9	540.5
40 44	209.6	239.3	284.4	347.1	424.1
45-49	175.5	199.7	228.9	273.3	334.9
50-54	138.5	165.2	188.9	217.6	261.0
55-59	110.2	127.8	153.4	176.4	204.4
60-64	84.8	98.5	115.1	139.2	161.3
65-69	62.2	71.7	84.1	99.3	121.4
70-74	39.5	48.0	56.2	66.8	80.0
75-79	22.6	26.5	32.9	39.3	47.6
80+	11.3	14.2	17.4	22.1	27.6
Total	5,661.8	6,725.3	8,073.4	9,758.3	1,1834.1

Source : Demographic projection, Central Statistical Office, Lusaka.

place. The increase in population has been estimated on the basis of high and constant fertility and declining mortality. The rate of natural increase is likely to increase from 3.4 per cent between 1980 and 1985 to 3.8 per cent between 1995 and 2000. The other demographic indication also predict about rapid population increase by A.D. 2000 (Table 9.2). The expectation of life for males and females is likely to increase

Table 9.2 : Demographic Indicators : 1980-2000

Population (in thousands)	*Medium Variant*				
	1980	*1985*	*High 1990*	*1995*	*2000*
Aged 15-64	2730.085	3280.705	3949.907	4734.033	5690.263
Women aged 15-49	1260.827	1513.771	1817.850	2160.782	1079.7
Dependency Ratio (per 1,000)	1073.9	1050.0	1043.9	1061.3	1079.7
Child/Women ratio (per woman)	.893	.880	.899	.992	.932
Sex ratio (per 1,000 females)	95.8	96.5	97.2	97.9	98.6
Medium Age (Years)	15.3	15.5	15.6	15.4	15.2
	1980-1985	1985-1990	1990-1995		1995-2000
Rate of National Increase (per 1,000)	34.34	36.44	37.80		38.45
Crude Birth Rate (per 1,000)	49.2	49.7	45.5		48.6
Crude death rate (per 1,000)	14.82	13.22	11.69		10.18
Births (in thousand)	1522.556	1837.475	2206.090		2626.221
Deaths (in thousand)	459.058	489.368	521.171		549.489
Gross reproduction Rate	3.448	3.448	3.448		3.448
Net reproduction	2.560	2.659	2.755		2.848
Total fertility (per 1,000 women)	7.000	7.000	7.000		7.000
General fertility (per 1,000 women)	219.5	220.6	221.8		221.8
Expectation of life (Males)	50.40	52.50	55.40		57.90
At birth (Females)	52.50	55.0	57.50		60.00
Infant mortality (Total)	100.52	89.56	79.04		68.97

Notes : Based on the Medium variant projections.
Source : C.S.O., Demographic Projections.

to 57.9 and 60.0 respectively. The increase in population will have adverse effects even in this underpopulated country if no steps are taken to meet the challenges. Additional population will have to be provided with food, shelter and work. The labour force will increase from 1.7 million in 1980 to 3.7 million in 2000 (Table 9.3). The ratio of unemployed to total labour force is already high: 23.5 per cent in Copperbelt and 13.8 in Lusaka provinces. Employment for additional 2 million persons will be required. The unemployment in urban areas is higher than rural areas. Obviously, the new sources of employment are to be found out in rural areas, particularly in agriculture sector. Agriculture is not only to be improved for generating employment or providing food, but also for redistributing population.

Table 9.3: Labour Force Projection (12+), 1980-2000

Sex	*1980*	*1985*	*1990*	*1995*	*2000*
Male	1,122,058	1,360,258	1,642,382	1,999,139	2,440,518
Female	622,126	743,464	884,675	1,046,972	1,241,779
Total	1,744,184	2,103,722	2,527,057	3,046,111	3,682,297

Source : Central Statistical Office, Lusaka.

Rural Scene

The nature of chiefs' headquarters, neighbourhood centres, villages, hamlets and homesteads can be studied in relation to the organisation of rural settlements.[6] Such organisations have close relationship with the economy, environmental resources and the land. On this framework developmental infrastructure is through agricultural camps, which is becoming important for the organisation of rural settlements. But, this infrastructure encouraged the growth of settlements along the old line-of-rail, while the settlements away from it continued to decay or remain stagnant.

The aim of the planned settlements in rural areas is to concentrate funds and energies of limited staff in specific model development schemes for which sites are chosen in relation to the broad national objectives. These schemes are located in the agricultural potential areas of Zambia, particularly in Central, Eastern, and Lusaka provinces. Since co-operative support the government development policies, they are integrated with such planned development as well. During the colonial period, the main pre-occupation affecting rural development were administrative expediency and religious conversion, and most of the centres which developed are a direct product of these circumstances.[7] Mungwi settlement scheme proved to be a failure. During the post-independence period, the national development plans were oriented for planned rural change and development. Miengewe Village Re-grouping Scheme and Kafubu Block have some degree of success. In the Second National Development Plan (1972-1976), Intensive Development Zones (IDZ) were created and other planned rural settlements, such as Chifwile were moulded into I.D.Z. concepts. Kalichero is a pattern of rural settlement planned on similar concept. The focus of this type of planning is oriented more towards the creation of agricultural growth poles rather than the existing urban centres.[8]

Urban Scene

The urban settlements in Zambia are the towns and cities which evolved with the advent on the colonial powers. These settlements have a long history of debacle and rejuvenation. Chipata, an early colonial town, has provision for the Indian population, while Mongu developed as a seat of indirect administration in the Barotseland Protectorate. The urban planning during the colonial period was influenced by cost, density and racial pattern of houses and shopping centres. The study of Kasama town indicates about taking advantage of an escarpment in planning such a pattern. Urban planning during the post-independence period is effected by the housing problem, which has forced urban population to find out an alternative solution to this problem.

The urban settlements can be classified into four groups. Mwinilunga a representative of *boma* towns (district headquarters towns), indicates the slow growth in vast rural districts. Mansa, an example of provincial headquarters towns, reflects the fast peri-urban growth. Livingstone, a town at the southern end of the old line-of-rail, has suffered impulses of growth and decay. Ndola city in Copperbelt is the distributive and commercial centre of Zambia and is a fast growing urban settlement. However, Lusaka the capital city is a unique example of its kind. The unplanned development is at a faster rate than the planned growth. It is the most intricate exercise of urban planning in Zambia.[9]

Squatter Population and Settlements

The squatter settlements in Zambia refers to the densely mushroomed hutment settlements within the council boundaries where the houses are below the minimum recognized standards and without legal rights. These settlements are associated with the urban centres in Zambia.[10] Their distribution is similar to the pattern of urban settlements. One of the most important factors for the growth of these settlements is owing to the colonial housing policies. After independence, the urban planning was motivated for upgrading these settlements, which as evinced from the case study of Ndola city, were developing at a faster rate than the low cost housing areas. The physical structure shows the dominancy of in-filling and out-growing processes in cyclic fashion.[11] The average density is about 30 huts per ha. In older settlements, the sex-ratio and number of children are balanced owing to the migration from areas away from the old line-of-rail. The residents are engaged more in blue-collar jobs, however, there are some self-employed persons as well. These settlements are temporary and loosely organised and more linked with the city/town centre. Squatter settlements, such as Garneton in the north and Malota in the south of old line-of-rail can be taken as sample cases. Garneton which was functionally linked with the nearby small-holdings, became associated with the Kitwe city centre with the passage of time. Malota, an old squatter settlements, has complications in the possession of plots which were once laid on grid-pattern.

Developmental Infrastructure

The planning framework in Zambia has been highlighted in the Second National Development Plan.[12] The Development Planning Division is the sole authority for Zambian planning which controls the Regional Planning Units, Provincial Units and the Department of Town and Country Planning. However, a modified way for the organising of Zambian settlements through growth poles can be suggested here. For such transformation it is imperative to study the environmental framework, administrative set-up, population, circulatory behaviour and nature of establishments. Though waterbasins play a vital role, planning through them is only partially applicable in Zambia. The roads, railway and settlement have developed on the water-sheds and high topography (Fig. 9.1). The ill-drained and lowlying areas below 1,500 m are infested by tsetse flies and human population are not found in such areas.[13] Population planning should be focused on the redistribution.[14] Heavy migration of 15-44 age-group towards the old line-of-rail has come in way of planning and development of settlements elsewhere.[15] The circulation of population is mainly along this line. The distribution of urban centres has shown a tilt towards Lusaka while other service centres are widely distributed. On this framework the country can be planned through the growth poles, growth centres, growth points, service centres and service points.

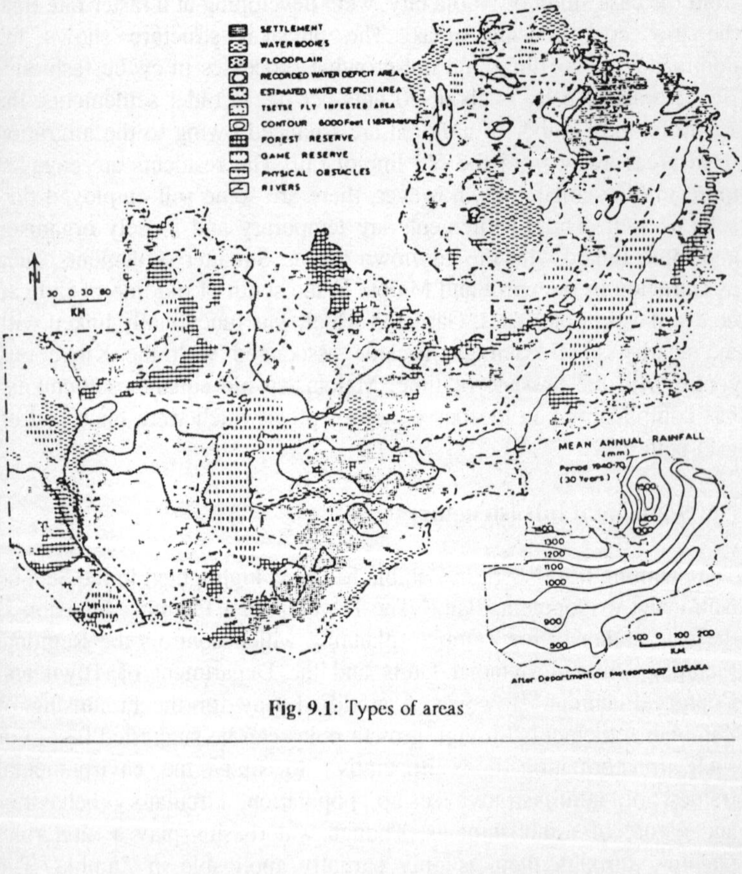

Fig. 9.1: Types of areas

framework of planning, it was found that with a few modification both the approaches are complimentary to each other. But, the development from below needs stability of rural settlements. Economic institutions as well as agricultural camps are to be incorporated with the hierarchy of poles. This arrangement of growth poles will develop a continuum of rural and urban settlements and the future labour force can be employed in these centres. Urban centres, especially away from the old line-of-rail, will become more attractive in the proposed arrangement. The total set-up will however discourage squatter settlements. The cost, density and racial bases of houses need to be changed in the future urban plans.[16]

Future Trends

Three types of the areas can be carved out in relation to human settlements. They are : (a) areas not available for settlements; (b) areas available for settlement; and (c) existing settled areas. The areas available for settlement can be classified into (i) high accessibility areas; and (ii) poor accessibility areas (Fig. 9.2). Contagious fashion of diffusion with former and hierarchical fashion with latter is the likely pattern of future Zambian population and settlements, and the poles are to be established on such dynamics (Fig.9.2). After recognizing the problems, prospects, economic trends and planning methodologies, a railway line based model can be suggested for Zambia. The new Tan-Zam railway line fits into this model which have already shown favourable results.

For a viable and dynamic settlement planning, based on the present administrative set-up, the above mentioned orders of settlements may be taken into account. It is possible to integrate the Second National Development Planning organisation with the growth pole hierarchy. A service centre with ward, growth point with district, and growth centre or growth pole with province can be equated. There is no administrative order equivalent to service point to serve a neighbourhood. In order to organise the settlements at lower order a ward may be divided either according to physical features, such as, water-basins; or by grouping service points. Further, such sub-ward areas can be organised by different forms of service points, such as (a) agricultural camps, (b) agricultural growth centres (settlement schemes), (c) sub-*bomas*, (d) small scale industrial settlement, (e) recreational points, (f) transport points, and (g) rural service centre. Only intensive co-ordination of settlements at grass-root will create a polarised space and hence poles will emerge on Zambian landscape. Treatment of settlements at different orders will integrate the spectrum of poles which would ultimately reverse the gears of the line-of-rail based population migration. This will check the growth of squatter population and deterioration of rural settlements.

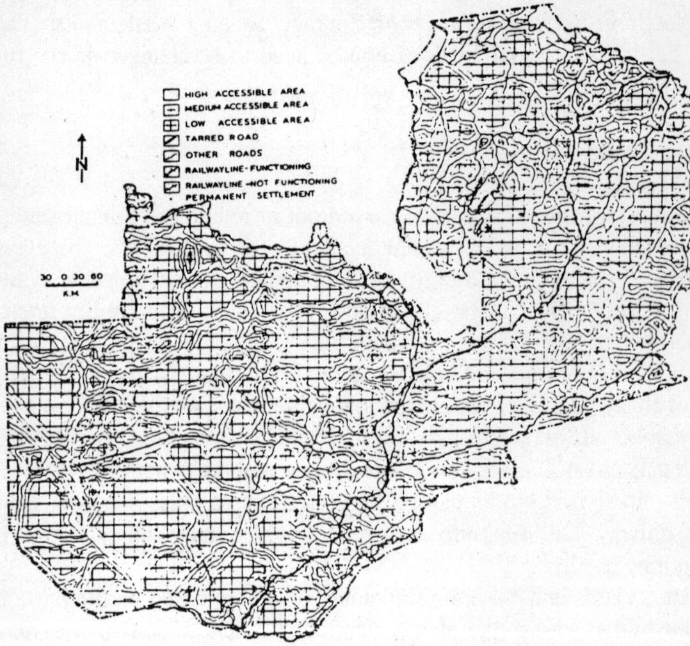

Fig. 9.2: Rail-road accessibility

The new Tan-Zam railway line is developing as a new corridor with a number of urban settlements. However, it is felt that there is a herculean task in front of the national planners to dilute the personality of the old line-of-rail even in the distant future. The only way out is to develop similar economic line throughout the country which will lead to diffusion and interaction of poles, balanced regional development and economic potency to individual rural and urban settlements. This will not only organise the human habitation but also integrate the country in one functional settlement system which aims at 'One Zambia One Nation'.

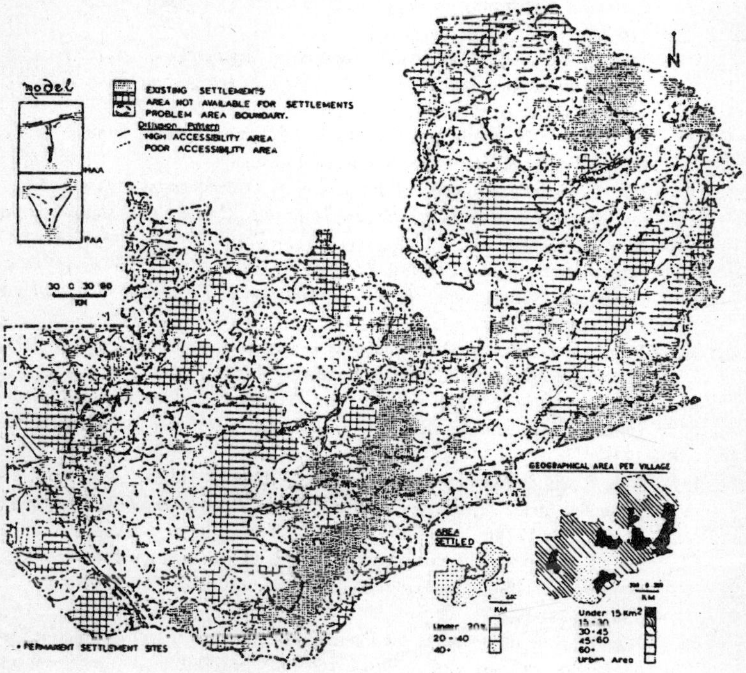

Fig. 9.3: Likely Diffusion Pattern of Population

4. Nag, P., Asian settlement in Zambia, *Africa Quarterly*, Vol. XVIII, April 1979, pp. 59-77.
5. *Census of Population and Housing, 1969 (First Report)*, Central Statistical Office, Lusaka.
6. Nag, P., Territorial Organisation of Zambian Settlements in T. Tanioka (ed.), *Historical Geography*, Konkon-Shoin Publishing Company, Tokyo, 1982, pp. 166-71.
7. Jauhari, A.S. and P. Nag, Rural development in an under-populated developing country of Africa : Zambia, in Singh, R.L. *et al.* (eds.) *Geographic Dimensions of Rural Settlements*, NGSI Publication, Varanasi, 1976, pp. 248-61.
8. Beaumont, A.N., Settlement Schemes and Policy Guidelines, Landuse Services, Ministry of Rural Development, Lusaka, Undated.
9. Nag, P., Lusaka : Problems of developing an African capital city, in Yadav C.S. (ed.) *International Series on Urban Geography*, Concept Publishing Company, New Delhi.
10. Nag, P., Squatter Population in Zambian Towns, in the *Proceedings of the pre-Conference Symposium of the IGU Commission on Population Geography*, Sao Paulo, pp. 113-26 (mimio).
11. *Low Cost Residential Development in Lusaka*, Department of Town & Country Planning, Research Unit, Lusaka, August 1972.
12. *Second National Develcpment Plan*, Ministry of Planning and National Guidance, Government Republic of Zambia, Government Printers, Lusaka, 1971.
13. Nag, P., Environmental hazards and their effect on Human settlements, paper presented in the *MAB/IGU Workshop on the Perception of the Environment*, Ibadan, July 1978.
14. Nag, P., Population Redistribution : Aspects of Zambian national development plans and programmes, *Geographical Review of India*, Vol. 43, No. 1, March 1981, pp. 41-9.
15. Nag, P., Role of women in the internal migration in Zambia, *Population Geography*, Special Issue, Vol. 5, Nos. 1 & 2, 1983, pp. 60-9.
16. Nag, P., Role of rural and urban centres in the transformation of rural habitat of Zambia, in Singh, R.L. *et al* (eds.), *Rural Habitat Transformation in World Frontiers*, NGSI Publication, Varanasi, 1980, pp. 424-34.

SELECT BIBLIOGRAPHY RELATED TO ZAMBIA

Published Work

Allan, W., African Land Usage, *RLJ*, No. 3, June, 1945.

Allan, W., *How much land does a man require?* RLP, No. 15, pp. 1-15.

Allan, W., *Studies in African Land Usages in Northern Rhodesia*, RLP, No. 15, Oxford Un Press, 1949.

Allan, W., *The African Husbandman*, Edinburgh, London, New York, 1967.

Allan, W., Gluckman, M., Peters, D.U. and Trapnell, C.G., *Land Holding and Land Usage among the Plateau Tonga of Mazabuka District : A Reconnaisance Survey*, R.L.P., No. 14, 1948; ISR, 1968.

Anthorpe, R.J. (Ed.), *Present Inter-relations in Central African Rural and Urban Life*-Rhodes-Livingstone Institute Conference Proceedings, 1956, 1961 and 1968.

Anthorpe, R.J., (Ed.), *From Tribal Rule to Modern Government*, Rhodes-Livingstone Institute Conference Proceedings, 1960 & 1966.

Anthorpe, R.J., and Mathews, D. (Eds.), *Social Relations in Central African Industry*, Rhodes-Livingstone Institute Conference Proceedings, 1958.

Baker, C., Non-African Population of the Federation of Rhodesia and Nyasaland, *Geography* , 1958, Vol. 43, pp. 132-4.

Baker, S.J.K. and White, R.J., "The Distribution of Native Population over South-East Central Africa", *GJ*, V-CVIII, 1946, p. 201.

Balwin, Robert E., Wage Policy in Dual Economy - The case of Northern Rhodesia, *Race*, Vol 4, pp. 73-87.

Barnes, H.B., *The Fort Rosebery District Notebook--Calendars of the District Notebooks (Luapula Province) 1798 - 1963*, National Archives of Zambia, Lusaka, V - 1.

Barnes, J.A., *Politics in a Changing Society*, MUP, 1967.

Barber, W.J., *The Economy of British Central Africa : A Case Study of Economic Development in a Dualistic Society*, London, 1961.

Bates, R.H., *Rural Responses to Industrialization: A Study of Village Zambia*, Yale University Press, New Haven and London, 1976.

Baxter, T.W., Slave Trader in North Eastern Rhodesia, *NRJ*, June, 1960.

Bellers, M. and Kingsburg, P., The Kafue Flats : An account of the Effects of the Kafue George Hydro-Electric Schemes on the Geography of the Flats, *ZGA*, Lusaka, 1971.

Berg, E.J., The Development of Labour Force in Sub-Saharan Africa, *EDCC*, Vol. 13, 1965, pp. 395-412.

Berger, Elena A., *Labour, Race and Colonial Rule : The Copperbelt from 1924 to Independence*, Clarendon Press, Oxford, 1974.

Bettison, D.G., *Numerical Data on African Dwellers in Lusaka, Northern Rhodesia*, RLC, No. 16 (mimiographed), 1959 and 1962.

Bisson, Michael Stephen, *The Prehistoric Coppermines of Zambia*, Ph.D. Thesis, University of California, Santa Barbara (Anthropology), Feb.1976, University Microfilms International, Ann Arbor, Michigon and London.

Bond, George S., *The Politics of Change in a Zambian Community*, The University of Chicago Press, Chicago and London, 1976.

Bradley, Kenneth, Company Days : The Rule of the British South African Company in Northern Rhodesia, *NRJ*, V-IV, 1961.

Brelsford, W.V., Fisherman of the Bangweulu Swamps : A Study of Fishing Activities of the Unga Tribe, *RLP*, No. 12, 1946, IAS 1972.

Brelsford, W.V., A Further Note on European Place Names, *NRJ*, No. VI, 1952.

Brelsford, W.V., Abandoned Bomas : A Consolidated list : Zambia, *NRJ*, V-VI,1965.

Brelsford, W.V., *The Tribes of Zambia*, G.P., Lusaka 1965 (2nd ed.) - Cowie, William James, *Changing Settlement Systems and Economic Development : The Case of Kanyanja Parish, Zambia*, Ph.D. Thesis, University of London, 1982.

Brooke, E. and V. Nyivenda (eds.), *Social Development in Zambia : Case Studies*, Studies in Zambian Society : 2, March 1977 (mimio).

Bruce Miller, F.U., A Few Historical Notes on Fiera and Zumbo, *Journal of the Royal African Society*, V-IX, 1910.

Bull, M., *Politics and Societies in 19th Century Zambia*, 1970.

Bulteel, S., Kafue Textiles of Zambia, *Z.G.A.*, 1970.

Butter, L.G., A Lusaka African Community : Chilenge, Part I, *NRJ*, V-II, 1958; Part II, *NRJ*, V-III, 1958.

Cape, Jonathan, *Lusaka - The New Capital of Northern Rhodesia*, Produced for Private circulation, London, 1935, (available in foreign & Commonwealth Office Library, London).

Chambers, Robert, *Settlement Schemes in Tropical Africa - A Study of Organizations and Development*, Routledge & Kegan Paul, London, 1969.

Chaplin, J.H., A Note on the Forts of the Eastern Provinces, *NRJ*, V-IV, 1961.

Clark, J.D., A Note on the Pre-Bantu Inhabitant of Northern Rhodesia and Nyasaland, *NRJ*, V-II, 1950.

Clark, J.D., *The Stone Age Cultures of Northern Rhodesia*, South African Archaeological Society, Cape Town, 1950.

Clark, J.D., The Portuguese Settlement : Fiera, Zambia-Northern Rhodesia Journal, V-VII, 1965.

Clay, G.C.R., *History of the Mankoya District*, RLC, No. 4, 1973.

Cohen, A., *British Policy in Changing Africa*, North-Western University, African Studies No.2, 1959.

Coleman, Francis L., *The Northern Rhodesian Copperbelt, 1899-1962*, Technological Development upto the end of Central African Federation, MUP, 1971.

Cole, Monica M., Kariba Project, *Geography*, 1960, Vol., 45, pp.98-105.

Collins, J., *Lusaka : The Myth of the Garden City*, Zambia Urban Studies (Special Series), The University of Zambia, Lusaka, 1969.

Colson, E., *Marriage and the Family among the Plateau Tonga of Northern Rhodesia*, MUP, 1958 & 1967.

Colson, E., *The Plateau Tonga of Northern Rhodesia (Zambia)*, MUP, 1966 & 1970.

Colson, E., and Gluckman, M., *Seven Tribes of British Central Africa*, MUP, 1968.

Colson, E., *The Social Consequences of Resettlement : The Impact of the Kariba Resettlement upon the Gwembe Tonga*, MUP, 1971.

Co-operatives – Part of our Culture, *Zambia Daily Mail*, Nov. 2, 1973.

Cunnison, I., *Kinship and Local Organisation on the Luapula: A preliminary Account of some Aspects of Luapula Social Organisation*, RLC, No. 5, 1950 & 1965.

Cunnison, I., Kazembe and the Portuguese, 1798-1832, *The Jl of African History*, V-III, No.1.

Cunnison, I., *The Luapula People of Northern Rhodesia*, MUP, 1967.

Cunnison, I., *History of the Luapula : An Essay on the Historical Nations of a Central African Tribe*, RLP, No. 21, 1969.

Dale, E.H., Some Geographical Aspects of African Land-Locked States, *AAAG*, V-58, 1968.

Darby, H., Clifford, Settlement in Northern Rhodesia, *GR*, V-XXI, 1931, pp. 559-73.

Davies, D.H., *Lusaka, Zambia : Some Town Planning Problems in an African Capital City at Independence*, Zambia Urban Studies (Special Series), University of Zambia, Lusaka, 1969.

Davies, D.H., (ed.), *Zambia in Maps*, University of London Press Ltd., 1971.

Deshler, W., Livestock Tryponosomiasis and Human Settlement in North-èastern Uganda, *GR*, V-50, 1960, pp. 541-554.

Drysdall, A.R., Johnson, R.L., Moore, T.A., and Thieme J.G., Outline of the Geology of Zambia, *Geoligien Mijnbouw*, V-51(3), 1972, pp. 265-276.

Europa Publication, *Africa : South of Sahara, 1982-83*, Europa Publication Ltd., 12th ed. pp. 1179-93.

Fagan, B.M. (ed.), *A Short History of Zambia*, Oxford University Press, 1970.

Fagan, B.M., Phillipson, D.W. and Daniels, S.G.H., *Iron Age Culture in Zambia*, V-2, National Museum of Zambia, Lusaka.

Fitzgerald, W., *Africa*, Methuen, London, 1961.

Fraser, R.H., *Land Settlement in the Eastern Province of Northern Rhodesia*, RLJ, No. 3, June, 1945.

Fryer, G., Mwamfuli's Village', The New Fulcrum of the Bangweulu Fish Trade, *NRJ*, V-III, 1958.QC

Gann, L., The End of the Slave Trade in British Central Africa, *RLJ*, No.16, 1954.

Gann, L.H., *The Birth of a Plural Society : The Development of Northern Rhodesia under the British South African Company 1894-1914*, MUP, 1959.

Gann, L.H., *A History of Northern Rhodesia*, Manchester, 1964.

Gouldsberg, C. and Sheame, H., *The Great Plateau of Northern Rhodesia*, London, 1911.

Gluckman, M., African Land Tenure, *RLJ*, No. 3, 1945.

Gluckman, M., *Order and Rebellion in Tribal Africa*, Cohen & West, London, 1963.

Gluckman, M., Economy of the Central Borotse Plain, *RLP*, 1941; *ISR*, 1968.

Gray, R., *The Two Nations: Aspects of Development of Race Relations in Rhodesia and Nyasaland*, London 1960.

Guler, Josep, On the Theory of Rural-Urban Migration : The Case of Sub-Saharan Africa, in Jackson, J.A. (ed.), *Migration*, Sociological Studies 2, Cambridge University Press, 1969.

Gupta, Anirudha, *Reporting Africa*, Peoples Publishing House, Delhi, Ahmedabad and Bombay, 1969.

Gupta, Anirudha, *Government and Politics in Africa*, Vikas Publishing House, 1975.

Ghai, Dharam (ed.), *Portrait of a Minority : Asians in East Africa*, O.U.P., 1965.

Griffiths, I.L., Zambian Coal : An example of Strategic Resource Development, *GR*, V-58, 1968, pp. 538-51.

Griffiths, I.L., Zambia's New Coalfields, *Geography*, Vol. 53, 1968, pp. 415-8.

Graham, Ivor, Notes on Transport in North-Eastern -Rhodesia, *NRJ*, V-V, 1962.

Grimstuedt, S., The Swedish Settlement in the Kasempa District, *NRJ*, V-III, 1956.

Hamilton, P., Population Pressure and Land Use in Chiweshe Reserve, *RLJ*, No. 36, Dec. 1964.

Harkema, R.C., The Production and Geographical Distribution of Tobacco in Zambia, *East African Geographical Review*, No. 11, 1972, pp. 51-64.

Harkema, R.C., *The Geographical Distribution of Cattle in Zambia*, ZGA, Lusaka, 1971.

Hazlewood, A., (ed.), *African Integration and Disintegration*, Oxford University Press, London, New York and Toronto, 1967.

Hellen, Anthony, Some Aspects of Landuse and Over Population in the Ngoni Reserves of Northern Rhodesia, *Sonderdruck ans, Erdkunde, Archivfur, Wissens Chaftliche Geographic*, Band XVI, Bonn, 1962, pp. 190-205.

Hellen, J.A., *Rural Economic Development in Zambia*, 1890-1964, Wilforum Berlag, Munchen, 1968.

Henderson, I., The Economic Origins of Decolonisation in Zambia, 1940-45, *Rhodesian History*, 1974, Vol. 5, pp. 49-66.

Herghese, A.J., Kin, Caste and Nation Among the Rhodesian Ndebele, *RLP*, No. 25, 1959.

Hollingsworth, L.W., *The Asians in East Africa*, Macmillan, 1960.

Hint, B.L., First European Church in North Eastern Rhodesia, *NRJ*, Vol. IV, 1960.

Howman, R., The Significance of Law for Native Administration in Africa, *RLJ*, 1949; *ISR* 1970.

Ismagilova, R.N., *Ethnic Problems of Tropical Africa. Can They be Solved?* Progress Publishers, Moscow, 1978.

Jackman, M., J.H. Case and P. Dow, *Geographical Distribution and Monuments of Tracer Project Participants*, Tracer Project, University of Zambia,1973.

Geographical Study of the Kaonde, Kesempa, District Zambia, Royal Tropical Institute, Amsterdam, 1981.

Jaspan, M.A., *The Ila-Tonga Peoples of North Western Rhodesia*, International African Institute, London, 1953.

Jauhari, A.S. and Nag, P., Rural Development in an Underpopulated Developing Country of Africa : Zambia in Singh, R.L. (ed.), *Geographic Dimensions of Rural Settlements*, NGSI, Varanasi, 1976.

Jayrajan, C.K., An Estimate of Future Needs and a Strategy for Training of Physical Planners and Planning Assistants in Zambia, D.T. & C.P.

John, R. and Show, R., Nkala : An Abandoned Mission on the Kafue Flats, *NRJ*, V-IV, 1961.

Johnwood, A. St., *Northern Rhodesia : The Human Background*, Pall Mall Press, London, 1961.

Jordon, E.K., Mungu in 1908, *NRJ*, V-II, 1954.

Kamarck, M., *The Economies of African Development*, Pall Mall Press, London, 1967.

Kapferer, B., *The Population of a Zambian Municipal Township : A Preliminary Report of a 1964 Social Survey of the Broken Hill Municipal Townships*, ISRC, No.1, 1966.

Kaunda, Kenneth, *Zambia Shall be Free*, London, 1966.

Kay, George, Land Apportionment in Northern Rhodesia, *NRJ*, V-IV, 1959.

Kay, G., *A Population Map (1:500,000) of the Luapula-Bangeweulu Region of Northern Rhodesia, with Notes on the Population*, RLC, No. 26, 1964.

Kay, G., Sources and Uses of Cash in Some Ushi Villages, Fort Roseberry, *RLJ*, No. 35, 1964.

Kay, G., *Social Aspects of Village Regrouping in Zambia*, ISR, Special Publication, 1967.

Kay, G., *Social Geography of Zambia*, London, 1967.

Kay, George, *A Social and Economic Study of Fort Rosebery*, RLC, No. 21, (Mimeo).

Keatley, Patrick, *The Politics of Partnership*, Peguin African Library, 1963.

King, R.B., *Land Resources of the Northern and Luapula Provinces, Zambia : A Reconnaisance Assessment*, Vol. 6. The Land System, Land Resource Division, Ministry of Overseas Development, Survey, 1976.

Kinross, K.S., Kasempa-Solwezi in 1920's, *NRJ*, V-V, 1964.

Knappert, J., *Myths and Legends of the Swahili*, Heinemann Educational Books, London, 1970.

Knight, C. Gregory, The Ecology of African Sleeping Sickness, *AAAC*, V-61, 1971, pp. 30-43.

Kuper, Adam, *Kalahari Village Politics : An African Democracy*, Cambridge, 1970.

Lancaster, D.G. and Brelsford, W.V., European Place Names of Majoi Geographical Features, *NRJ*, Dec. 1950.

Langworthy, H.W., *Zambia Before 1890*, Longmans, London, 1972.

Legum, Coln (ed.), *Zambia - Independence and Beyond - The Speeches of Kenneth Kaunda*, Nelson, London, 1966.

Livingstone, D., *Missionary Travels and Researches in South Africa*, Murry, London, 1857.

Logan, W.M., Native Administration in Northern Rhodesia, *Race Relations*, Vol. VI, No. 2, 1939, pp. 50-9.

Lombard, C.S., *The Growth of Co-operatives in Zambia : 1914-71*, MUP, Z.P., No. 6, 1971.

Long, M., *Social Change and the Individual : A Study of the Social and Religious Response to Innovation in a Zambian Rural Community*, IAS, 1971.

Lundgren, T., Schlyter, A. and Schlyter, T., *Kapwepwe Compound : A Study of an Unauthorised Settlement*, University of Lund, Deptt. of Architecture - II, B., Sweden.

Mac Cullock, M., *A Social Survey of the African Population of Livingstone*, RLP, No. 6, 1968.

Mackel, R., *The Physiographic Regions of Zambia*, ZGA, No. 19, 1972.

Mackel, R., *The Changing Chibola : A Village Survey*, ZGA, No.14, 1971.

Maclean, H.A.M., *An Agricultural Stock Taking of Barotseland*, GP., Lusaka, 1965.

Mainga, M., *Bulozi Under the Luyana Kings*, Longman, 1973.

Mainga, M., *A History of Lozi People to 1900*, Lusaka, 1969.

Mansfield, J.E., *Summary of Geonomic Research, Zambia*, Supplementary Report 7, Land Resource Division, Tolworth Tower, Survey, England, 1973.

Mansfield, J.E., *et al., Land Resources of the Northern Provinces, Zambia : A Reconnaisance Assessment* ; Volume 4; Conclusion and Recommendations, Foreign and Commonwealth Office, Overseas Development Administration, Survey, England, 1973.

Marter, Alan and David Honeybone, The Economic Resources of Rural Households, and its distribution of Agricultural Development, *Rural Development Studies Bureau*, University of Zambia, December 1976.

Mason, P., *The Birth of a Dilemma*, Oxford University Press, 1958.

Meebela, H., *Reaction to Colonialism : A Prelude to the Politics of Independence in Northern Zambia : 1893-1939*, IAS, 1971.

Mendelzohn, F., (ed.), *The Geology of the Northern Rhodesia Copperbelt*, Macdonald, London, 1961.

Mihalyi, L., *Charcoal in Zambia*, ZGA, No.16, 1971.

Millum, T., *Chipata - A Study of Some Problems of Rural Development*, ZGA, Lusaka, No.18, 1972.

Mitchell, J.C., *African Urbanization in Ndola and Luanshya*, RLC, No. 5, 1961.

Mitchell, J.C., Structural Plurality, Urbanization and Labour Circulation in Southern Rhodesia, in Jackson, J.A. (ed.), *Migration*, Sociological Series No. 2, Cambridge University Press, 1969.

Mitchell, J.C., *A Note on the Urbanization of Africans on the Copperbelt*, RLJ, No. 2, 1970.

Mitchell, J.C., *Social Network in Urban Situations : An Analysis of Personal Relationships in Centrl African Towns*, IAS, 1971.

Mitchell, J.C., *The Yao Village : A Study in the Social Structure of Nyasaland Tribe*, IAS, 1971.

Mocral, F.B., History of Mporokose District, *NRJ*, V-III, 1956.

Muhone, B., What's in a name? A Lot Says Chiwala, *Zambia Daily Mail*, 28-2-1974.

Muntemba, Maud Shimwaayi, Expectation Unfulfilled : The Underdevelopment of Peasant Agriculture in Zambia; The Case of Kabwe Rural District, 1964-70, *Journal of Southern African Studies*, Vol. 5, No. 1, Oct. 1978, pp. 59-85.

Mvula, Albert, Zambians Look at NAMBoard : Can it get out of the Red?, *Zambia Daily Mail*, 6.2.1974.

Mwaziona : A Study of an Unofficial Housing Area, DT2C.P., Research Unit, Lusaka, 1973.

Nag, P., Basis of Zambian Settlements, *Africa Quarterly*, Indian Centre for Africa, Vol. XVII, July 1977, pp. 59-77. Also published in Dzienwonski, K. (ed.), *National Settlement Systems : Topical and National Reports*, Institute of Geography and Spatial Organisation, Polish Academy of Sciences, Warszawa, 1980, pp. 445-462.

Nag, P., Asian Settlement in Zambia, *Africa Quarterly*, Indian Centre for Africa, Vol. XVIII, April 1979, pp. 59-77.

Nag, P., Territorial Organisation of Zambian Settlements, in Tanioka, T. (ed), *Historical Geography*, Konkon-Shoin Publishing Company, Tokyo, 1982, pp. 166-71.

Nag, P., Alternative Approach for the Indentification of Randomness in Point Patterns, *Geographical Review of India*, Vol. 39, 1978, pp. 193-4.

Nag, P., Lusaka : Problems of Developing an African Capital City, in Yadav, C.S. (ed), *International Series on Urban Geography*, Concept Publishing Company, New Delhi, 1987.

Nag, P., Squatter Population in Zambian Towns, in the *Proceedings of the pre-Conference Symposium of the IGU Commission on Population Geography*, Sao Paulo, 1982, pp.113-26 (mimio).

Nag, P., Environmental Hazards and their Effect on Human Settlements, Paper presented in the MAB/IGU Workshop on the Perception of the Environment, Ibadan, July 1978 (unpublished).

Nag, P., Population Redistribution : Aspects of Zambian National Development Plans and Programmes, *Geographical Review of India*, Vol. 43, No. 1, March 1981, pp. 41-9.

Nag, P., Role of Women in the Internal Migration of Zambia, *Population Geography*, Vol. 5, No. 1 & 2, June-December 1983, Special Issue (Guest Editor : Maria Luisa Gentileschi), pp. 60-9.

Nag, P., Role of Rural and Urban Centres in the Transformation of Rural Habitat of Zambia, in Singh, R.L. *et al* (eds.), *Rural Habitat Transformation in World Frontiers*, NGSI Publication, Varanasi, 1980, pp. 424-34.

Nag, P., Geography of the Zambian Settlements, *Philippine Geographical Journal*, Vol. XXVIII, Nos. 3 & 4, July-December 1984, pp.110-8.

Nag, P., Historical Types of Spatial Organisation in Zambia, in Rosciszewski, Marcin (ed), *Transition from Spontaneous to Regulated Spatial Organisation*, Institute of Geography and Spatial Organisation, Polish Academy of Science, Warszawa, 1984, pp.117-25.

Nag, P., Zambian Settlements : A Study in Diffusion Pattern, in Mukhopadhyay, S.C. (ed), *Geographical Mosaic*, Professor K.G. Bagchi felicitation volume, Calcutta, 1984, pp. 393-8.

Nag, P., Quantitative Analysis of Zambian Rural Settlements, *Rural Systems*, Vol. 1, No. 4, 1983, pp. 295-300.

Nag, P., *Zambia : A Geographical Analysis of Settlement Planning*, unpublished Ph.D. Thesis, Banaras Hindu University, Varanasi, 1976.

Nag, P., India, Indian Ocean and Africa : Historical and Geographical Factors, in Chandra, Satish (ed), *Indian Ocean : Exploration Commerce, Politics and History*, Sage International New Delhi (in press).

Nieuwolt, S., *The Climate of Zambia*, ZGA, 1970.

Ohadike, P.O., *Development and Factors in the Employment of African Migrants in the Copper Mines of Zambia : 1940-66*, Z.P., No. 4, ISR, 1969.

Ohadike, P.O., *Some Demographic Measurements for Africans in Zambia : In Appraisal of 1963 Administration and Results*, I.S.R., Lusaka, 1969.

Omer-Copper, J., *Kingdoms and Villages : A Possible New Perspective in African History*, ISR, 1972.

Ominde, S.H., (ed), *Studies in East African Geography and Development*, Heinemann, London, Nairobi and Ibadan, 1971.

Page, Thomas, Early Days in Fort Jameson, *NRJ*, V-III, 1956.

Paine, Denis, *Lake Mweru - Its Fish and Fishing Industry*, NRJ, No. 11, 1950.

Palmer, Robin (ed), *Zambian Land and Labour Studies*, Vol. III, National Archives Occasional Paper No. 2, 1976.

Pasteur, D., *Financial Resources for Urban Services and Development in Lusaka : A Case Study and an Exercise*, Development Administration Group, Institute of Local Government Studies, University of Birmingham, 1978.

Pelekamayo, J., *Economic and Social Activities in Minga Area in the Petauke District*, ZGA, No. 14, April, 1971.

Peters, D.V., *Land Usage in Seranji District*, RLP, No. 19, 1950.

Peters, D.V., *Land Usage in Barotse Land*, RLC, No. 19, 1973.

Powdermaker, H., *Copper Town : Changing Africa*, Harper & Row, New York, 1962.

Prescott, J.R.V., Migrant Labour in the Central African Federation, *GR*, Vol. 49, 1959, 424-7.

Prustley, M.J.S.W. and Greening, P., *Ngoni Land Utilization Survey : 1954-1955*, G.P. Lusaka, 1956.

Pullan, R.A. (ed), *Mansa*, ZGA, Conference Handbook, Lusaka, 1972.

Pullan, R.A., *A First Check List of the Published Maps of Northern Rhodesia 1890-1949*, Zambia Geographical Association, Bibliography 3, Lusaka, 1978.

Rakodi, Carole and Ann Schlyter, *Upgrading in Lusaka : Participation and Physical Changes*, The National Swedish Institute for Building Research, Gavle, 1981.

Ranger, T.O., *The Agricultural History of Zambia*, The Historical Association of Zambia, National Educational Company of Zambia, 1971.

Reeve, W.H., *The Geology and Mineral Resources of Northern Rhodesia*, GP, Lusaka, 1963.

Reeve, W.H., Progress and Geographical Significance of the Kaviba Dam, *GJ*, V-CXXVI, Part 2, 1960, pp.140-6.

Richards, A.I., *Bemba Marriage and Present Economic Conditions*, RLP, No. 4; ISR, 1969.

Richards, A.I., *Land, Labour and Diet in Northern Rhodesia*, Oxford University Press, 1961.

Richardson, B.M., *Aushi Village Structure in the Fort Rosebery District of Northern Rhodesia*, RLC, No. 13, IAS, 1959.

Roberts, R.A.J., *The Role of Money in the Development of Farming in the Mumbwa and Katete Areas of Zambia*, University of Nottingham, Deptt. of Agriculture and Horticulture, Farm Management Bulletin No. 1, Loughborough, Oct.1972.

Roberts, A.D., *Pre-Colonial Trade in Zambia*, ASR, No. 10, 1970.

Rodney, Walter, *How Europe Underdeveloped Africa*, London, Dar-es-Salaam, 1972.

Rotberg, Robert I., *Black Heart : Gore-Browne and the Politics of Multiracial Zambia*, University of California Press, Berkeley, Los Angeles and London, 1977.

Rothman, N., *African Urban Development in Colonial Period : A Study of Lusaka, 1905-64*, Ph.D. Thesis, Northwestern University, Illinois, 1972 (History), Microfilm Ann Arbor, Michigan.

Subbagh, M.B., Some Geographical Characteristic of a Plural Society : Apartheid in S.A., *GR*, V-58, 1968, p.1-28.

Sampson, Richard, *So This Was Lusakas*, Multimedia Publication, Lusaka, 1971.

Sendder, T., *The Ecology of the Gwembe Tonga*, MUP, 1962.

Shaw, J.R., The European Settlement, *NRJ*, No.VI, 1952.

Shaw, Timothy, M., *Dependence and Underdevelopment : The Development and Foreign Policies of Zambia*, Centre for International Studies, Ohio University, papers in International Studies, Africa Series, No. 28, 1976.

Siddle, D.J., Rural Development in Zambia : A Spatial Analysis, *The Journal of Modern African Studies*, V-8, 1970, pp. 271-284.

Simmance, Alan J.F., *Urbanization in Zambia*, International Urbanization Survey, The Ford Foundation, 1973.

Soremekun, Fole, The Challenge of Nation Building, *Africa Quarterly*, Indian Council for Africa, New Delhi, V-XII, No. 3, 1972.

Steel, R.W., Land and Population in British Tropical Africa, *Geography*, V-XL, 1955, p. 13.

Steel, R.W., Copperbelt of Northern Rhodesia, *Geography*, Vol. 42, 1957, pp. 83-92.

Stockers, E.T. and Brown, R., *The Zambesian Past : Studies in Central African History*, MUP, 1966.

Stone, J.C., Early Maps as a Demographic Sources : The Case of Zambia, in Fyfe, C. and D.McMaster (eds.), *African Historical Demography*, African Studies Centre, University of Edinburgh, 1977, pp. 453-73.

Stone, J.C., *A Guide to the Administrative Boundaries of Northern Rhodesia*, Department of Geography, University of Aberdeen, O'dell Memorial Monograph No. 7, 1979.

Tanguy, Fr., Kayambi : The First White Father Mission in Northern Rhodesia, *NRJ*, V - 11, 1954.

Thann, L.H. and Duignan, P., *White Settlement in Tropical Africa*, Peguin African Series, 1962.

Thomas, J.B., Memories of Abandoned Bomas : Chiengi, *NRJ*, V-II, 1955.

Todd, Dave, *Small Scale Manufacturing in Lusaka : A Comparison of Markets and Small-Scale Industry Sites*, Urban Community Reports No. 2, IAS, Lusaka, Sep.1980 (mimio).

Todd, Dave, Alfred Mulenga and Chris Muplmpila, *Marketeers and Urban Growth A Study of Five Lusaka Markets in 1978*, Urban Community Reports No. 1, IAS, Lusaka.

Todd, Dave, and Chistopher Shaw, *Education Employment and the Informal Sector in Zambia*, Urban Community Research Unit, Report No. 2, IAS, Lusaka.

Tordoff, William (ed), *Administration in Zambia*, Manchester University Press, and University of Wisconsin Press, 1980.

Trewartha, G.T., New Population Maps of Uganda, Kenya, Nyasaland and Gold Coast, *AAAG*, V-42, 1957, pp.41-58.

Tuthil, D.F., John, A. Williams and Forter, P.W., *The Structure of Shifting Agriculture in Two Chewa Villages*, University of Maryland, Miscellaneous Publication 629, 1968.

Turner, V.W., *Schism and Continuity in an African Society : A Study of Ndembu Village Life*, MUP, 1964, IAS, 1971.

Van Den Berg, L.M., *Central Place Theory*, Occasional Studies No. 5, ZGA, Lusaka, 1972.

Vaux, H., Unusual Aspects of Native Land Tenure in the Mazabuka District, *NRJ*, V-II, 1953.

Velsen, J. Van, Labour Migration as a Positive Factor in the Continuity of Tonga Tribal Society, *EDCC*, Vol. 8, 1960, pp. 256-78.

Velsen, J. Van, *The Politics of Kinship : A Study in Social Manipulation Among the Lakeside Tonga*, MUP 1964, IAS, 1971.

Verboom, W.C., *Planned Rural Development in the Northern Province of Northern Rhodesia*, Delft, The Netherlands, 1961.

Vogel, J., *Kumadzula : An Early Iron Age Village Site in Southern Zambia*, Zambia Museum Papers 3, Oxford University Press, 1971.

Vyas, C.L., *I Have a Point*, Department of Cultural Services of Zambia, 1971.

Watson, W., *Tribal Cohesion in a Money Economy*, MUP, 1958.

Wells, F.B., Transportation in Rhodesian Copperbelt, *Geography*, 1957, Vol. 42, pp. 93-5.

White, C.M.N., *A Preliminary Survey of Luvale Rural Economy*, RLP, No. 29, ISR, 1968.

White, C.M.N., *An Outline of Luvale Social and Political Organization*, RLP, No. 30, ISR, 1968.

White, C.M.N., *The Baluvale Peoples and Their Historical Background*, RLJ, 1949, ISR, 1970.

Wheteley, W., *The Bemba and Related Peoples of Northern Rhodesia*, International African Institute, 1951.

Williams, G.D.B., Some Early Mail Runner Service, *NRJ*, V-IV, 1961.

Williams, G.J., *A Bibliography of Geographical Writings on Zambia, 1900-79*, Zambia Geographical Association, Bibliography No. 4, Lusaka, 1982.

Williams, J.L., Measure of Change in Rural Settlement: A Statistical Approach, ZGA, July 1973.

Wilson, Elizabeth, Lusaka : A City of Tropical Africa, *Geography*, Vol. 48, 1963, 411-4.

Wilson, Fox, H., The Development of Rhodesia from a Geographical Standpoint, *Geographical Journal*, Oct. 1916, pp. 289-310.

Wilson, G., *An Essay on the Economics of Detribalization in Northern Rhodesia*, RLP, Part Land II, ISR, 1968.

Woldring, Klaas, Chibwe Chibaye *et al.*, *Beyond Political Independence : Zambia's Development Predicament in the 1980's*, Mounton Publishers, Berlin, New York, Amsterdam, 1984.

Wood, A.P., Population Trends in Zambia : A Review of the 1980 Census, in Findlay, A. (ed), *Recent National Population Change*, Population Geography Study Group, Durham, Institute of British Geographers, 1982, pp. 102-25.

Wood, A.P., Demographic data for Socio-economic Planning, in Ncube, P.(ed), *Agricultural Data for Planning in Zambia*, National Commission Development Planning, University of Zambia, Lusaka, 1983, pp. 80-129.

Wood, A.P., Zambia, in Nag, P. (ed), *Census Mapping Survey*, IGU Commission on Population Geography, Concept Publishing Company, 1984, pp. 232-51.

Wood, A.P., A Century of Development Measures and Population Redistribution Along the Upper Zambezi, in Clarke, John I., Mustafa Khogali and L.A. Kosinski (eds), *Population and Development Projects in Africa*, Cambridge University Press, 1985, pp. 163-75.

University of Zambia, National Conference on Population and Development (Report), 13-14 December 1974, Extra Mural Studies Department, Lusaka.

Ziche, J., Beharrel, B., and Hartman, T.T., Relative Importance of Labour Input in Agricultural Development : The Zambian Case, *Journal of Rural Development*, 1974, pp. 111-41.

Government Reports/U.N. Reports/Unpublished Literature on Zambia

African Agricultural Development, U.N., F.A.O., E/CN.14/342, New York, 1966.

Agricultural and Pastoral Production, 1968, C.S.O.,1968.

Annual Report : Mount Makulu Research Station, Lusaka, 1971.

Annual Report : Land Use Service - 1972, MRD, Lusaka.

Annual Report : Eastern Province 1 Oct. 1972 - 30 Sept. 1973, Deptt. of Agriculture, Chipata.

A New Strategy for Rural Development in Zambia, Report of a Seminar on Rural Development in Lusaka, MRD, 1970.

ASCO, *Ndola Development Plan : Phase I*, Lusaka.

ASCO, *Mansa Development Plan - Preliminary Report*, Lusaka, Dec., 1969.

ASCO, *Kasama Development Plan - Preliminary Report*, ASCO-House, Lusaka, 1969.

ASCO, *Development Trends for the Ndola and Luanshya Regions*, M.L.G.H., Lusaka, 1972.

ASCO, *Site Selection of 4,000 Plots for the City Council of Ndola*, M.L.G.H., Lusaka, 1972.

ASCO, *Site Selection of 2,500 Plots of the Municipal Council of Livingstone*, M.L.G.H., Lusaka, 1972.

A Sociological Survey of Selected Types and Occupants, The Research Units, Deptt. of Community Development, Lusaka, 1968.

Barnett, P. and Henery, J.A., *Katete Settlement* , LUS, MRD, Chipata, 1972.

Beanmont, A.N., *Settlement Schemes and Policy Guidelines*, M.R.D., LUS, Lusaka.

Bcruimans, J.D., *Settlement Schemes in Zambia : A Brief Appraisal and Inventory*, LUS, MRD, 1972, (Official Paper).

Bourne, T.E. and Wilson, M.J., *Jimoli Commercial Farm Settlement*, LUS, MRD, Chipata, 1976.

Calendars of the District Note Books (Luapula Province) : 1798-1963, V-1, National Archives of Zambia, Lusaka (Compiled by P.M. Mukula).

Case Studies in Development, Research Project on Administration for Rural Development, NIPA, Lusaka.

Census of Population and Housing, 1969, CSO, Lusaka, 1970.

Chipata Development Plan 1971 -2000, D.T. & C.P., 1972.

Chakravarthy, D.N., *Annual Report for Luapula Regional Research Station*, Mansa.

Clothier, J.N., *A Report on the Agricultural Possibilities in Selected Areas on the Copperbelt*, G.P., Lusaka, 1936.

Copperbelt Development Plan, Lusaka, Copperbelt Planning Authority, Ministry of Lands & Natural Resources, G.P., Lusaka, 1965.

Coster, R.N., *Peasant Farming*, Agricultural Bulletin No.15, G.P., Lusaka, 1958.

C.S.O., *Census of Population and Housing, 1969*, Lusaka, 1970.

C.S.O., *Population, Projections for Zambia, 1969-99*, Lusaka, Jan. 1975.

C.S.O., *Projections of the Labour Force, 1969-84*, Population Monograph No. 3, Lusaka, March, 1976.

C.S.O., *Manpower Survey*, (Second Quarter, 1975), Lusaka, February 1978.

C.S.O., *1980 Census of Population and Housing*, Preliminary Report, Lusaka, January 1981.

C.S.O., *Monthly Digest of Statistics*, Vol. XVII, No. 4 to 6, April/June, 1982, Lusaka.

C.S.O., *Demographic Situation in Zambia*, Lusaka, 1985 (mimio).

C.S.O., *Demographic Projection*, Lusaka 1985 (mimio).

Dawtrey, B., *Miengwe Village Regrouping Scheme*, LUS, Ministry of Agriculture, Lusaka, Revised Version, Sept.1969.

Dawtrey, B., *Machiya Development Plan*, LUS, MRD, Ndola, 1972.

Dawtrey, B., *Annual Report - Copperbelt Province - Farming Settlement Schemes*, MRD, Ndola, 1973.

Department of Cooperatives - *Annual Report - 1970*, MRD, G.P., 1972.

Department of Cooperatives, *Annual Report - 1968*, MRD, G.P., 1969.

Doxiadis Associates, *Ntambu*, DOX-ZAM-A33, Lusaka, Dec. 1968.

Doxiadis Associates, *Mongu Development Plan*, DOX-ZAM-A26.

Doxiadis Associates, *Urban Centres : Selection of Site and Programme* , DOX-ZAM-A52, July, 1969.

Doxiadis Associates, *Kafue Master Plan and Communities Layout : Final Report*, DOX-ZAM-A9, Sept. 1967.

Doxiadis Associates, *Lusaka - Existing Conditions*, DOX-ZAM-A38, Lusaka.

Eccler, L.W.G., *Report on Land Development on the Copperbelt*, Unpublished, 1939.

Economic Development in Zambia, UN, ECA, FAO, Ndola, 1964

Economic Report, 1970, G.P., Lusaka, 1971.

First National Development Plan , Ministry of National Development and Planning, G.P., Lusaka, 1966.

Final Report of the May/June 1963 Census of Africans, C.S.O., Lusaka, Jan., 1968.

Friso, H.B.J., Proposal for the Determination of the Basic Ground Rental on Farms Leased by Government to Farmers, MRD, Nov. 1973.

F.R.N., *Population of the Federation of Rhodesia and Nyasaland*, (1:2.5 million), Federal Atlas Sheet No. 9, Federal Department of Trignometrical and Topographical Surveys, Salisburg, 1960.

F.R.N., *Census of Population*, C.S.O., Salisburg, 1960.

General List of Chiefs, G.P., Lusaka, 1973.

Godel, G.L., *An Analysis of Zambian Agriculture Camps*, July 15, 1972, MRD, Lusaka.

Godel, G.L., *An Analysis of Zambian Agriculture*, Planning Unit, MRD, Lusaka, 1972.

Green, R.N., *Regional Plan for the S.E. Chipangali Area in the Fort Jameson District*, LUS, MRD, Chipata.

G.R.Z., *Third National Development Plan*, Office of the President, National Commission for Development Planning, Lusaka, 1979.

Harvey R.H., Some Determinants of the Agricultural Productivity of Rural Households - Report of a Survey in Kalichero District, Eastern Province, Msekera Regional Research Station, MRD, Chipata, April,1973.

Harvey, R.H., *Zemba One Acre Virgenia Tobacco Scheme*, Msekera Regional Research Station, MRD, Feb., 1973.

History About Zambia, ZIS, Lusaka.

Hydrological Year Book : 1956-60, G.P., Lusaka, 1971.

Kabwe - Quinquennial Review of Development Plan, 1967.

Kalimeta Settlement, LUS, MRD,Chipata.

Karve, C.D., *Report on Blind and Handicapped Farms-Mushota, Kazembe and Lumini*, MRD, Mansa.

Kaunda, K.D., *A Path for the Future*, Mulungushi, 8th May, 1971.

Kaunda, K.D., *Humanism in Zambia and a Guide to its Implementation*, ZIS, Lusaka, 1971.

Kaunda, K.D., *The Imperative of Human Dignity*, ZIS, Lusaka, 1969.

Kaunda, K.D., *Take up the Challenge*, ZIS, Lusaka, 1970.

Kaunda, K.D., *Complete Independence : Zambia is Yours*, G.P., Lusaka, 1971.

Kaunda, K.D., *The Road to Positive Response*, G.P., Lusaka, 1971.

Kaunda, K.D., *Economic Reforms*, ZIS, Lusaka, 1968.

Kaunda, K.D., *This Complete Economic Reforms : Now Zambia is Ours*, ZIS, Lusaka, 1970.

Kaunda, K.D., *Zambia's Guideline for Next Decade*, ZIS, Lusaka, 1968.

Kaunda, K.D., *On Mobilization of the Masses for Rural Reconstruction and Development*, An Address, Nov., 5, 1971.

Lilje, B., *Zambezi Training Farm Settlement Scheme*, LUS, MRD, Kabwe, June 1973.

Lodgers and Houses in New Kanyama : A Survey, The Research Unit, Deptt. of Community Development, Lusaka, 1966.

Low Cost Residential Development in Lusaka, D.T.&C.P., Research Unit, Lusaka, Aug. 1972.

Lundgren, Thomas, Schlyter, Ann and Schlyter, Thomas, *Kapwepwe Compound : A Study of an Unauthorised Settlement*, University of Lund, Deptt. of Architecture IIB, Sweden, 1969.

Magoye Unit Farm Report 1966-71, Magoye Research Station, MRD, Oct., 1971.

Migration Statistic - 1968, C.S.O., Lusaka, 1969.

Mongu Development Plan : 1973-2000, D.T. & C.P., Lusaka, 1973.

Multipurpose Survey of the Kafue River Basin - Zambia, Final Report, V-1, General U.N. Development Programme, F.A.O./SF:35/Zam, 1968.

Mwaziona : A Study of an Unofficial Housing Area, D.T.&C.P., Research Unit, 1973.

National Housing Authorities, *Greater Kitwe Development Plan*, Lusaka.

National Council for Scientific Research, *Atlas of the Population of Zambia*, Lusaka, 1977.

National Housing Authority, *Self-help in Action - A Study of Site and Service Schemes in Zambia*, Research Study No. 2, June 1975.

Non-African Census : 1911-1961, C.S.O., Lusaka.

Northern Rhodesia : Urban African Local Government Committee, G.P., Lusaka, 1950.

Notes on Family Farms Ltd., LUS, MRD, Lusaka.

Pattern of Social Welfare Organisation and Administration in Africa, U.N.Publication, E/CN.14/SWSA/2, 1963.

Policy Matters for Discussion and Approval : Chifwile and Kapatu Settlement Schemes, MRD, Lusaka.

Regional Reports and Settlement Schemes - Ngwezi, D.T. & C.P., Lusaka.

Report of the Second National Convention on Rural Development, Incomes, Wages and Prices in Zambia : Policy and Machinery, ZIS, Lusaka, 1970.

Report of Soil and Landuse Survey of the Copperbelt, Deptt. of Agriculture , G.P., Lusaka, 1956.

Review of Economic Activity in Africa 1950 to 1954, U.N. Publication, 1963.

Sama Pande, J.K., *Town Planning*, Talk to Zambian Geographical Association.

Second National Development Plan, Ministry of Development Planning and National Guidance, Lusaka, 1971.

Simmance, A.J.F., *et al.*, *Report of the Working Party to Review the System of Decentralised Administration*, G.P., Lusaka.

Snead, Paul G., *Settlement Scheme Repayment*, S623/73, M.R.D., Lusaka, Official Paper.

Social Reconstruction in the Newly Independent Countries of East Africa, U.N. Publication, E/CN.13/SWSA/4.

Spain, E.S., *Investigation into Frequency of Thunderstorm Days in Zambia*, Deptt. of Meteorology, Lusaka, 1970.

Statistical Year Book, 1969, CSO, Lusaka 1970.

Stokes, J.C.A., *Ngwezi Settlement : Extension B - Mazabuka District*, LUS, MRD, 1970.

Totals of Monthly and Annual Rainfall : Season 1968-69, Deptt. of Meteorology, Lusaka, 1970.

The Land, River and Lakes, ZIS, Lusaka, 1970.

The Rufunsa Area : A Socio-Economic Survey for Village Regrouping, Research Unit, Deptt. of Community Development, Lusaka.

The Luapula Province : Agricultural Stock Taking, Mansa, April, 1965.

The Eastern Province of Zambia : Provincial Stock Taking for Rural Development - Fort Jameson, Chipata, 1965.

The Ntembe Area : A Semi Socio-Economic Survey, Research Unit, Deptt. of Community Development, Lusaka, 1968.

The People of Zambia City, Research Unit, Deptt. of Community Development, Lusaka, 1966.

Transport Statistics, January-March, 1971, CSO, Lusaka, 1971.

Trapnell, C.G., *The Soils, Vegetation and Agriculture of North-Eastern Rhodesia*, G.P.Lusaka, 1953.

Trapnell, C.G., and Clothier, J.N., *The Soils, Vegetation and Agricultureal Systems of North - Western Rhodesia*, G.P., Lusaka, 1957.

Verboom, W.C. and Bowles, I.B., *Rukuzye Regional Plan in Fort Jameson District of Northern Rhodesia*, LUS, MRD, Chipata.

Village Productivity and Ward Development Committees : A Pocket Manual, G.P., Lusaka, 1971.

Wilson, M.J., Bourne, T.E., and Vande Poll, B.W., *Zambia One-Acre Virginia Tobacco Scheme*, LUS, MRD, 1970.

Witola, Zeilter, *A Socio-Economic Survey of Kalingalinga*, Lusaka.

Zambia in Brief, ZIS, Lusaka, 1970.

INDEX

Accelerated rural development, 87
Acephalous societies, 63
Administration, 113, 148
Administrative framework, 8-10
African Affairs Committee, 168
African rural development, 89; urban community, 113; urbanization, 112-14
Agglomeration, 84
Agricultural growth centres, 58, 205; output, 10; camp, 190
Amenities, 190
America, 141
Angola, 2
Animal husbandry, 58
Area development units, 180

Banyan Quarters, 111
Basic villages, 190
Bisa, 18
Blue collar labour force, 164
Bomas, 108, 109; settlement, 64; towns, 202
Boost agricultural production, 100
Bowling plan, implementation of, 111-12
British missionaries, 21
British South African Company (BSAC), 22, 125

Caste system, 198
Catchment and Conservation Plans (CCP), 92
Central functions, 185
Central place development, 182-83
Challenges, 202
Cheap accommodation, 164
Chewa (tribes), 19
Chienji, 109
Chifwile mixed farming scheme, 97, 100
Chitemene systems, 66, 89
Civil service housing, 115
Colonial policies, 112-14; organisation, 198
Constraints, 10-11
Copperbelt, 22, 23, 32; province, 114, 117, 143; squatter settlement in, 148-49; urban complex, 55, 100; urban regions, 117-22
Credit Organization of Zambia (COZ), 102
Crops, 83
Crown land, 22, 23-25, 198

Dambos, 2, 14
Development constraints, 10-12; infrastructure, 176, 203-204
Development Planning Division (DPD), 180
District Development Committee, 27
Doxiadis associates, 183
Dry farming-semi-commercial schemes, 102
Dwelling units, 143; ownership pattern of, 145-46

Early Iron Age, 15
Early Stone Age, 14
Early town plans, 110
Economic activity, 117; crisis, 197
Employment, 11, 156, 157, 158, 159, 178, 201; opportunities, 48, 96; status, 58; structure, 163-65
Environmental factors, 88
Ethnic population, 9

European agricultural techniques, 88
Existing conditions, 183-84
Explicit policies, 177-78
Exploitation, 66, 96

Fairview, 111
Farming land, 22
Farming settlement schemes, 102, 108
Female migration, 55-56
Fertility and Mortality, 45-46
First National Development Plan (FNDP), 10, 92, 114, 178-79
Fort Jameson Reserves, 88
Fort Rosebery, 109, 111
Functional systems, aspects of, 180-82, 207-208
Functionaries, 19-20
Future trends, 205-206

Gandhi, Mahatma, 1
Gardiner, John, 120
Gossner Service Team (GST), 102
Grass Root, 205
Grid-pattern, 125-26
Group housing scheme, 92
Growth centre, 191; foci, 189; point, 191; poles, 182-83, 187, 192-93
Gugler, J., 48

Hamlets and Homestead, 66-67
High accessibility areas, 205
High density residential areas, 124-25, 147
Housing problems, 141-76
Households, composition of, 41-42
Hutton, C.R., 48

Ikelenga - Kalene Complex, 71
Illiterate migrants, 162
Implicit policies, 177-78
Income, additional sources of, 81
Increasing housing problems, 114
Intensive Development Zone (IDZ), 96, 202
International Labour migration, 48
Interrelated issues, 183
Israeli settlement schemes, 93
Issues in development, 181-82
Itimpi small-holding, 149

Jauhori, A.S., 183
Job opportunities, 192

Kabwe, 122
Kafubu Block, 201
Kalichero Area-Intensive Development Zone, 96-100
Katumbi, 109
Kaunda, K., 183
Katange (Zaire), 15
Kay, G., 183
Koka, 109

Land reform steps, 26-27
Land use services, 102, 180
Languages, 7-8
Large Urban Areas (LUA), 135
Late Stone Age, 15
Laupula Valley, 18, 128
Line-of-rail urban system, 8
Literacy and education levels, 40-41
Little englands, 23
Livingstone, 37, 108, 111, 112, 152
Local level policy programmes, 193
Lords of Land, 62
Low cost housing areas, 115, 147-55
Low density residential areas, 123-24
Lozi administration, 18
Luba, 15
Lubemba, 18
Lunda, 15
Lusaka, 32, 122; planned and unplanned housing areas, 167-72; social action in, 154

Malawi, 2
Male-female population distribution, 37
Malota, oldest African residential area, 151-53
Mapepela village regrouping scheme, 92
Marital status, 43-45
Mass migration, 26
Matrilineal rural society, 60
Medical facilities, 47
Mictchell, J.C., 48
Middle Stone Age, 14

Miengewe village regrouping scheme, 93-94, 202
Migration and movement, 47-48; pattern of, 54-55
Mindola Dam settlement, 164
Model development scheme, 201
Modern agricultural community, 101
Modern transportation, 176
Modernization, 176
Mozambique, 2
Multi-functional settlement, 111
Multi-nuclai settlement, 111
Mungwi settlement scheme, 89-90
Municipal corporation ordinance, 23; location, 147
Mwanza, J.M., 48
Mwomboshi, 109

Nag, P., 183
Nalolo, 109
National Agricultural Marketing Boards (NAM-Boards), 28, 64
National Development Plan, 177-180
National Housing Authority, 27, 115
Native reserves, 198; trust land, 22, 23, 198
Natural environmental condition, 71
Nature of centres, 189
Ndola, 52, 122; council houses in, 158; housing units and waiting list in, 157-58
Ndola Rural Council, 93
New Tan-Zam Rail line, 32, 51, 205, 206
Ngoni (tribes), 21
Nodol development scheme, 91-92
Non-centralised scheme, 63
North Charterland Exploration Company (NCEC), 22, 88, 101
Nsenga (tribes), 19

Occupation, sources of, 59-60
Official self help scheme, 154
Old-line-of-rail, 32, 50, 51, 60,. 87, 100, 103, 122, 134, 176, 206
One Party Participatory Democracy, 9, 176, 198
Out migration, 169

Peasant Farming scheme, 89
Permanent villages, 17
Peri urban areas, population growth in, 127-29
Petauke Reserves, 88
Pole and dagga, 143
Political nuclai, 17; organization, 17; territorial organization, 21
Polygamy, 80
Population change, 100; distribution pattern, 32-36; projection, 199; redistribution of, 87-106; shifting of, 32, 60; trends, 201; and dwelling, 146-47
Poor accessibility areas, 205
Portuguese, 21, 198
Poses problems, 87
Prospects, problems of, 197-98
Provincial development committees, 27
Provincial Planning Units (PPU), 180
Pseudo planned housing sector, 115-16

Raiding territories, 63-64
Railway line model, 192
Random values, distribution pattern, 73
Recent population trends, 59; urbanization, 133-34
Recepitulation, 28-29
Receiving tribute labour, 63
Recreation points, 205
Regional Planning Units (RPU), 180
Regionalization scheme, 2-3
Rejuvenation, 108
Reserves lands, 22, 88
Rhodesia, 20
Richardson, E.M., 76
River Zambezi, 108, 109
Rural areas, cultural settlement in, 96, 100; job opportunities, 192
Rural development, 87-106; approaches, 90-91; colonial period, 87-89; post independence period, 90-91
Rural Health Centre (RHC), 64
Rural settlement system, 62-85; neighbouring units, 65-66; organization of, 201; pattern of, 67-68; quantitative analysis of, 71-74; tribo-territorial bases of, 62-64; villages in, 65-66
Rural-urban migration, 4, 60; pattern of, 133-34; population growth of, 38-39

Rural service centre, 201, 206

Sample villages characteristics of, 83-84
Second National Development Plan (SNDP), 94, 115, 178, 202
Second World War, 89
Secondary functions, 190
Semi-compect settlement pattern, 67-68
Service centres, 190-91; points, 190
Settlement and production units, 92
Siddle, D.J., 183
Site and service programme, 154, 197
Skilled and educated manpower, 11
Slave-traders, 21, 198
Small Scale industries settlement, 205
Social factors, 76; obligation, 113
Spinkled settlement, 71
Squatter households, composition of, 160-61
Squatter population, 141-77, 203; after independence, 153-54; crash programme, 154; growth of, 155-56
Squatter settlement, 50-51; distribution of, 146-47; informal activities in, 165-67; upgrading of, 115-16
State farms and ranches, 92
Swahilis, 198
Swahili Native Reserve, 21-24

Tanzania, 2
Ten Year Plan, 177
Third National Development Plan (TNDP), 179
Tobacco Board of Zambia (TBZ), 102
Towns, colonial pattern of, 114-15
Town and country planning, 115
Township ordinance, 23
Tractor mechanization scheme, 90, 92, 102
Traditional - tribal hierarchy, 63
Traditional village system, 19, 62
Transformation, proposed process of, 187-88; rural settlement process of, 98-100; stages of, 188-89
Transitional development plan, 178
Transportation facilities, 51, 87, 103, 194, 205
Tribute labour, 62
Tripoli, 147
Tsetse fly infestation, 101

Unemployment, 60, 162, 163, 201
United Bus Service of Zambia (UBZ), 52
Unplanned habitat, 98
Urban centres, distribution of, 116-17
Urban scene, 202-203; housing problems, 142, 168; settlement, origin of, 108-10
Urban social system, 182

Van-Dan Berg, L.M., 183
Veterinary and Tsetse control services, 180
Villa Elisabetta, 111
Village, accommodation, 81-82; economy of, 76; territorial unit, 66
Village Productivity Committee (VPC), 19, 27

Ward Development Committee (WDC), 9, 27
Water Bodies, 71
Watson, W., 48
Weekly markets, 190
Wilson, Godfrey, 113
Working population, 56-58

Zambezi system, 2
Zambia, chiefs territories, 26-27; in 18th century, 20-21; general landuse and social set-up, 4-8; independence, 1; industrial areas, 126-28; mineral and natural wealth, 22-23; physiography, 2-4; population and settlement, growth of, 14-30; squatter population and settlements, 141, 203-204; urban development, 108-10
Zambian towns, morphology, 122-23; labour force, 48; society, 40, 62
Zaire, 2, 122
Zimbabwe, 2